Unchanged Trebles

Unchanged Trebles

*What Boy Choirs Teach Us About
Motherhood and Masculinity*

REBEKAH PEEPLES

RUTGERS UNIVERSITY PRESS
NEW BRUNSWICK, CAMDEN, AND NEWARK, NEW JERSEY
LONDON

Rutgers University Press is a department of Rutgers, The State University of New Jersey, one of the leading public research universities in the nation. By publishing worldwide, it furthers the University's mission of dedication to excellence in teaching, scholarship, research, and clinical care.

Library of Congress Cataloging-in-Publication Data

Names: Peeples, Rebekah, author.
Title: Unchanged trebles: what boy choirs teach us about motherhood and masculinity / Rebekah Peeples.
Description: New Brunswick: Rutgers University Press, 2025. | Includes bibliographical references.
Identifiers: LCCN 2024060854 (print) | LCCN 2024060855 (ebook) | ISBN 9781978844568 (hardcover) | ISBN 9781978844575 (epub)
Subjects: LCSH: Boys' choirs—Social aspects. | Boys—Psychology. | Boys—Social life and customs. | Sex role in children. | Gender identity in children. | Masculinity.
Classification: LCC ML3838 .P33 2025 (print) | LCC ML3838 (ebook) | DDC 782.7/9111—dc23/eng/20250131
LC record available at https://lccn.loc.gov/2024060854
LC ebook record available at https://lccn.loc.gov/2024060855

A British Cataloging-in-Publication record for this book is available from the British Library.

Copyright © 2026 by Rebekah Peeples

All rights reserved

No part of this book may be reproduced or utilized in any form or by any means, electronic or mechanical, or by any information storage and retrieval system, without written permission from the publisher. Please contact Rutgers University Press, 106 Somerset Street, New Brunswick, NJ 08901. The only exception to this prohibition is "fair use" as defined by U.S. copyright law.

References to internet websites (URLs) were accurate at the time of writing. Neither the author nor Rutgers University Press is responsible for URLs that may have expired or changed since the manuscript was prepared.

♾ The paper used in this publication meets the requirements of the American National Standard for Information Sciences—Permanence of Paper for Printed Library Materials, ANSI Z39.48-1992.

rutgersuniversitypress.org

*For my daughter Margaret,
who understood from a very early age that
gender is a social construct*

Contents

Introduction 1

1. Do You Know a Boy Who Loves to Sing? 11
2. It's Like a Finishing School for Boys 39
3. Unchanged Trebles 67
4. Don't You Want to See the World? 97
5. Draw the Circle Wide 119
6. Closets 143
7. A Ceremony of Discipline 171
8. Mother Nature Has Them by the Throat 197
9. The Child is Father of the Man 227

Acknowledgments 247
Notes 249
Index 261

Unchanged Trebles

Introduction

The boys have spent months practicing for this moment. They're the crown jewel of this musical offering, even if they're currently crowded together in a cramped huddle at the back of the Gothic sanctuary. Their individual names aren't listed in any program, but a few moments from now an audience of millions will tune in to hear them sing. The BBC's red light sits on the floor next to the choristers' feet, flashing for twenty seconds at three o'clock sharp while the broadcast is introduced. One boy will be picked to sing the opening solo, although he won't know this until moments before the service begins. The choirmaster will tap him on the shoulder with an approving nod, and the boy will step out of the huddle to sing alone and unaccompanied, just as other boys have done before him for more than a century on this day. The organist will have been improvising for a few minutes, hovering around the opening pitches—D, F#, G—so that the potential soloist can begin to imagine the starting pitch he'll need to locate out of thin air. If he gets it wrong, the organist will need to transpose the rest of the hymn when the congregation joins in; there's no room for error for these singers, and especially not today. Even the youngest boys, who are only eight or nine, understand the stakes.

This "Festival of Nine Lessons and Carols" has been offered for more than one hundred years at the chapel at King's College, Cambridge. If boy choirs were baseball teams, then the boys in the choir at King's would be the Yankees, with the Christmas Eve service akin to the World Series. Because the performance is simultaneously broadcast live on television and radio, some estimate that the King's College Christmas Eve service is the most watched and listened to BBC broadcast of the year. Audiences appreciate the familiar aspects of this traditional Anglican service. A new carol is commissioned for the chapel each year, but the scripture readings have been unchanged since the service's beginning in 1918. Of course, the boy choir itself predates the service by centuries. Founded in 1456, the choir has sung nearly continuously since that time, save for a few disruptions owing to war along with British monarchical and ecclesial disputes, and, a few years ago, the global pandemic caused by COVID-19. For much of its history, the choir school was a vehicle of upward mobility (or at least some promise of formal education and semireliable free meals) for musically talented boys of meager circumstances. Generations of families sent their sons away to choir schools like King's all across England, hoping that somehow the experience they found there would offer them a better life, preparing them for all of the unknowable challenges and opportunities that would surely lie ahead.

Things are different nowadays, of course. For one thing, few all-boy choral schools remain, even in England. Parents are less inclined to send eight-year-olds away to boarding school, especially to focus exclusively on music. Perhaps more profoundly, it's also getting harder to justify the all-boy composition of these groups in a cultural moment that increasingly sees gender as a component of individual expression rather than a predetermined category of exclusion. Just down the road from King's in Cambridge, the Saint John's chapel choir has recently begun admitting girls to its "top line" of treble voices.[1] Many have cheered this move as a step toward gender equality. Others worry quietly that inviting girls into the mix will diminish future boys' interest, accelerating the disappearance of a tradition that is already in decline. Their concerns stem from one persistent observation: that boys want to sing only when they can do so with *other boys*. Some are just too embarrassed to sing in their treble voices around girls. Others might especially enjoy feeling like "one of the boys" even if they're doing something that's not particularly masculine. Or maybe they just want to feel special for their fleeting, transient gift—the ability to enchant an audience with an otherworldly, angelic sound broadcast worldwide on Christmas Eve.

When the red light goes off, the organist stops. About ten seconds of silence follows before the red light comes back on, which means the broadcast is live. After the chosen boy has been tapped on the shoulder, he steps forward from the others to sing the familiar words: "Once in royal David's city / Stood a lowly cattle shed / Where a mother laid her baby / in a manger for his bed." Being chosen like this means that he doesn't ever have a chance to get nervous, even though he's been training for years for this single, fleeting moment, hoping that his voice won't change before it's his turn to be picked. The whole thing lasts for about forty-five seconds, before the boys file into the chapel, two by two, ready to lead the world in song.

As an American, I've only ever listened to this service of "Lessons and Carols" over the radio. But I'm still transfixed by the boy choir sound—its unmistakable clarity, its ability to communicate pure and unguarded vulnerability. I've always wondered about the boys *in* the choir—and of course, about each year's soloist—and how they came to attend the choir school, if they always enjoy singing, and if they miss their mothers. But this book comes out of questions that interested me even more: what it means for a boy to have and use his treble voice, and in the tradition that supports the boys who do so. What happens when their voices start to change? After all, no one grows up to be a boy soprano. And if the shifting range of the human voice is a metaphor for how male and female qualities can coexist in one body, then does some piece of that voice—a more vulnerable, feminine piece—live on within them, even after they pass through adolescence? What would it take for our society to recognize and nurture this kind of vulnerability in all our boys and men?

Although this is a book about boy sopranos like those at King's College in Cambridge, it's also a story about gender and adolescence and what it means to be the mother of a boy in a society that has yet to offer many viable models of healthy masculinity. But while it's partly a meditation on motherhood and a lament for masculinity's limits, it is also an argument about the potential of the arts for helping today's boys and men learn to express their emotions and embrace more fully the vulnerability that makes us all human. This book also outlines the potential of same-gender spaces for helping all of us to embrace more expansive notions of gender, especially boys in the formative years of early adolescence.

It began in a place that was unexpected for me: my own son's sudden entry into the world of boy choirs at eleven years old. Although he didn't attend a boarding choir school like King's—those schools have all but disappeared in the United States—many features of a boy choir performance remain constant across varied formats and continents. The defining feature of these groups is a collection of boys between the ages of eight and fourteen singing in their treble voices, usually dressed in uniforms of jackets, ties, and neatly pressed slacks. At a personal level, my son's entry into a community boy choir set the two of us on a series of intensive, often all-consuming commitments to rehearsal and performance. I also became increasingly interested in understanding the deeper questions about masculinity and motherhood that this experience ignited, a curiosity that spurred me to learn more about the boy choir tradition and what its future might hold. In particular, I wondered how an all-boy tradition would fare in a cultural moment in which children and their parents are thinking about gender in radically transformed ways—where identifying as a boy, as a girl, or as queer or nonbinary is increasingly seen as an individual choice rather than biological destiny. At the same time, I couldn't help but observe how the gender-specific needs of boys and men seemed an evergreen topic of cultural and scholarly concern. How can families, culture, and institutions best help boys embrace an understanding of masculinity that values care, vulnerability, and emotional expression? And are gender-segregated spaces necessarily at odds with the goals of gender inclusion?

Asking questions like this is what I am trained to do as a sociologist. I'm always interested in the deeper meanings attached to quotidian aspects of daily life and eager to probe the contradictions and inconsistencies that underlie taken-for-granted rituals and traditions. But in addition to being a social scientist, I am also the mother of a boy, and this book grew out of my own personal journey to address the worries that increasingly accompany the complicated work of raising sons. One could easily fill a bookshelf with recent titles that either chronicle the struggles and bad behavior of boys and men or promise expert advice on how to parent boys so as to avoid these concerning outcomes.[2]

And parents of boys do have reason to be worried. A substantial body of data highlights the many negative consequences of traditional masculinity—a constellation of behaviors and attitudes that emphasize, among other things, dominating others, constrained emotional expression, and eschewing any and everything deemed "feminine."[3] By the time they reach adulthood, far too many men are adrift and lonely: As many as 15 percent say they don't have any close friends, and the portion of young men who say they could ask a friend for help during a difficult time has declined by half since 1990.[4] Boys and men make up the majority of the "deaths of despair" that result from addiction or suicide.[5] A preoccupation with violence—whether the real world of gun culture or the fantasy world of video games—engulfs too many boys in a toxic marinade of isolation and extremism. A handful even go on to shoot up schools, churches, and supermarkets.

At the same time, strident public personalities like Tucker Carlson and Joe Rogan protest that men are suffering precisely *because* traditional forms of masculinity are under attack. Although these doomsday warnings have been soundly debunked by the mainstream media, the persistent following they enjoy attests to the widespread appeal of these perspectives.[6] And these fears do testify to the enduring fragility of masculinity as a category, along with the dislocation and uncertainty that men increasingly encounter in a society that has, in many ways, shifted markedly in its expectations of men over the past thirty years.[7] To that end, researchers like Richard Reeves warn of an identity crisis among men whose traditional role as providers and protectors has undergone a sudden and unprecedented revision. Wherever one falls on the political spectrum, we can probably all agree on this: we are deeply divided about the kind of men we want in our society and how we can best help boys to become them.

This book doesn't propose easy answers to those questions, but it does explore the deeper meanings attached to boyhood and the innovative ways that parents, teachers, and other adults can help boys negotiate between these ever-present conflicts as they approach manhood. As I learned firsthand as the mother of a boy soprano, waiting for the voice change also means paying special attention to the physical and emotional transformations that accompany male adolescence. My son's experience in a boy choir therefore gave me a singular opportunity to think carefully and deliberately about aspects of male puberty that we're generally tempted to overlook. These years are undeniably awkward and uncomfortable for everyone, but I think mothers are particularly inclined to look away from the spectacle of male puberty. We don't quite know how to respond to the physical transitions that render our boys unrecognizable in their new, almost-man form, bringing with it a new kind of emotional distance and discomfort. I can't count the number of times I've sat with a group of women talking about their teenaged boys, shuddering as they recount how much their sons repulse them now—how they won't get a proper haircut, think they don't need deodorant, and respond to text messages only with one-word, dismissive answers. The same bodies that we used to cuddle and comfort become alien to us as they inch, haltingly and uncertainly, toward the strange new world of manhood. It feels like a journey they must make alone. Casting mother aside along the way is part and parcel of their duty.

My use of terms like "boy," "mother," and "son" in the preceding paragraphs is intentional, although I use these terms cautiously knowing how easily they can become politicized. My goal in these pages is neither to reify a gender binary nor to argue for its erasure. Rather, my research into these questions around the significance of gender in adolescence only underscores how desperately we need more expansive ways of thinking about what it can mean to be a boy or a girl, a man or a woman, binary or nonbinary in a society that is currently engaged in battle over what these categories can and should mean. The centuries-old boy choir tradition also illustrates quite pointedly how the characteristics we consider masculine or feminine, male or female, have long been intertwined across blurry boundaries that escape our notice.

At the same time, most of us live our daily lives in ways that are still firmly rooted in a binary gender structure. Therefore, I chose to write this book using mostly binary terms because these are the ones used by the people whose lives are portrayed in its pages. Singing is unavoidably rooted in the body, which makes it difficult to avoid discussions of the relationship between gender and embodiment. Sociologists are often reluctant to engage with the biological dimensions of a binary gender structure, even though doing so can actually offer findings that don't privilege a binary outcome.[8] Indeed, one irony of the boy choir tradition is how the all-male composition of these groups can actually encourage boys to engage in far more expansive performances of gender than might be possible in similar settings that include both boys and girls. While most boy choirs do restrict membership to children who identify as boys, the kinds of singing and emotional expression that they require are things that our larger society generally views as effeminate, or at the very least "not masculine."

I also use these gender-specific terms because my relationship with my son during his teenaged years was shaped in profound ways by the gendered aspects of our relationship as mother and son. True, we are both cisgender and heterosexual and enter society with all the privileges that those identities entail. But as his adolescent years unfolded, I realized that many of our interactions with each other were influenced by the prevailing norms of masculinity and femininity that animated our family life, along with my ongoing attempts to find new and unconventional ways to develop within him an understanding of manhood that might self-consciously recognize and even renounce male privilege. So although my story begins in a place of our gender specificity, it is also unquestionably relevant to all parents, whether they identify as mothers or fathers, or are parents of boys, girls, or gender-nonbinary children. My specific interest is in boy choirs, but the larger lessons are about the potential of same-sex spaces to help boys learn a more expansive way to enter manhood from the parents, teachers, coaches, and music directors who care about them and their emotional well-being.

And much depends on our ability to transcend these limiting assumptions. The most recent election underscored just how many American voters, especially those under the age of thirty, seem to increasingly view the political process through a gendered lens. The MAGA movement's unabashedly hypermasculine appeal to disaffected male voters capitalized on a current of angry misogyny that ricocheted across right-wing podcasts and social media influencers. Suburban mothers looked askance at the notion of children choosing their pronouns and transwomen competing in women's sports, even as reproductive rights were at stake in the election too. Regardless of how one cast one's vote, conflicting ideas about what it means to be a man or a woman, masculine or feminine were as important to voters as their pocketbook concerns about the economy.

As a sociologist, I'm instinctually suspicious of attempts to use individual observations to generate reliable, broad-scale conclusions. The ensuing chapters therefore draw upon more than sixty interviews conducted mostly with boy choir directors and former boy choristers in the contemporary United States. I supplement these perspectives with insights from girl choir and mixed-gender choral directors as well as a handful of parents. Most interviews lasted an hour or more; some people I spoke with multiple times either to clarify their earlier comments or to learn how things were going in their choirs as they started to emerge from the pandemic in 2021. The majority of respondents quoted in this book gave me explicit permission to identify them by name. This is partly because the boy choir world is admittedly small, and most would have easily recognized each other through the thin veil of a sociologist's pseudonym (though if a respondent chose to use a pseudonym, I note that in the narrative). But more importantly, they are proud of their work and their insights and eager to be associated publicly with their perspectives. Most of them have spent their lifetimes working with boys between the ages of eight and fourteen or reflecting on key moments of their own experiences during those years, and they have learned things that the rest of us would do well to pay attention to.

Over the years in which I was conducting this research, I was continually astounded by the ability of these mostly male respondents to speak with an uninhibited understanding of their emotional world as well as their own misgivings about the constraining expectations of conventional masculinity. Some are openly gay, but most are straight; many have children of their own now, which means that like me they are wrestling with these questions in their own nuclear families. It's impossible to know whether or not the things that made them so willing to talk about feelings of vulnerability—like shame and loss, or even uninhibited joy—were the same things that led them to pursue these aspects of vocal performance. It's also possible that those experiences have somehow changed them and kept their emotional receptors alive during a part of the life course when our society tends to extinguish them in boys and young men. But either way, I came away from this research convinced that there's a strong relationship between participating in the arts, especially choral singing, and being an emotionally aware man.

In the pages that follow, I endeavor to be clear about my own role in this story, as author, researcher, and most of all a mother. But it is admittedly unconventional for a work of social science to offer as much first-person narrative as I include in this book. Early on in my writing I planned to constrain my experience as a "boy choir mom" to a few paragraphs in an introduction or the occasional footnote. But as the research unfolded, I realized that to deny my own role in this story would be to excise some of the deepest thinking and interpretation that my research inspired. I will leave it to readers to evaluate my arguments and, perhaps, also my mothering. On that point, I tell my son's part of the story with his explicit permission; over the years that I was writing this book he would read chapter drafts, offer his insights, and flag any details that he wasn't comfortable sharing publicly (though this was rare). I also reviewed relevant portions of the manuscript with other family members, who also gave me permission to write about them publicly in this way.

Finally, although this story is partly about my own family, I hope that readers will see that it's really about much more than us. A foundational principle of sociology is that private experiences and individual lives are inextricably connected to the social world in which they exist and that they are both constrained and enabled by that larger social context. This book charts my journey between those realms, offering an unflinching look at the challenges inherent in contemporary boyhood as well as the possibilities we all have before us if we truly want to build a different kind of future.

CHAPTER 1

Do You Know a Boy Who Loves to Sing?

"He stole a laptop," I said to Ellen, prickly tears springing up behind my eyes.

The only reason I was able to avoid a full-on breakdown is that Ellen and I were running together on a Sunday morning and crying would mean stopping to walk, something that we try not to do very often.

"He didn't steal it, really," she countered. "I mean, it wasn't like he put the laptop in his backpack and tried to walk out of the school with it."

Ellen is my best friend, and among her many admirable qualities is the way she frames the challenges I experience with my children in a slightly more optimistic light than I do. Case in point: I was currently imagining my eleven-year-old son being carted off to prison, and she was envisioning a destination more along the lines of the school counselor's office. And of course, she was right. Haydon hadn't stolen the laptop . . . at least, not exactly. He had just taken it off of a teacher's cart, without permission, when he was waiting in a classroom backstage during an all-day dress rehearsal for the elementary school musical. That year the musical at our neighborhood elementary school was *Annie* and Haydon had the starring role of Oliver Warbucks. He had been explicitly instructed not to do this backstage at least one time before, and yet he had done it again anyway.

I had learned about this the previous day when the head of the drama club, a kind but demanding teacher named Mr. Kane, sent me an email with the subject line "The Two Haydons." The moment the email arrived, I knew without opening it the gist of what it would contain—Mr. Kane was going to tell me that Haydon was smart, talented, and gregarious. Then he would go on to tell me that his behavior was problematic.

And indeed, this is what the email said: that Mr. Kane had been impressed all year by how well Haydon performed onstage; how he so naturally embodied the starring role of Daddy Warbucks; how he had locked down the lines and handled the blocking instructions with ease; how the show's musical director was consistently impressed with Haydon's voice, which was always on point and never needed more than one rehearsal to lock in the notes and rhythms.

But backstage, he was a total disaster—playing with the props on the prop table, roughhousing with other boys in the hallways, forgetting to turn his microphone off when he exited the stage. And finally, stealing a laptop from Mr. Kane's cart.

Truth be told, I had been waiting for this email for weeks. Haydon's relationships with teachers often generated emails like this, and his fifth-grade year had produced a bumper crop. Before Mr. Kane's missive, I had been fielding similar correspondence from the school music teacher, who had been trying in vain to keep Haydon practicing for the National Children's Choir (NCC), a yearly convention for which school music teachers from around the country nominate student participants for a national audition. He had auditioned only by accident because he was tagging along with a new friend in the early weeks of the school year. Haydon aced the audition; his friend did not. In fact, no boys from his school successfully placed into the choir, something that had diminished Haydon's interest considerably. As preparation for NCC continued, Haydon's attitude toward the entire project became increasingly disinterested—especially since rehearsing for NCC meant staying in at recess in order to practice a relatively demanding choral repertoire—with girls. To make matters even worse, as a first soprano, he had the highest voice in the group; the girls were all second sopranos and altos.

As the weeks went on, Haydon had started avoiding choir practice during recess, "forgetting" the obligation and heading out to the field to play kickball with his friends instead. And when he was in rehearsal, he often refused to sing the music and was deliberately obstructionist. The increasingly frequent phone calls and emails from the choir director were another variation on "The Two Haydons" theme: Haydon is a very talented singer, but also a highly disruptive presence. After several rounds of emails and at least one contentious phone conversation with the choir director, Haydon had finally bellowed "I DON'T WANT TO DO THE NATIONAL CHILDREN'S CHOIR." His dad and I decided to let him quit, reasoning that managing the drama club and the NCC was perhaps more than he could reasonably take on at the same time. After all, he was only eleven.

But now we were five days out before the opening weekend of *Annie*, with Mr. Kane still worried that Haydon could effectively ruin the entire show for the rest of the cast. The email was all that I could think about in the tense days that followed. My husband and I saw our marriage therapist the following Tuesday and spent the entire forty-five minutes talking about our oldest child. This had become yet another thing we saw differently: he thought Haydon just needed more boundaries, more discipline, while I was convinced we should work harder to understand his emotions. Only then could we understand and address why he so often ended up in trouble. I was also overcome with the feeling that I, too, was being evaluated, as if I were in a show called "Parenting Successfully" and my children were the performers. Actually, I wasn't sure if I was directing the production or just playing a leading role, but either way the audience was the wider world, waiting to render its critical judgment. Mr. Kane's email ignited in me a sense of failure so profound that I could not meet his eyes the next time that I walked into the school. I'd spent my life pleasing teachers like Mr. Kane. For reasons I could not understand, my son seemed utterly unconcerned about doing the same.

In the days following the Two Haydons email, Mr. Kane and I agreed that I would join him in his classroom backstage with Haydon, at least until the show started, to ensure he wasn't getting himself or anyone else into trouble. This meant that I ended up supervising all of the boys who were in the show, which was easier than I expected because there were only four of them. Being backstage required the cast to get changed into their costumes, and for that reason the boys and the girls had been separated into two different classrooms along the same wing of the school. One classroom had at least two dozen girls spilling out of it, little groups of orphans in adorably ragtag costumes. They were clearly excited about how much makeup they got to wear in order to be onstage, their nervous energy flowing between them like an electric current that produced only smiles and laughter.

The boys, however, were a different story. There were only four of them, after all—Haydon as Daddy Warbucks, his butler Drake, and two other boys playing relatively minor roles as a police officer and a laundry deliveryman. In fact, there were so many girls who wanted to be in the play that some of them had ended up playing male roles, like Ms. Hannigan's brother Rooster. The air in this room felt very different than the one down the hall and wasn't just because the boys weren't as excited about wearing makeup. I couldn't quite put my finger on it, but it almost seemed that they were waiting to see who would be the one to get things started, to come up with something to pass the time. The boys were keyed up with nerves of their own, but they weren't talking gregariously like their female classmates down the hall. In fact, they seemed loath to interact with each other at all, which meant they were looking for something to release the tension, waiting for one of them to come up with a game that might allow them to interact without bearing the burden of talking. If they had been outside with a basketball they'd surely be shooting hoops by now or doing something even more chaotic, like tackling each other in a spirited round of tag. Inside the confining walls of a classroom, however, they were casting about for a way to burn off their nervous energy. At one point I had to reprimand Haydon for trying to initiate a game of keep-away with the police officer's hat, suggesting in my best no-nonsense voice that they play hangman on the blackboard instead. Of course, no one was especially interested in this idea, because it bordered on having educational value, because a mom suggested it, or both.

Finally, the show started and I slipped into the audience next to the rest of my family. We sat on uncomfortable aluminum chairs in the un-air-conditioned gym, but I was sure I'd be sweating even without the heat. My heart pounded each time that Haydon came onto the stage, and I breathed a little sigh of relief with every scene that was completed successfully, every time that he remembered to turn off his microphone when he exited the stage. Miraculously, no props went missing backstage. I felt little stabs of guilt for not forcing him into a bald cap—this may have been the first production of *Annie* in which Oliver Warbucks had a full head of dark brown curls—but no one else seemed to be bothered by this detail. I was almost too nervous to watch his solo in "N.Y.C.," but every single pitch was on target, every note pristine and clear. When the number ended, I finally felt myself exhale.

After the show there was a blur of people in the hallway: "Your son! His voice!" I heard them say. I smiled and tried to enact parental modesty with a casual wave of my hand. "Who knew he could sing?" I shrugged, acting as if I was as surprised as anyone. No one knew about the stolen laptop, at least. I felt like the mother of a star, not a future felon.

The next week Ellen and I went running again, and we talked more about the laptop incident. I told her about the environment in the boys' classroom backstage and about how Haydon himself still couldn't seem to articulate exactly why he took it. Ellen offered up her own hypothesis: "Do you think that maybe he was trying to impress the others?" she asked. She reasoned that perhaps Haydon was jockeying for position in the eyes of the other boys, wanting to cross a line and earn their admiration by doing so. After all, being backstage involves a lot of waiting, which is boring, and perhaps Haydon wanted to look cool by figuring out how to entertain his male castmates by logging on to YouTube.

This was worth considering, although it cast the notion of performance in a slightly different light. Ellen's hypothesis suggested that the boys were performing for each other, even when they were technically backstage. This was a different kind of performance—they may not have even realized they were doing it, after all—but just like the school play it had roles, a script, and an audience. It's ironic that Ellen was the one who came up with this explanation because she's a writer, while I'm a sociologist. It should have been obvious to me that this was part of what was going on with the laptop, but I'm rarely objective when it comes to evaluating my own life and relationships. Ellen was also not the mother of a laptop-stealer, so perhaps she had a bit more critical distance.

Hers was a fair point, and one that started to make sense the more that I allowed myself to think about it. The later elementary school years are precisely the time when kids start to turn up the volume on their performance of the gender-specific behaviors they expect will impress others.[1] This peer-group posturing happens for kids of all genders, but masculinity is notoriously harder to prove and easier to lose, which means this can take on particular urgency for boys. And the kind of behaviors esteemed by boys at these ages aren't exactly the traits that win approval from teachers—for instance, taking risks, being funny or even obnoxious and disruptive, and establishing themselves as a dominating presence among their peers.[2] The jockeying for status that starts in elementary school funnels boys into status hierarchies that privilege other stereotypically masculine traits by the time they get to middle school—athletic ability, emotional detachment, confidence, and toughness.[3] I reasoned that perhaps Haydon's actions were an attempt to establish his supremacy in a bizarre male pecking order that made little sense to me, as his mother—an eleven-year-old's version of suggesting to his fraternity brothers that perhaps it would be a good idea to try jumping off the roof into the backyard pool.

I'd been aware of the challenges that come with raising a boy in a culture that still esteems toxic models of masculine expression since the moment I found out that I was pregnant with a child who had XY chromosomes. For my part, I had been determined to raise a son who didn't express the worst stereotypes of masculinity—emotional detachment, physical aggression, disengagement with school, misogyny. Instead, I wanted to raise an emotionally attuned son who could cry during movies and proudly call himself a feminist—and not just because he knew that doing this would appeal to girls. As someone who works on a college campus, I'd sat with enough students after an allegation of sexual assault, both male and female, to know that I wanted to raise a son who would find the drunk girl at the party and walk her safely home.

My belief that raising an empathetic, emotionally attuned man was within my control stemmed in part from my training as a sociologist, which takes for granted the notion that gender is a social construct. This means that I generally see the meanings attached to being male or female as ones that come not from the biological sex assigned at birth but instead from institutions and social interactions that attach distinct social meanings to being male or female. In other words, the reason that the boys and girls in the classrooms backstage behave differently is because from the moment they were born they've absorbed countless messages about how they *should* behave that fall along gendered lines. For instance, the girls have learned that having close relationships and expressing their feelings are desirable traits, even things that are expected of them, while the boys have learned to perform emotional detachment, hiding their fear and anxiety before they go onstage. Expectations like these become taken-for-granted ideas about how men and women (or boys and girls) *should be*—for instance, a "real boy" is one who doesn't show vulnerability or engage in open displays of emotion.[4]

The good news, in my mind, was that if gender was a social construction, I could help to deconstruct it by raising my son, and a few years later my daughter, to consciously reject the societal stereotypes that we so often associate with masculinity and femininity. Instead, I could help them incorporate the best socially constructed features that are associated with the opposite gender into their own performance of the meanings attached to their biological sex. My daughter could become a confident, assertive woman and my son could be an empathetic, expressive man. I thought of these not necessarily as gendered outcomes but as larger goals that I would desire for all human beings, regardless of gender. In the hubris of early parenthood, I convinced myself that this would be a relatively straightforward project in which I, as a parent, would have nearly complete control.

Of course, carrying out these goals within my own nuclear family was infinitely more complicated than I expected. On one hand, before my husband and I married we'd negotiated plans for what would eventually become a fairly egalitarian partnership—my husband was typically on duty after school, since he had a more flexible work schedule than I did, and he'd been a consistently equal partner in the hands-on aspects of child-rearing from the beginning, like changing diapers, giving baths, going to the playground, or driving to and from activities. For most of our marriage we'd also earned similar salaries, which helped ensure a system of structural equality within our family.

But I was completely unprepared for how much of being a parent concerned emotional labor, a set of relational intangibles for which I found myself consistently responsible—defusing a tantrum, for instance, or negotiating a reconciliation when the kids were arguing with each other. When it was time to soothe hurt feelings or help a child "use your words," I generally found myself the primary parent on duty. This also meant that we ended up modeling fairly stereotypical performances of gender within our family, in which mothers carry out the bulk of a family's emotional labor, even if dads are equal partners in many of the household and child-rearing chores. We were reproducing gendered patterns and performances in our daily interpersonal interactions, even if other aspects of our family life were explicitly organized around structural egalitarianism.

My hopes for dismantling the social construction of gender were also complicated by the fact that from the moment my son became a toddler he did what I can best describe as stereotypically "boy things." We had plenty of dolls and stuffed animals, but he preferred things with wheels.

He also liked to throw stuff, to find sticks in the yard and then use them to hit things. He wasn't angry, just energetic and often impulsive—qualities that made him entertaining to be around but sometimes pushed the boundaries with teachers and other adults. "He sure is all boy, isn't he?" friends and neighbors would say, a refrain that managed to combine sympathy, praise, and some measure of judgment all at once.

My plan was also thwarted by the fact that in general children don't always do what we want. "Being a parent would be so much easier," I often found myself saying to Ellen, "if they would just do exactly what you tell them to." Ten years of trying to explain to Haydon why he needed to sit still and follow adults' instructions hadn't exactly produced full compliance. It also wasn't lost on me that many of my interactions with my son involved me, a woman, trying to manage and limit the expression of impulses that our society often considers "masculine." *I need for you to sit quietly now. Do not throw that rock that's in your hand. If I get another call from your teacher about disruptions during class then there will be no more video games this week.* Curbing the impulses of masculinity inevitably meant giving up some of his power—to me, a woman.

It's worth noting that we don't ask the same thing of girls when we encourage them to move beyond the confines associated with being feminine. I felt this contradiction most acutely when I compared my son's experience in extracurricular activities with his sister's, who was only two years younger. When it came to sports, for instance, the messages available to girls seemed self-consciously designed to challenge the cultural ideal of docile, submissive femininity. In fact, my daughter's experience in youth sports seemed entirely oriented around encouraging girls to develop physical strength and become aggressive competitors, traits that clearly challenge many of those associated with femininity. The same messages conveyed in youth sports for boys, on the other hand, seemed only to endorse and entrench existing understanding of masculinity. "Be aggressive!" parents yelled at their ten-year-old boys from the sidelines of the lacrosse field—while they chased after each other wearing armor and carrying sticks. If I was looking for help in raising an emotionally attuned, empathetic son, youth sports didn't seem like a place to find solutions.

Now that Haydon was on the cusp of puberty I felt as though my ability to constrain and direct his behavior was becoming ever more difficult—just at the same time that the consequences for his occasional impulsivity and defiance of authority were going to become even more significant. And as we had learned backstage during *Annie*, he was finding ways to perform some of the undesirable features of masculinity in the midst of something that others might consider feminine—being in the elementary school drama club. No wonder only four boys had signed up. After all, it involved wearing makeup.

A few weeks later I was in my office at work, having a meeting with Gabriel Crouch, director of the Princeton University Glee Club. He wanted to talk with me about revising the university's program in music performance to make it possible for singers to earn a certificate in what he called vocal consort singing—that is, vocal performance that is not the work of soloists. I'd spent enough time around Princeton students to know that they're excellent at just about everything, so I was surprised to learn that there were singers on campus who didn't want to be solo performers. Gabriel explained that he conducts plenty of singers who want to sing only as part of an ensemble—either because their voices aren't quite soloist quality or because they simply prefer to sing with other people. He added that he actually puts himself in this group, as he has always preferred to be a member of an ensemble, something that started when he was a boy in England and attended the choir school at Westminster Abbey in the 1980s. "My mum wanted me to have violin lessons," he said, "but she knew she couldn't afford them. The choir school was the way she made sure I got a musical education." He didn't end up focusing much on the violin, but he did become a professional musician. He was eight years old when he left for school.

Gabriel has an exceedingly kind and friendly demeanor, and as our conversation continued I found myself talking about eleven-year-old

Haydon and the saga with the NCC, how he didn't want to sing with girls, and my general exasperation with the challenges of raising a boy. "Maybe we should think about sending him to a boy choir school," I joked, but Gabriel didn't think this was a joke at all. In fact, he said that his wife worked for the American Boychoir, a choir boarding school located just down the road from the university. I had heard about the American Boychoir School, but hadn't given it a thought until now; the school's name had more recently been associated with scandal, when it became the subject of an expansive lawsuit that alleged widespread sexual abuse of boys at the hands of school staff, particularly one charismatic, pedophilic choirmaster in the 1970s.

Gabriel suggested that perhaps my son would consider an audition; the choir was always looking for boys who excelled at singing, although it was becoming a much harder sell these days. When I asked him why, he explained that it was partly about the legacy of the sexual abuse lawsuits, but that this was not the whole story. After all, the school had radically revised its child protection policies in the intervening years—they had long had a "two adults in a room" rule that ensured that no adult was ever alone with a child. Instead, he hypothesized that choir schools were becoming extinct because of widespread social changes in how we think about childhood. "Parents today want to live their children's lives with them," he said, adding that the kind of experience he had as a boy chorister was slowly disappearing, even in his home country of England. "Every minute of a choir school of prescribed," he explained, "but not by the parents." In his view, contemporary parents wanted to carefully manage their children's activities but would view it as an abdication of their responsibility to hand over all of the discipline and control to one institution.

When Gabriel left my office, I impulsively looked up the American Boychoir School. I knew that we probably wouldn't really consider sending Haydon to a choir school, but I did notice that they offered a weeklong summer camp that started after our school year ended. "Do You Know a Boy Who Loves to Sing?" the web page queried, in a big, colorful flyer. It occurred to me that I wasn't quite sure if my boy loved to sing, exactly, but I did know that he seemed to be pretty good at it. The camp flyer explained that boys could be day campers or they could spend the week on a nearby secondary school campus in Princeton where they would eat all of their meals in the school dining hall and stay in one of the dormitories. The cost of the overnight option was only slightly more than the day camper version, and I thought of how we had set some money aside for the NCC, which could now be diverted to a different musical project. Perhaps this would be a way to address more than one goal—we needed summer child care for that week anyway, and we could find out if Haydon really did like to sing.

However, I knew I had to sell it the right way to all of the males in my household. I decided to start with Haydon, and the conversation went something like this:

"So, I found out about this weeklong camp for boys who like to sing."

"Mom, I told you, I didn't want to do the National Children's Choir."

"Well, this wouldn't be the same thing," I countered. "This would be just with boys. Actually, boys come from all over the country for this camp."

"Do they take everyone who signs up?"

"No—actually, you would have to do an audition."

He pondered this for a moment. The competition and status associated with this arrangement is clearly something that fell into the plus column for him.

"Is it overnight?" he asked.

"You can stay overnight if you want to." I explained that the camp was held at a nearby boarding school campus, which meant that he would be able to eat in their cafeteria and enjoy all the pizza and French fries he wanted for the week.

This part clearly held some appeal. "And it's *only* for boys?" He paused to confirm this last part one more time, adding, "Do you think that the boys who go to the camp would also play sports?"

"Sure!" I said (though truth be told, I was not at all sure about this).

He thought about it for a moment and then agreed that he was willing to audition.

His father, on the other hand, was highly skeptical. "Didn't some boys get molested at the American Boychoir School?" he asked.

"That was like, forty years ago," I said, exasperated. "And anyway, they have a 'two adults in the room' rule now."

The fear of sexual abuse was not the only concern, however. In my husband's view, not only was the week at boy choir camp a potential risk, it was a week that could have been better spent honing Haydon's ability on some kind of sports field. "I think Haydon is better off doing a week of strenuous activity than sitting around in a room singing all day," he objected. "What's going to happen when he's stuck in a choir room and he sees kids at lacrosse camp outside?"

I was tempted to admit that he had a point, but wasn't ready to concede my position, at least not yet. While my husband had been a stellar athlete in his youth, I'd spent my time in the school band and at the piano, and I was increasingly invested in the notion that my son might follow in those artistic footsteps, too. So I secured Haydon a phone audition the following week with the camp's admission director, who reassured me that Haydon didn't need to prepare or practice anything. They were looking for boys with a good natural ear, she explained, regardless of whether or not they could read music. As promised, the audition was low-stakes; Haydon sang "Happy Birthday," sang a few scales, and was then asked to listen and sing back the notes in some broken chords played on the piano. She thanked him for his singing, after which she asked if she could talk with me privately. "I hear a lot of boys sing," she said to me once Haydon was out of earshot. "And your son is really, really talented." I heard those words and allowed them to settle in for a moment. They felt like a salve that promised to heal over all of our shortcomings—the trouble at school, the stolen laptop, my failing marriage. The "Parenting Successfully" show was back on—this time envisioned as a musical, one that promised to silence all of the critics, especially the ones inside my own head.

I had hoped that this verdict about Haydon's musical talent would help to persuade his father that this was a worthwhile project, but he still harbored doubts that this was a worthwhile use of time or money. This disagreement was only the latest one in a long-standing struggle with my husband, where a contest of wills often made us feel like adversaries—two equally ranked generals who disagreed about the battle plan, facing off against each other instead of the shared enemy. The ever-present sense that our lives needed to be oriented around the "Parenting Successfully" performance had become an all-consuming distraction from the intractable problems and disappointments of our own adult lives.

Amid all these worries, the choir opportunity somehow seemed to me like a potential intervention. Perhaps the discipline would be good for Haydon—being in a choir involved a lot of sitting, standing, and waiting—and the fact that it was all boys might relax the sense of punitive surveillance that had mostly characterized his school experiences thus far. I thought it might also help his self-esteem to stand out in an activity like this, since most of his experiences in school seemed to involve getting in trouble, at least as of late. And unlike his father, I saw the opportunity to develop an interest other than athletics as something that was highly desirable for a boy—it felt unusual, even countercultural to promote an activity for boys that was so explicitly organized around artistic expression. In the end, I won the argument with his father by playing the ultimate trump card. "Well," I said, "if you don't think that he should go to the ABS summer camp, then perhaps you can find another camp opportunity for him to do that week?" The enormity of that potential task was enough to silence the opposition. It was decided: Haydon would do the camp.

The last week of June finally arrived, and I helped my son pack his suitcase, which included black pants, black shoes and socks, a white oxford shirt, and a tie to wear at the concert, and drove the twenty-five minutes to the campus on a Sunday afternoon. There was a check-in spot, where

Haydon got a lanyard with his ABS Summer Experience name tag, waited in line for a "voice check" with the director, who was stationed at a piano just inside the school's main lobby, and was then permitted to unpack his things in his dorm room.

As we walked across the campus I looked nervously around at the other boys who would be joining my son for the next five days, feeling a stirring in the pit of my stomach. His father felt it too, slipping me disgruntled sideways glances every so often, so as to send telepathic jabs like "These are not the boys you would want on your dodgeball team." Haydon felt it, too, whispering nervously in my ear, "What if I don't like this?"

"Oh, it's going to be fun!" I said cheerily, though thoroughly unconvinced myself.

We said our goodbyes, exchanged hugs, and then walked slowly back to the car.

The ensuing week inched along like an eternity, although my nervousness had faded a bit since we'd left Haydon at camp the previous weekend—in the intervening days we'd had a few phone calls, which were all positive. One night when he was in a particularly good mood I asked why his spirits were so high, to which responded pleasantly, "I don't know. I guess we're just getting a lot of good work done on the music." He paused, then added, "I can't wait for you to hear it."

Finally, it was time for the Saturday afternoon concert that represented the culmination of the summer camp. We waited with other families outside of the Princeton Theological Seminary chapel for admittance to the venue where the boys' final concert would be held. I peeked in through the windows at the back of the hall and could see the boys, practicing their movements on and off of the risers, looking pristine in their black pants, white shirts, and ties.

When we were finally allowed into the hall, the parents and families filed into the austere, wooden pews of the chapel and readied ourselves for the concert. A rush of cool air greeted us as we moved out of one, big, sweaty crowd and into the open space of the chapel, with its vaulted ceilings and imposing pipe organ. The program clearly stated that no recordings or videos were permitted, but one particularly brazen father proceeded to set up his tripod and digital recorder off to the side. I wasn't so brave, choosing instead to keep my phone on the pew next to me, readying myself to record a few excerpts surreptitiously as voice memos. Eventually we were welcomed by ABS director Fernando Malvar-Ruiz, who gave an overview of the week at camp, ending with this inspiring conclusion: "Training our singers is a way of educating the boy—music is not the end goal, it is just a tool. So, we hope that when your boy goes home with you today, that perhaps you notice that he stands a little bit taller, that he pushes his chair in after dinner, or perhaps he tidies his room without being asked. Maybe you will notice that he's more confident, more respectful, more eager to learn and engage." Listening to this speech, I couldn't help but acknowledge internally that apparently, I hadn't needed to worry at all about Haydon's behavior that week; he seemed to have managed himself in this context without any difficulties that rose to the level of "call a parent." Maybe when he was in a setting of all boys the pressure to misbehave was less pronounced, or maybe misbehavior simply looked different in a setting of all boys.

As the concert began, I spotted Haydon on one of the top rows—he saw us as well, giving us a beaming smile. I also noticed that, while the boys were clearly instructed to wear black socks and black shoes, Haydon had instead chosen to wear neon green Nike socks that stuck out amid a sea of black in the boys' lower extremities. I wanted to hold up a sign that said, "I packed black socks in his suitcase, I promise!" but it didn't matter, because when the music began I was no longer paying attention to his feet, focusing instead on my son's face. I couldn't decide what surprised me more—the quality of the singing or the expression around his eyes and his mouth. On the former, the boys sounded unlike any children's choir that I'd ever heard before in church or in school. I was astounded at the quality of the music that these boys were able to produce after just five days of rehearsal. The notes were clear and crisp, all the "t's" and "ck's" annunciated with precision, the group perfectly on pitch with every single boy staring straight at the director and focused on his every cue. But more than that, my son—*my son!!*—was positively beaming. His eyes were full of life and his chin held so high that it seemed his entire body was powered by joy. I found myself wondering how he was able to sing while he smiled so widely, so full of emotion and expression.

His father noticed it too and seemed willing to admit, at least tentatively, that I had been right about all of this.

"I've never seen his face look like that before," he said plainly.

The display of emotion that we saw on Haydon's face that day *was* unusual—not just for him, but for many boys in general. One of the earliest lessons that boys in our culture learn is that showing certain emotions can be risky—especially those that can make them feel vulnerable, like uninhibited joy. Boys learn what is and isn't off-limits earlier than we might think. In fact, Stanford psychologist Judy Chu finds that these lessons seep into boys' lives in early childhood, even before they start kindergarten.[5] Over a year spent observing children in one preschool class in a middle-class, suburban community, Chu found that four- and five-year-old boys began to distance themselves from the unguarded emotions they had previously displayed without self-consciousness. Chu emphasizes that it's not so much that the boys forgot how to be connected, empathetic, and vulnerable with each other as that they began to realize that there was a social cost to displaying those qualities in public. The more authentic and engaged relationships that she observed among the boys at the start of their prekindergarten year became more performative as the year went on, and thus, she suggests, more *in*attentive, *in*articulate, and *in*authentic.

One particular lesson that the boys learned was that being masculine meant *not* doing or valuing the things that were associated with girls and women. This was best illustrated by a group that the boys themselves called the Mean Team, an informal social construction that existed primarily to bother other children, especially girls, and disrupt their play in ways that were generally harmless, but still annoying. The Mean Team allowed only boys to be members and threatened boys with being "fired" from the team if they abandoned its goals. A boy who was "fired" would be forced to be on the Nice Team, which in practice meant playing with the girls and being cut off from the other boys. Chu is careful to show how this behavior wasn't exactly antisocial; in fact, the Mean Team offered boys a way of feeling a part of the group, even though the price of membership was behaving in ways that individual boys could find emotionally constraining. As she writes, "It was primarily through and within their interpersonal relationships that messages about masculinity and pressures to conform to masculine norms were introduced, reinforced, incorporated, and perpetuated in ways that became personally meaningful and directly consequential to these boys."[6] Even though the Mean Team was partly about exercising power, it was also something that offered the boys connection with each other in the larger social organization of a mixed-gender classroom.

Chu's findings echo those of other researchers who have studied the performance of masculinity, particularly among older boys and men. For instance, C. J. Pascoe's study of boys at an American high school shows how boys (and some girls) consistently perform masculinity by enacting dominance over one another. At the center of these performances is what Pascoe calls "fag discourse," in which boys use this epithet to shame, criticize, and demean each other. What's interesting is that boys don't use this word to refer to other boys who are actually gay but deploy it instead as an insult whenever a member of the group shows weakness, displays vulnerability, or otherwise fails to live up to masculine ideals.[7] Just like being "fired" from the Mean Team in preschool, the consequences of not being masculine enough for older boys can mean being too feminine, and therefore not "one of the guys."

If being masculine is that which is *not* feminine, then a significant part of the difference between these two extremes has to do with the regulation of emotion—or more precisely, the contexts in which certain emotions can be expressed publicly. Of course, all human beings can feel and exhibit emotion, but the ideals of masculinity and femininity can limit the emotions that our society views as acceptable expressions based on one's gender. For example, emotions that communicate a desire for power, like anger and aggression, generally provoke more positive receptions when they are exhibited by men than by women. On the other hand, men who express emotions that convey vulnerability—sadness, fear, even love—may be met with disapproval or, worse, ridicule.

It's tempting to conclude that boys and men simply aren't good at this kind of emotional expression or that these are natural outcomes of biological differences. The truth, of course, is more complicated. For starters, our expectations about how boys typically behave means that we often ignore the moments when boys *do* show their emotions, like Haydon did in the choir performance, which means that we forgo opportunities to encourage this kind of emotional expression in childhood and adolescence.[8] Psychologist Niobe Way, who studies adolescent boys and their friendships, also emphasizes the negative role of "our cultural equation of emotional vulnerability with being gay and girlish" along with our larger "fear of making our boys into girls or gay."[9] Way notes that in a partially gender-integrated society such as ours—where women and men socialize freely, but where homosexuality is often still stigmatized—many men feel compelled to demonstrate their masculine credentials, for fear of being misgendered or having their sexual orientation misunderstood. Yet her research with adolescent boys repeatedly shows how much they still express desire for close connection and emotionally rich friendships— as she says, "wanting the very thing that we assume they don't want or need naturally."[10]

We all pay a high price for dismissing the emotional needs of boys and men. The emotional constraints of masculinity can mean alienating teachers in elementary school and avoiding close friendships with women as they become teenagers. Male adolescents, and later men, who endorse more stereotypically masculine modes of thinking also report higher levels of depression and more frequently say they use drugs, alcohol, and tobacco. Not only are these attitudes also associated with higher levels of misogyny (since so much of what it means to be "masculine" means denigrating anything "feminine"), these stereotypical constructions of masculinity are bad for boys' and men's emotional and physical health.[11]

One model for reforming these damaging cultural constructions is what sociologist Eric Anderson calls "inclusive masculinity."[12] Inclusive masculinity proposes an alternative to the concept of hegemonic masculinity—the toxic notion that views the most desirable presentation of a "real man" as someone who is physically competitive, heterosexually dominant, emotionally detached, and misogynistic.[13] Social and cultural theorists have long proposed that homophobia is a central part of what perpetuates this ideal since hegemonic masculinity defines any deviations from this norm as culturally deficient.[14] But Anderson offers the hopeful prediction that in settings where homophobia begins to decline, boys and men won't worry so much about reassuring each other that they aren't gay.[15] This makes it more possible for men to express and embody other forms of masculinity that don't rely upon this exclusively heterosexual, patriarchal manifestation of manhood. Instead, men can be more comfortable being open and expressive with each other—qualities coded as "feminine"—and because the group can't sanction this behavior as trending "gay," hegemonic masculinity loses some of its power. Not only do close relationships between men begin to form, but men can also create nonsexualized close relationships with women. Anderson even goes so far as to argue that this movement is one that could potentially topple a binary system of gender altogether and, with it, the patriarchy.

Anderson's vision may be overly optimistic for many reasons, one of which is the persistent backlash that these ideas still invite. Encouraging men to be more emotionally expressive is not always a welcome project;

recent conflicts over teaching things like social-emotional learning in public schools illustrate how these initiatives can activate much deeper fears about dismantling various forms of privilege.[16] This echoes other, ongoing debates about how schools and parents shape children's views of themselves and their gender; by their very existence, these controversies acknowledge that much of how we learn about gender comes not just from our parents but also from institutions and how we learn to act within them. This is why sociologists take pains to emphasize that gender is not something we *accomplish* but something we *continually do*—often at the risk of being sanctioned when we do it in ways that others consider inadequate or even subversive.[17] Whether in a preschool classroom, on a stage in the school musical, on a sports field, or in a locker room, we are often performing what we think our gender means as well as what we think other people want or expect to see. And like all performances, things vary depending on the location of the stage and the composition of the audience.

When we think about boy choirs in this kind of larger, sociological context, they turn out to be a unique place in which to think about the performance of gender.[18] To begin with, boys who sing are doing something gender-transgressive by defying conventional expectations of how boys should behave. Singing itself is something that makes one vulnerable—after all, it requires using the body to communicate artistic and emotional expression in front of others, which may be one of the main reasons for the persistent social stereotype that boys who are drawn to the arts are more likely to be gay. In addition, singing in a treble voice means that boy choristers sound like girls or women, which is another reason this kind of performance could potentially be seen as emasculating for boys and young men. But even so, there's something about the all-male composition of a boy choir that changes the meaning of the performance; in my son's case, the most striking transformation was how it made him willing and able to express his feelings in ways that looked very different from his experiences with music in a mixed-gender setting. And perhaps without the pressure to distinguish himself as a "real boy," the behavioral problems that he sometimes displayed at school had seemed to evaporate, too.

There are also plenty of reasons to think that boys would feel more pressured to perform masculinity when they're around girls, where the assumed backdrop of heterosexuality can pressure both boys and girls to play up the behaviors they assume would be attractive to the opposite sex. For instance, when Haydon was practicing for the NCC, and being expected to miss recess to sing with girls, he was being asked to perform his gender in a particular way: as a lone boy singing in a treble voice and alongside other girls, one of whom I suspected was the object of a full-blown crush. The fact that the rehearsal was being led by a woman probably didn't add to his enthusiasm for the activity, which almost certainly made him feel emasculated in front of a romantic target and also excluded him from what the boys were doing at the same time during their recess period. It's as if the Mean Team and the Nice Team from Chu's preschool classroom study had been reconstituted into the kids who play kickball at recess (the boys) and the kids who stay inside to practice singing (the girls, who now included Haydon). In retrospect, it's no surprise that he didn't want to participate—he wanted desperately to be seen as a boy, a boundary that the group's focus and composition had blurred.

Things might have felt quite different to Haydon, however, when the singing happened just among boys, as with the American Boychoir School summer camp. Not only is the activity one that is made prestigious through the required audition, but there were hardly any girls or women to be found there—once the mothers had gone, that is. The two choral directors were men, the accompanist was a man, and the camp counselors were all former alums of the American Boychoir School (also all teenaged boys or young men). And only boys were in the choir, which meant that there just weren't many opportunities for the boys to end up feeling like girls or to compare their actions or expressions so explicitly to norms of femininity. Something about the all-boy composition of the program meant that the boys were better able to set aside a fear of appearing feminine—or at least, not masculine—and instead felt more comfortable showing their emotions.

Of course, it's also undeniable that putting a bunch of boys and men in one place doesn't always produce healthy forms of vulnerability and emotional expression. We need only look at the stories about fraternity hazing and sexual assault on college campuses for abundant evidence to the contrary. Locker rooms and fraternity houses are, unfortunately, places where some of the most misogynistic and sexually abusive forms of discourse and practice unfold.[19] Not surprisingly, all-male spaces like these are often places where heterosexuality is assumed, and where girls and women are tacitly understood to be objects of sexual conquest. But groups like boy choirs could represent something different—a chance for boys to be together and just be boys, whether straight or gay or simply too young to even be thinking about their sexual orientation. In settings where boys can escape or transcend concerns about sexuality, they might be able to more freely expand their ideas about what masculinity means.

This is one reason that educators have long pointed to the benefits of same-sex schooling, especially for boys. Without the need to impress girls on a daily basis or worry about being aligned with girls socially, boys in these environments may feel more at ease participating in activities like music and drama, which would otherwise be seen as feminine pursuits.[20] Choral directors often reiterate this same perspective, insisting that boys between the ages of eleven and fifteen are often too embarrassed to sing in their treble register when girls are around because it showcases their emotional vulnerability through the expressive act of soprano-range singing, something that is seen as feminine and therefore potentially emasculating. Establishing boy-only choral groups helps create an environment in which boys can do things that might otherwise prompt teasing and ridicule from their peers. Within these male-only spaces, they argue, preteen and adolescent boys can learn to display emotion freely and be at ease with other boys who, together, are not conforming to the societal pressures of traditional masculinity.

Opportunities to celebrate these more feminine components of boyhood are few and far between in our society—and in fact, they are often virulently opposed. Incorporating feminine impulses into masculine identities is more complicated than importing masculinity into stereotypically feminine forms of expression. There's no clear male equivalent of the "tomboy," for instance—a generally positive archetype that celebrates masculine impulses in girlhood.[21] Part of what makes the tomboy socially acceptable is how this archetype uses key features of masculinity to demonstrate power—for instance, to dominate other girls or to gain access to male groups where other girls remain excluded.[22] At the same time, boys who express more feminine characteristics during their boyhoods may be seen as actually giving up power, choosing instead to forgo masculine dominance.

Together, these may be good reasons to think that boys need a particular kind of space in which to embody and express these impulses, one that draws the boundaries slightly differently than the safe spaces that are usually conceived as a resource for people claiming identities that have been historically marginalized, such as women, sexual minorities, or people of color. The backlash against this notion tends to call for an equivalent arena of protection for the mostly white, heterosexual, cisgender men who protest that they now feel under assault as aggressors and demand a place to air their sense of grievance and perceived persecution. Instead, a safe space for the feminine aspects of boyhood would represent something very different—an expansive arena in which ideas about what it means to be masculine might be imbued with new and broader meanings. Raising emotionally attuned boys requires reassuring them that they can both identify as boys *and* do things that our society has coded as feminine. This requires not that boys claim victimhood for their male identity, but rather that we as a society pay careful attention to how hegemonic masculinity can wound and cripple boys, too. In the process, we could create not just better boys and men, but better humans.

Boy choir directors have another reason to insist that boys should sing separately from girls in early adolescence: many believe that the voices of boys and girls are simply biologically different. In fact, the choral world distinguishes between boys and girls in their childhood years; boys who can still access soprano and alto notes have a special name—"unchanged trebles"—a term that emphasizes the fleeting nature of their soprano voices. Many choir directors insist that the physical changes that boys experience in early puberty create a unique vocal sound by age twelve or thirteen—when boy choristers have enough musical training to have good vocal control but can still access their treble notes with the added power and breath support that comes with their growing, adolescent bodies. In fact, conventional wisdom suggests that the voice of an unchanged treble is *most* beautiful right before the change—as journalist Elizabeth Weil has written, like flowers at the peak of their bloom.[23] This is, in essence, a biological argument for keeping boys' singing segregated from girls'—there's something unique about their adolescent vocal development that comes from having XY chromosomes.

As a mother and audience member, I don't need much convincing to agree that the voices of unchanged trebles are something special. But as a sociologist, I tend to view the reasons that are offered for gender segregation with a healthy dose of skepticism, since these justifications typically have a way of perpetuating men's privilege.[24] This is the kind of argument made most publicly by English soprano Lesley Garrett, an outspoken critic of the British choral school model that has been training boy choristers for centuries. By endorsing a biological argument for sex segregation, Garrett worries, girls do not have equal access to the kind of musical training and high-profile performance opportunities enjoyed by boys-only organizations with longer histories and established positions of prestige.[25] In 2018, Garrett publicly challenged the new director of music at King's

College Cambridge to start including girls.[26] Anticipating the yearly broadcast of "Lessons and Carols" on Christmas Eve and hearing a boy sing the first verse of "Once in Royal David's City," Garrett told *Radio Times*, "I will certainly be watching the BBC's broadcast because this is an occasion I wouldn't miss. But I'll also be wondering to myself this year, as I do every year: where are the girls? Girls' voices are just as pure, just as sweet and just as sonorous."[27]

These biological arguments also raise important questions about how boy-only choirs might alternately create or deny gender-affirming experiences for trans young people. Sociologist Tey Meadow's study of trans children and their families finds that organizations like these can play a key role in supporting both the social and psychological aspects of individual gender transitions, which are legitimized when institutions like schools and recreational groups officially recognize a child's decision to live and identify with a gender category that falls outside of the biological sex assigned to them at birth.[28] But would boy choirs be keen to welcome singers born female who wanted to live and identify as boys? Or would they present yet another obstacle to inclusion, particularly if they insisted that the voices of children born male were biologically distinct and, by extension, superior? These questions also offer a different way of thinking about the issues at stake in similar conversations about trans athletes, which generally worry about protecting females from being disadvantaged in contests against participants who were born male.

As I continued to reflect on Haydon's experience with the American Boychoir School, it still wasn't clear to me where all-male organizations like these should fall in a society that was simultaneously pursuing gender inclusion while also increasingly worried about the negative effects of toxic masculinity. Were boys-only choirs training grounds for future gender-based entitlement, or heralds of a new, more expressive form of masculinity? Were these groups doing something revolutionary, or just perpetuating long-standing forms of privilege and hierarchy? And what could they tell us about any potential role for same-gender groups in a society pursuing gender equality?

One of the final songs on the program at the ABS summer concert was an arrangement of an upbeat number called "Feel Good" by gospel composers Craig Scott and Leonard Tyson. It began with a jazzy piano riff interspersed with claps from the singers, the lyrics proclaiming, "There's joy down in my soul, I can't explain. I gotta tell everybody, I feel good!" Weeks later, I still couldn't forget how my son had looked as he sang those words. It was as if he was actually feeling joy that simply couldn't be contained any longer, radiating into his face, his eyes, and even his hands as they clapped at the appropriate moments. This performance was so different from what I usually saw from my son, whose attitude toward music at school was more often studied disengagement and whose most vocal emotional displays came when he was playing video games. Something about it felt like a buried treasure that we'd stumbled upon by accident and was now waiting to be fully unearthed.

"I want to find a way to keep him singing," I said to Ellen later that summer. "But I'm not sure if it's the right thing to do."

Ellen is a very practical person, which meant that she was slightly less concerned about the ethical dimensions of this dilemma. She reminded me that there are plenty of boys who play sports, but not so many who sing in boy choirs. "Maybe you can keep him in it until he applies to college," she suggested matter-of-factly, no doubt imagining the potential to impress college admissions officers with a memorable hook.

I had to admit that this might be true, but mainly I was thrilled that he'd had such an amazing musical experience and wanted Haydon to be able to continue singing for as long as he would remain an unchanged treble. I started to wonder if we could find other opportunities for him to sing alongside other boys, especially if it meant that he might become more consistently comfortable showing his emotions.

But as a feminist, I wasn't sure if this would make me part of the solution or part of the problem. Would I just be shoring up the patriarchy by enrolling my male child in an all-male organization? Or would I be dismantling some of it if what he learned there was about a different, more inclusive way to be a man?

I knew that I wasn't sure of the answers. But as a sociologist, I also knew that I had tools at my disposal to get to the bottom of these questions—or at least to begin to sketch out more complicated answers than "yes" or "no."

Couldn't I do both—be a mother and a researcher, both participant and observer? I wasn't exactly sure what I would find, but I knew that I could ask the right questions. And as a mother, I knew what I wanted, partly for him, and definitely for me:

I wanted to keep him singing.

CHAPTER 2

It's Like a Finishing School for Boys

A few months later, Haydon and I stood outside the offices of the Philadelphia Boys Choir and Chorale, waiting to enter for an audition. It's one of the country's most prestigious boy choirs, with their trademark red jackets a well-known symbol of Philadelphia pride. We'd heard a boy from the choir sing at our church a few months before that—he'd sung the boy soprano part in Mendelssohn's *Elijah* with the church choir—and his bright red jacket was almost as memorable as his pristine treble voice. So when I started to cast around for an opportunity for Haydon to join a community boy choir, the PBC quickly jumped to the top of the list. Their long-standing reputation as a cultural institution in Philadelphia meant that they regularly performed with the city's other arts organizations and sang the national anthem with the city's professional sports teams. Although he wasn't exactly begging me to find him an opportunity to keep singing in a community choir, Haydon seemed open to the idea, with two conditions: the choir had to be good, and it had to be all boys.

For my part, this visit was an attempt to regain the joy we saw at the American Boychoir School summer camp, to keep it going for another year or two—three if we were really lucky. Haydon was about to turn twelve, and so we didn't know how much time he had left in that pristine treble register. A sense of urgency, of time's fleetingness, of the inevitability of the Change animates the world of boy choirs throughout. "Mother Nature has them by the throat," they say—as if somewhere there lurked an all-powerful, maternal figure whose goal was to institute a kind of reverse castration on these boys' vocal folds, disemboweling their pure, treble notes and replacing them with the hoarse and honking register of adolescence. Nature's unknowable deadline animated this errand with even more urgency than was typical for a hypercontrolling parent like me.

The entryway to one of the city's most celebrated cultural institutions turned out to be a relatively nondescript glass storefront nestled between other unmemorable buildings on the edge of Philadelphia's bustling downtown. We opened the door and walked inside to a small, open waiting area flanked on one side by a rehearsal room and on the other by a lounge full of tables. Most of the space was decidedly unremarkable, but the walls of the foyer provided plenty to look at—large, poster-sized pictures of boys in white pants and red jackets posing in uniformed splendor with famous people or in particularly striking settings: on the set of *Good Morning America*, with Christmas lights glittering in the background; in the Galapagos Islands, accompanied by an enormous tortoise; outside of the Acropolis; standing around Barack Obama.

Haydon and I pondered these photos in silence for a moment, until Jeff Smith, the choir's artistic director, emerged from an office down the hall and strode over quickly to introduce himself. "So, you must be Haydon," he said, offering his hand to my son. "You're the one who was just at the American Boychoir School summer camp, is that right?" Haydon nodded, with a ready smile. Smith explained that he would take Haydon in for a quick audition and that I was free to have a seat in the parents' lounge. It occurred to me that aside from his brief solo in the school musical and the phone audition for the ABS summer camp, I've not heard Haydon sing by himself all that much, and I was a bit disappointed that I couldn't sit in on the audition as its lone audience member. Haydon disappeared with Smith while I found myself a chair, listening to the faint sounds of a distant piano moving through a series of chord progressions, inching up into the very top of the soprano register as a woman sang through a set of scales.

After a bit, Haydon and Smith returned, and Smith settled into a chair across from where I was sitting at one of the tables. It occurred to me then that the singing I'd been hearing had stopped, and I put the pieces together. "Was that you singing down the hall just now?" I asked Haydon. "I assumed there was a woman having a voice lesson somewhere else in this building."

Haydon beamed in response, while Smith laughed and dropped a stack of photocopied music onto the table that sat between us. "He can go straight into the concert choir," Smith said, adding that there are plenty of boys who can sing as high as Haydon, but that they're often just reluctant to do so.

"He wouldn't need to do the trainer choir first, like your website says? Why not?" I asked. My brief experience in the world of boy choirs had already taught me a few things, one of which is that regardless of size, boy choirs almost always require singers to enter through a training or preparatory choir in which they learn fundamental musical skills, like matching pitch and watching the conductor. Entry into the top choir for unchanged voices—the one that would perform on tour, for instance—typically requires that boys spend at least a few months on the farm team.

"Well, he has a very good ear," Smith explained. "And then there's also his age—he's almost twelve. We don't know how much time he has. It could just be months, or perhaps just this coming year. The older boys also tend to have a bit more maturity, and so they don't always need the training and socialization that comes from being in the training choir."

There was a great deal to think about with this offer. There would definitely be opportunities to sing with the Philadelphia Ballet—twenty-six performances of the *Nutcracker*, to be exact—the Philadelphia Orchestra, the Philadelphia Pops, and of course all those international tours that the photographs on the walls document. But there was also the stack of music on the table in front of us—Haydon would need to learn all of this repertoire independently and commit it to memory so that he could earn his spot in the choir. Smith assured us that there were listening tracks available and added that there was a day camp later in August during which some of the newer boys would be getting together to go over some of the music. This was an option, too—although it came with a price tag of several hundred dollars. And then there was the cost of being in the choir—that would be about twelve hundred dollars for the year, and the cost of the tours would be additional, to the tune of thousands more dollars. The rehearsals would be twice a week, Wednesdays and Saturdays, in downtown Philadelphia. This would mean a solid hour or more of driving each way from where we live, a leafy exurb that is far closer to New Jersey than any corner of Philadelphia.

The sheer enormity of the logistical operation that would be required to get him to rehearsals and performances immediately gave me pause. Smith assured me that families carpool but cautioned that he wasn't sure there were currently any choristers living near us. It was inspiring to discover that there were other families who had found their way into this strange new world, but apparently our ability to pull this off would depend on at least some of them living nearby. We left the audition without making a commitment—I promised to do some more research, give it some thought, and be back in touch within a week.

The Philadelphia Boys Choir is not unusual in this irony—being a boy choir named for a city that now draws many of its choristers from the surrounding suburbs, with boys driven into the city by beleaguered parents who have just gotten home from work (sometimes from those same urban centers of business and commerce). Like other city boy choirs founded midcentury, the Philadelphia Boys Choir had early roots in the Philadelphia Public School system, as what was then called the All Philadelphia Elementary School Boys Choir.[1] A *Philadelphia Inquirer* story from 1968 celebrated the young group's achievements just as a select group drawn from the three hundred boys in the choir—sixty boys known as the Ensemble—prepared to represent the city in a trip abroad to Wales "to show the people of that melodic country how youngsters do it here."[2] Two years later they were off to Moscow, and the *Philadelphia Tribune* declared the group "a Philadelphia institution" with a broad range of choristers that exemplified the city's religious and ethnic diversity. The boys in the red jackets were also portrayed as good American boys with impeccable patriotism: "Besides talented, they are mature, dedicated, personable and proud—proud to be Philadelphians and proud to be Americans." And if there were any doubts about their masculinity, readers were reassured that "most of the youngsters are regular participants on Little League teams and members of the Boy Scouts of America."[3] By the late 1980s the Philadelphia Boys Choir became the first American ensemble to sing in East Berlin, where they shared the stage with the Moscow Boys Choir, an accomplishment that earned them coverage in a local documentary.[4] By the end of the century, the choir had toured in more than forty countries—including Australia, South Africa, and a U.S.-sanctioned goodwill visit to Cuba. As they prepared to head to Havana in the spring of 1999, the Philadelphia institution known as "America's Ambassadors of Song" brought with them ninety baseball gloves donated from across the city along with 120 baseballs autographed by the Phillies.[5]

My friend Ellen was right to point out that the boys who sing in choirs are few and far between, especially compared to the portion of boys who participate in youth sports. American families' commitment to the arts lags far behind athletics; a 2015 Pew Research Center report found that 73 percent of families said their school-age kids were involved in athletics, while just over half reported that their kids had taken any music, art, or dance lessons.[6] And boys are overrepresented in sports relative to girls; in 2021 the Aspen Institute estimated that 45 percent of male children between the ages of thirteen and seventeen played a sport on a regular, organized basis, compared to 37 percent of female children of the same age.[7] The pressure to pursue athletics is particularly pronounced for boys, since sports have long played a role assuaging the societal anxieties that surround boys' journeys into manhood, beginning with the sports craze that gripped Americans at the turn of the twentieth century, with sports like tennis, golf, boxing—and of course baseball—gaining new and widespread fandom.[8] These pastimes promised boys benefits like physical fitness, self-control, and teamwork as they assumed the mantle of masculinity. "In short," one scholar writes of athletics during this time period, "sports made boys into men."[9] Although the motivations that drive boys to athletics are different now—for instance, the idea that sports are one way to develop a healthy, well-rounded child, regardless of gender—the pressure that boys still feel to prove their masculinity through athletics persists.[10]

There are other reasons that kids, especially boys, aren't likely to sing in choirs during childhood and adolescence. The traditional avenues that led boys to choral singing generations ago—expansive public school music programs during the week, religious attendance and church choirs on weekends—have declined in the decades since organizations like the Philadelphia Boys Choir were founded. Fears about kids' safety don't help, either; just weeks after Haydon's choral audition in Philadelphia we learned that the American Boychoir School would close its doors after eighty years, due in part to the financial consequences of litigating sexual abuse lawsuits. Add to that a once-in-a-century pandemic that made group singing a public health risk, and these groups are in a place of serious vulnerability today.

Given these challenges, it's astounding that boy choirs persist at all.

And yet my son and I were learning that boy choirs still carry a cultural and regional imprimatur that makes at least some parents willing to get back into the car after their evening commute—the performances with the Philadelphia Ballet, a chance to sing "America the Beautiful" at the Phillies' opening day, an invitation to greet the Pope in song—these are opportunities that don't come with athletics, regardless of the prestige that accompanies a club sports team. Travel soccer doesn't qualify you to join the welcome wagon that represents your city at a head of state's visit. For the small number of boys and families who commit to this intensive activity, boy choirs promise them elite access to localized cultural prestige, the chance to represent their city or state at local and even national venues of performance. Even though they're constantly teetering on the edge of extinction, community boy choirs offer a rare form of communal cultural status that's different from what kids can get from sports.

We would also go on to learn something else: that even as they embody a local place of pride, boy choirs are also propagating a new vision of masculinity that conveys the same values that were promised by sports in the early twentieth century, such as self-control, character, teamwork, and leadership. The celebration of these civilized, genteel virtues intersects with a forward-looking understanding of what it means to be twenty-first-century men—one that looks quite different from the sometimes aggressive, win-at-all-costs model of masculinity that can permeate youth sports, especially for boys. Although it unfolds in an all-male setting steeped in tradition, the new masculinity that boy choirs endorse teaches boys to embrace empathy, vulnerability, and the ability to show emotion in public. Though rooted in the past, boy choirs seek to build men for the future.

Most of the American boy choirs that are still in existence were founded between the middle of the twentieth century and the 1970s. These are the choirs with names we can easily place and locate—the Texas Boys Choir (1946), the Phoenix Boys Choir (1947), the San Francisco Boys Chorus (1948), the Minnesota Boychoir (1962), the Cincinnati Boychoir (1965), and Florida's Singing Sons (1975), to name a few. The Tucson Boys Chorus in Arizona is among the oldest, founded in 1939 by Eduardo Caso, an English tenor who, as the chorus's website boasts, "carried to the West the dream of a boys choir rooted in the European tradition but uniquely American in sound and repertoire."[11] True to form, the Tucson Boys Chorus continues to celebrate its connection to the American West, with a performance set that involves the boys donning cowboy hats and executing roping tricks. Their distinctive flair for representing their city and state once earned them an invitation to the White House for its annual Christmas tree lighting ceremony.

The local cultural capital that boy choirs wield—along with the promise of prestigious travel to represent their city on tour—is one reason that they still manage to attract singers. Even though parents may ultimately be the ones won over by these benefits, recruitment is frequently initiated by networks of school music teachers who are aware of the local boy choir and eager to refer boys with promising voices for these opportunities. Unlike sports, where a parent may have had a youth sports experience that they want to re-create or enjoy along with their child, a boy's musical ability often presents itself as something completely distinct from a parent's interests or accomplishments. Although some boy choir parents are musicians who consciously seek out these experiences for their sons, many boys in choirs have found their way there through happenstance, like we did—an encouraging school music teacher or perhaps a referral from a friend or neighbor. Finding out about a boy's aptitude for music can feel like a special discovery of talent by an outside, neutral authenticator—yet another contrast with kids' sports, which many parents approach as a compulsory rite of passage in contemporary American childhood. Middle-class parents increasingly assume that their evenings and weekends will be spent shuffling kids to fields and courts in the hopes that their offspring will reveal an affinity for a particular sport, and even if they don't, parents convince themselves that the life lessons promised by recreational athletics justify this investment.[12]

But music is different. This is partly because the skills that suggest that a child might be a good singer are ones that do often exist naturally, without any adult intervention. This isn't to say that athletic talent doesn't present itself automatically—obviously, it does—but I suspect that kids' sports are simply so widespread that there's a language of practice and effort that legitimizes athletic activity and reassures the slow and uncoordinated (or at least their parents) that with enough practice, they too can become proficient athletes. In contrast, we tend to think of musical ability as something that comes as a natural gift, that can't necessarily be learned or developed. Although a training choir will often accept any interested boy who can carry a tune, elite performing choirs are looking for boys whose natural abilities are already well developed—boys who can hear harmonies easily and match pitch on the first try. Boys who are recommended for a choir don't even need to be able to read formal musical notation—particularly since choirs are ideally recruiting younger boys who are eight or nine years old, directors know that with time and training they'll be able to teach boys the precise skills they'll need to know in order to sing and perform at a very high level.

Choir directors also look to fill their risers through other local social networks, as in when existing choristers are encouraged to bring a friend to rehearsal or parents are asked to post fliers or invite neighbors to a concert. This means that the boys who are recruited for boy choirs aren't necessarily the boys who enjoy choir at school, either. One director of a chorus in the Northeast told me that the boys in her group often prefer the boy choir over their school music programs (something that didn't surprise me, based on my own son's experience). But she was also quick to dispel the notion that they were being bullied at school for liking music. "I think it's more so that they want that challenge," she explained, adding, "They're looking for something more. And I think that they feel really comfortable being around people who love it as much as they do." Daniel Bates, director of the Fort Lauderdale–based Florida Singing Sons, said that the boys who are recommended for his group by school music teachers find that they enjoy being part of an ensemble in which other boys have the same high level of interest in singing that they do. Ironically, the boys who primarily want to be soloists don't always stay in choirs; they are often more likely to join the drama club and explore musical theater. The boys who find their niche in choirs are looking to blend in—all the more reason that they are often discovered by someone else.

A recruitment system that relies heavily on these strategies is one reason that these groups often struggle to maintain racial and economic diversity. In 2021 I spoke with Jason Alexander Holmes, then-director of the Cincinnati Boychoir, who explained that much like the Philadelphia Boys Choir his group was founded as an extension of the Cincinnati public schools in the mid-sixties, with a membership composed of three boys from each elementary school in the city. Then called the Cincinnati All-City Boys Chorus, the group also accessed rehearsal space from the Cincinnati school district.[13] Holmes noted that the group was much more diverse during that time period since it intentionally recruited from all schools in the city. However, in the late 1970s a tax levy failed and the group lost its district support and had to be reorganized as a private nonprofit. The shift to nonprofit status also included a tuition requirement and made the choir open to boys outside of the Cincinnati city limits. Holmes said that the significance of this change is best chronicled through the choir's photographic archives: "When I look at pictures from that time, it's like, 'Whoa, it went from being a diverse array of children' to 'It's really white.'" The group has continued to make racial and ethnic diversity a priority in recruitment; Holmes sees this as particularly important given the choir's history and its claim to represent the city. In recent years the choir has had some notable success in achieving a level of racial representation that approximates the greater Cincinnati area's demographics. But Holmes admitted that representation from the city of Cincinnati—where the group's rehearsal space is actually located—is still lacking. This means that the group can appear diverse "if you're looking at race only in terms of color of skin," even though the boys in the choir disproportionately come from the city's suburbs.

As a result of this kind of networks-based recruiting, Holmes observed that the Cincinnati Boychoir overrepresents the schools and districts that have particularly strong music programs—schools that fall mostly in the suburbs. One suburban district, in particular, was so large that it had a dedicated music teacher for third grade who sent the recruitment materials home with dozens of boys. In contrast, some of the schools in Cincinnati proper might have music only every other week, which makes it more difficult for teachers to identify boys with an aptitude for choir and more difficult for children to recognize their own interest in singing.

As with so many things that are distinctly American, boy choirs embody the enduring patterns of residential segregation that convey the legacy of the white flight of the 1970s. The inordinate amounts of time spent in the car driving to rehearsals and performances are a direct result of the racialized patterns of development and construction that are distinctly American in character. I live in a quiet suburb that promised good schools and easy access to the major arteries required to access the cultural institutions associated with a major city. And all the while, the children who live near those cultural institutions—who in Philadelphia, like many major urban centers, are mostly Black—are underrepresented within them.

The group's origins aside, the sheer enormity of the transportation problem was enough to stall our developing relationship with the Philadelphia Boys Choir. As many different ways as I tried to imagine how we could get Haydon to rehearsals, I came to the same conclusion: this would push us over the edge. Not only did his father and I both work full-time, but we already had a full slate of after-school and weekend activities—there was basketball in the winter, lacrosse in the spring, piano lessons on Tuesdays, and church on Sundays. Haydon's younger sister had a similar array of commitments, although she had recently given up the piano in favor of the double bass. Like so many modern American families, we moved to this place exclusively for our jobs, which meant that we didn't have an extensive network of family members nearby who could help transport children to those commitments or occasionally come by the house to put a lasagna in the oven so that there would be something to eat when we all got home.

But around this time, a knowledgeable contact suggested to me that we look at a different boy choir in the Philadelphia area, one called the Keystone State Boychoir, or KSB for short. It was slightly closer to us—in Northwest Philadelphia—which meant that the drive would only be about

45 minutes each way, without traffic. I'd never heard of it, but it was actually just as big as the Philadelphia Boys Choir, with around two hundred boys ages eight to eighteen (like many groups, KSB encouraged boys with changed voices to keep singing in an ensemble composed of boys in high school). It was a younger, upstart challenger to the decades-old Philadelphia Boys Choir. Not surprisingly, both choirs had distinctive, if coincidental, ways to underline their connection to the city's professional sports teams. While the Philadelphia Boys Choir wore trademark red blazers and white pants (the same colors as the Phillies), the KSB boys' jackets were the same dark green as the Philadelphia Eagles.

In fact, KSB's cofounders, Joseph Fitzmartin and Steve Fisher, were both employed by the Philadelphia Boys Choir when they decided to leave it with the explicit goal of founding a choir that approached its training somewhat differently. At the time of the cofounding, Fitzmartin (affectionately known as "Mr. Fitz") had been the associate director of the Philadelphia Boys Choir for twenty-one years, a tenure that allowed him time to both conduct and compose for the group. The composition work, in particular, was one of the highlights of the job; as Mr. Fitz told me, "It was one of the finest choirs in the city giving me carte blanche to write anything I wanted, for any instrumentation, and have it performed. And then it would be taken on tour—it was beyond belief!" Fisher, then a young and idealistic recent college graduate, joined him as another associate director for the last eight years of that tenure, and the two men became fast friends through their shared work as associate directors.

Among the things they shared were growing personal and professional differences with the choir's longtime director, Bob Hamilton. On this point, Fisher liked to tell a story about how Hamilton once reprimanded then-chorister Benj Pasek for "sticking out" with his enthusiastic, emotional expression while singing. (Pasek would go on to become an award-winning songwriter with credits like *Dear Evan Hansen*, *La La Land*, and *The Greatest Showman*.) Fisher and Fitzmartin were becoming increasingly aligned in their conviction that the boys should be encouraged to sing with emotion, something that the PBC had generally discouraged. In fact, the Philadelphia Boys Choir had long embraced a physical posture that made it difficult for its choristers to use their bodies while singing—standing still with their fingers locked behind their backs. Although this created a uniform look throughout the choir, it also kept the boys from showing an embodied connection to the music or lyrics of a song that they were performing.

Fitzmartin believes that the ability to move one's body during singing is a fundamental component of musical expression and that this makes singing different from other kinds of musical performance. "For a singer, your body is your instrument," he explained to me, adding that playing that instrument involves more than just moving one's lips and mouth. Instead, it's a connection that a singer can feel and show using their entire body, something that Mr. Fitz calls "choral-ography." This kind of movement is not rehearsed or prescribed, he clarified, adding that "it's more subjective and informal than that." In his view, boys should just be free to show their feelings with their bodies in ways that are natural expressions of the emotional connections they feel with the music.

This wasn't to say that the Philadelphia Boys Choir never moved while singing—they had some standard songs that involved choreography, Fitzmartin noted—but that he and Fisher wanted the boys to be able to feel moved by the music and to show the feelings that they were experiencing when they performed rather than executing formal motions contrived by someone else. This difference gets to the heart of the kind of openness and vulnerability that the two men wanted to encourage among their choristers. "There is nothing between the performer and the listener for a singer," Fitzmartin emphasized. "There is nothing but your body." This kind of openness and expression was a key goal that they wanted to pursue when the two men decided to found what they called "a different kind of boy choir."

Fisher also wanted more opportunities for the boys to encounter repertoire that at the time would have been called "World Music"—folk songs from South Africa, Islamic chants, other works that fell outside of the

Western canon. He'd spent time on the African continent and was eager to develop some of the things he'd experienced there musically. The two men also wanted more opportunities for boys from underresourced public schools to encounter music education in their community, so they chose to rent space for the choir at a Presbyterian church in Germantown, an older Philadelphia neighborhood that had been majority-Black since the seventies. A 2013 YouTube video captures much of what the two men had hoped to build when they left the Philadelphia Boys Choir in 2001—a medley of South African songs performed a cappella by a diverse group of boys of all ages in a packed church sanctuary. The various songs all have accompanying hand and body motions that the boys embrace with gusto, swaying their entire bodies back and forth to the accompaniment of two djembe drums, played by middle school boys.[14]

The choir and the culture that Fisher and Fitzmartin built in KSB was one that proved remarkably successful—over two decades the choir grew from an idea birthed by two disillusioned Philadelphia Boys Choir directors into a well-organized enterprise that had managed to perform on all seven continents. A sister choir for girls, called the Pennsylvania Girlchoir, was founded a few years later, and the two choirs were governed by one board. One of the highlights of their joint venture was the visit of Pope Francis to Philadelphia in 2015. Both choirs were among the groups invited to sing at the city's Festival of Families when one of KSB's soloists, Bobby Hill, offered an impromptu performance of Andrew Lloyd Webber's "Pie Jesu" when a last-minute set change prevailed upon the choir to fill an empty sixty seconds. Hill's performance went viral, leading to interviews a few days later on *Today*, CNN, and *Fox & Friends*.

By 2016, KSB had five different ensembles, three of which were for boys with soprano voices: A Trainers and Apprentices group for the youngest boys, a Concert Choir, and the Towne Choir, which was the highest level for boys with unchanged voices. Joining both the Concert and Towne Choirs required boys to spend a full semester as candidates, when they would learn and perform (from memory) a common repertoire while also completing a music theory workbook. Boys with changed voices could likewise become members of the Graduate Choir and also had the option of auditioning for an even more exclusive changed-voice Chamber Choir, provided they were willing to commit to additional weekly rehearsals. As with the ensembles for unchanged trebles, the Graduate and Chamber Choirs also required a semester of candidacy that involved learning new repertoire and continuing music theory education.

I first learned all of this in a friendly conversation with KSB's program director, whom I initially spoke with about scheduling an audition for Haydon. She explained that Haydon could come for an audition in late August to join the Concert Choir. Since he was going into sixth grade, he was on the older side for the Concert Choir, which was mostly boys in fourth and fifth grades, but if he made good progress in the spring he might be able to move into the Towne Choir, where there would be more boys his age and where he could sing more challenging music. And while the cost was about the same as the Philadelphia Boys Choir, he wouldn't be expected to learn all of the repertoire on his own. Instead, he would be able to practice the songs with a group of other candidates throughout the semester.

When we came to the church for the audition, she greeted me warmly and took us upstairs to the choir room where Mr. Fitz was performing voice checks with current singers. She also had some encouraging news—another boy from our area was likely joining the choir, which meant that we might be able to form a carpool to get to rehearsals. If he was accepted, Haydon would have a required singer-musicianship session on Wednesdays for ninety minutes and Saturday morning rehearsals that would last anywhere from ninety minutes to three and a half hours, depending on the Saturday. The schedule for the elite Towne Choir was even more rigorous—rehearsals on Wednesday nights for an hour and a half, the same Saturday rehearsals as the Concert Choir, plus a Sunday evening rehearsal twice a month for another ninety minutes while he was a candidate.

I took some notes while the program manager explained these dizzying logistics, along with some of the ceremonial details of the ways that boys progressed through the organization. For all of the freedom conveyed in the boys' emotional expression while singing, the choir itself was highly structured. Some of this discipline even mimicked the military: For starters, boys were distinguished by their rank with differences in uniform. The youngest trainers and apprentices wore only the uniform of black pants, white shirt, green tie, and a green sweater until they were successfully incorporated into the Concert Choir. The other ensembles replaced the sweater with a green jacket, but the boys who were candidates for the Concert Choir were not even allowed to try on a green jacket until they had learned all of their music—almost twenty different pieces, no less—completed their theory requirements, and satisfactorily attended all rehearsals for the semester. Only then were they included in the category of "jacketed trebles." Fisher was fond of repeating the catch phrase, "you can't just yearn it, you have to earn it," of the coveted green jacket, which was awarded to the boys at the group's December holiday concert. Decorative pins affixed to the lapels of the green jackets charted boys' progression in the ranks—a "T" for Towne Choir, a small star for the Graduate Choir. Each year completed with the choir also earned a bar that decorated their lapels; participation in an international tour earned a pin with the country's flag.

As Haydon went in to complete his audition I sat outside the choir room with some of the other parents, who were there for their sons' twice-yearly voice check. I was clearly the only newbie, and they talked with each other in a manner that suggested they'd spent plenty of time chatting while waiting on their boys at rehearsal. They were friendly enough, asking where I lived and where my son went to school. When I said the name of my town one dad said, "Oh, that's far," but then added that his own journey to the church for rehearsals can take up to forty-five minutes each way due to rush hour traffic, even though he lives much closer. And in his opinion, the commitment was worth it: his son had already been on two international tours and recorded a voice track for a major video game. Another mom reassured me that being in the Concert Choir wasn't too overwhelming—there were the rehearsals to think about, but the Concert Choir didn't perform nearly as often as the Towne Choir. "Towne Choir is a little bit insane," she admitted, enumerating the frequency with which they were called to perform. "But I like to remind myself of something another parent told me a few years ago—that this is like a finishing school for boys!"

I asked her what she meant by this, and she was quick to offer a thorough explanation. First of all, there was the simple fact that the boys learned tons of music for performances, much of which was classical in nature—the kind of thing most kids don't get exposed to on their own, unless their parents happen to be avid consumers of classical music or professional musicians themselves. And when the boys weren't singing at performances, they were often sitting through repertoire performed by other ensembles, which meant they were listening to even more music. The tours took them to other continents where they perform in famous cathedrals and toured cultural sites of interest, often singing music that was connected to the place to which they were traveling. Then there were the uniforms, which involved a coat and tie and a shirt tucked in—the kind of clothes my son currently wore only to church, and even then, just on high holy days like Easter. And finally, there was the discipline—they had to sit or stand quietly at rehearsals; all of the adults in charge were addressed as "Mr." or as "Ms.," and when the group was touring or otherwise performing publicly, they were constantly reminded of how their individual behavior reflected on the group, which had high standards for politeness and interpersonal interaction. Learning the music for each step of candidacy—for the Concert Choir, the Towne Choir, and (if they stayed in after the voice change) the Graduate Choir—meant that they had to learn and memorize new repertoire, taking the initiative to do so on their own. And there was one more benefit—no technology was allowed at rehearsals. Phones were not to be found; when the boys had breaks during rehearsal they sat at tables and talked, eating snacks or playing cards or a board game.

I had to admit that the finishing school conversation was what I was still thinking of a few days later when the program manager emailed me to say that Haydon had been offered a spot as a Concert Choir candidate. The idea that my son might spend hours each week learning to stand still, that he would learn musical repertoire spanning both time and place, and that he would do it (at least during performances) while wearing a jacket and a tie and a shirt tucked in seemed infinitely preferable to the ways that he would prefer to spend his time, most of which involved wearing something with an elastic waistband in some form of competition—whether a video game or recreational sports. The boy choir offered both discipline and collaboration. And the idea that he could do this with boys—*just boys*—gave me hope that perhaps he would find some of the civilizing scaffolding that was missing for boys in our day-to-day life, an antidote to the confused picture of masculinity circulating in our current culture—one that eschews toxic masculinity but still struggles to offer boys something identifiable to replace it.

That dreamy vision was enough to persuade me that we could manage the drive, the music, the commitment. KSB would help me mold my son into a man.

I wrote back immediately: we were in.

———

Although KSB professed to be a different kind of boy choir, my conversations with boy choir directors from around the country suggest that many of the innovations that Fisher and Fitzmartin created after they left the Philadelphia Boys Choir are ones that other groups have incorporated too. They don't mention Eric Anderson's concept of "inclusive masculinity," of course, but many of their innovations seem lifted directly out of that playbook. More than anything, they want boys to know that it's okay to be emotionally vulnerable, and these directors repeatedly emphasized how they seek to make their choirs a safe place for boys who aren't stereotypically masculine, including boys who might be gay. At the same time, they also emphasized the importance of discipline, structure, and otherwise traditional expectations for public male civility, like wearing jackets and ties and greeting adults with respect. The twin goals of encouraging both "old-fashioned" discipline and emotional expression are closely intertwined: it's precisely because boy choirs embrace these traditional expressions of masculinity that they can simultaneously endorse things that would otherwise be viewed as feminine. The all-male structure of these groups also provides a protective backdrop—what sociologists would call "border work"—against which directors can articulate a broader vision of what it means to be a man.[15] This kind of inclusive masculinity doesn't need to be explicit; set in the context of a group that's only for boys, these messages are communicated subtly and obliquely, reassuring boys that it's okay to show emotion and express themselves in front of an audience.

A big part of this work depends on younger boys' tendency to look up to their older peers, which creates an implicit way of reassuring the younger boys that singing itself is a desirable thing for boys to do. Organizations like KSB—and particularly those choirs that keep older boys after their voices have changed—function as stepping stones for growth and achievement, usually leading to the top performing choir for unchanged voices or sometimes to a changed-voice ensemble for boys in high school. Keeping boys with changed voices has a number of benefits. At a practical level, it means that large groups can perform music written for SATB (soprano, alto, tenor, bass) sung entirely by boys, which expands considerably the repertoire available for performance. More importantly, however, it gives boys a structure in which they can look up to older boys and take cues from them about how to behave and conduct themselves. Joyce Keil, the founding director of the Silicon Valley–based boys' chorus Ragazzi, believes that keeping older boys in the mix is key for maintaining commitment and investment among boys in middle school grades—precisely the time when boys may start to worry about appearing too feminine when they continue to sing as unchanged trebles. "Boys look up to older boys," she said plainly; therefore, showing middle school boys that their older counterparts continue to sing makes it "an acceptable thing for a male to do."

A growing group of boy choirs make this kind of mentoring an explicit feature of their programming, for instance by assigning boys who are new to the choir a "big brother" or designated buddy in the ensemble they're joining. Julian Ackerly, who has directed the Tucson Boys Chorus for over forty years, described the ways that older boys in his chorus mentor younger boys in the group—not just by being role models but also by teaching younger boys actual skills, like the roping routines that the boys perform. The leadership philosophy he endorses is not one of deference to authority— for instance, the kind of relationship that pledges might have with an older brother in a fraternity. Instead, Ackerly emphasizes to the boys that "you lead by example, you don't lead by words, and you don't lead by commanding somebody." This means that the older boys should approach the younger ones with a posture that signals an invitation, saying, "look what I'm doing, you can be a part of this team." In his case, the boys do have to teach each other tangible skills—there are a dozen different roping tricks that they must become proficient in for their performances—but the rest of the relationship is about simply modeling what it looks like to be a good chorister.

Being a good chorister can mean many things, but it starts by being obedient, showing respect, and following directions. Mark Johnson of the Minnesota Boychoir has a set of rituals that boys in his choir learn to repeat when they enter the rehearsal space—they start by checking their "music mailbox" (the place they would receive new music or other information), putting their sheet music in order for rehearsal, and finding their assigned chair. Boys also learn to manage the physical restraint that rehearsals require—boys in the youngest training choirs start with learning to sit still when they're not singing, to refrain from talking, and to let the director do the work of correcting another singer's mistakes. The bodies of choristers themselves must also be adapted so that the look of the entire choir is visually consistent—KSB, for instance, trained boys to have "heavy hands" on the risers, keeping their arms still and at their sides rather than fiddling anxiously with their coat buttons or sticking their hands idly into their pockets. (More than one director told me that they had advised parents to sew the pants pockets closed on their sons' uniforms so that they wouldn't be tempted to use them onstage.)

This discipline isn't just something performed for the audience's benefit; it also facilitates productive rehearsals in which the boys need to get through a substantial repertoire in a relatively short period of time. It's typical for the highest levels of treble choirs to rehearse for at least three hours a week; some groups might rehearse for as many as five or six. And with an investment like this, it's hard for the boys not to become proficient singers, provided that they have a baseline sense of musicality at the outset. These high expectations are also essential to ensuring that an ensemble is one that boys will want to invest in, even if it requires some sacrifices. As one director told me, "At the end of the day, it has to be front and center an amazing musical product. And you can't get that without commitment." He continued, "There's all this talk in the choral community about recruitment," but in his view "the best retention of all is an amazing musical experience." This means it's imperative to hold high standards—like Saturday morning rehearsals that seem endless—and make peace with the fact that some kids will fall away because they aren't willing to make that investment. "In the long term," he said, "if you lower your standard, then it's going to really hurt you." In addition to creating an outstanding musical product, Houston director Carole Nelson sees these high expectations as crucial to building character because membership requires a high level of accountability on the part of individual singers. For instance, they must memorize their music, show up on time, and be kind and courteous to others. Beyond that, Nelson adds, "It's work, it's a job," because the choir is paid for their performances. This means that the boys "get to think of themselves as professionals and we try to work at a professional level."

Within this spirit of collaborative achievement, it's common for choirs to advertise the social and emotional abilities that boys can develop—self-discipline, accountability, restraint, politeness—through singing. Wes Martin, of the All-American Boys Chorus in Santa Ana, California, told me that their rehearsal space has a sign that reads, "We're only as good as our discipline," reminding the boys to "always put forth their best effort and work hard." Part of this discipline is animated by a traditional understanding of masculinity that carries within it echoes of citizenship and public virtue; as Martin explained, "we talk about [discipline] in the traditional sense of working hard, going after something. Don't be lazy, help the guys next to you." Directors don't see these as explicitly masculine qualities, however; Carole Nelson sees them as "human qualities" that all people should strive to inhabit. But Nelson worries that it's harder for children now—both boys and girls—to grow up in a culture that is so unabashedly competitive and in which violence is commonplace, whether dramatized in recreational sports and video games or enacted in real-life school shootings. She concluded, "Perhaps these boys need [music] more than ever, because of that. Maybe they need someplace that's civilized and calm, and has words that go with it."

Nelson's remarks were ones that I heard echoed throughout my interviews with boy choir directors, in particular the idea that boys' emotional needs require explicit acknowledgment. Prioritizing boys' emotional development is the starting point for an inclusive vision of manhood, one that endorses emotional vulnerability through practices that are fundamental to artmaking. The fact that choral music is oriented around text is one way that emotion enters performance—this differentiates singing from other kinds of musical performance, like playing the piano or guitar or being a part of a band or orchestra. For instance, Daniel Bates of the Florida Singing Sons is intentional about asking boys to think about the meaning of the words in the repertoire that they prepare, prompting them to think through what the composer meant in choosing those words, what they mean to the singers, and how the audience is likely to interpret them.

This is an embodiment of empathy—asking boys to think about the different feelings that have been expressed by others and their role in responding to and, in some cases, translating them. He explained that while orchestral music is designed to elicit feelings, the texts that animate choral music offer an audience "even more tangible things to grab," which gives young singers—and listeners in the audience—an easier path into music appreciation.

Nothing about the practice of empathy through singing is explicitly gendered, of course—boys, girls, and nonbinary kids all make music with the same part of their body. But the all-male composition of a boy choir implicitly endorses this kind of empathetic exchange as something that can be considered masculine—or put another way, it legitimizes these things as being *not* feminine because girls are just not a part of the mix. An all-male environment sanctions forms of interaction and self-presentation that would not necessarily be legitimized in a mixed-gender environment, where boys might feel the pressure to perform and defend their masculinity. Director Jason Holmes of the Cincinnati Boy Choir, who is Black, initially wrestled with the implications of leading a male-only group, particularly given that many people associate boy choirs with prestige and exclusion. For him, the benefit of a boys-only choir comes from the ways in which it allows boys to embrace a wider understanding of masculinity that is made possible only in a same-sex environment. He explained it by comparing gender to race:

> Over the past couple of years, I've been envious of people who went to HBCUs, because in both of my college experiences I was "The Black Guy" in the class. And that was a major social variant that people noticed, partially because you can see it. But I hear stories of colleagues who went to HBCUs, and they talk about all of this variance, where you can be the Black guy who is a classics major, and the Black guy who plays the piano for the gospel choir. And you might be the same Black person, but Blackness is the norm.

In Holmes's view, the major benefit of excluding girls from boy choirs is that it highlights the various ways that gender can be expressed among boys in a setting where simply being a boy is a common starting place. As he explained, "The boy who wears sparkly shoes is there and part of the team just as much as the boy who comes in stinking to high heaven" because he just came from a sports practice. Amid this diversity of gender expression, "they're all there, and they're all working towards a similar goal." As a director, Holmes wants to create an ensemble "where we recognize that there are many ways to be boys," which gives room for every boy to feel "like they can be themselves and that they don't have this sense of needing to save face." Ideas of masculinity are still in the mix, but the group can broaden their shared understanding of what it means to be a man and cultivate an environment of respect in the process.

It's true that some of the benefits that boys can get from being in a choir look similar to the ones that come from participating in athletics—like working hard, being accountable to other members of the team, and showing up on time. But cultivating a wider understanding of a respectful, inclusive masculinity is sometimes difficult in youth sports, particularly since so many sports that are explicitly marketed to boys are ones that prioritize toughness and sanction violence.[16] Moreover, my experience as a parent had witnessed plenty of behaviors during youth athletics that were the *opposite* of inclusion and respect, as when players—or just as often, their coaches or parents—yelled at referees or scolded other players for mistakes.[17] Sports also prioritize winning—winning games, attention from college recruiters, and (for the chosen few) those coveted college scholarships. Choirs are doing something refreshingly different. There's no yelling or coaching from the sidelines, for starters, and what matters is the final group product and the experience it creates for the people who are participating in it, either as singers or as members of the audience.

This also means that there's not the same pressure placed on children to demonstrate their exceptionalism in a choir as on a sports team. A choir might have forty or fifty singers, only one or two of whom are called upon to sing the occasional solo. In contrast, youth sports—at least, as I had experienced them thus far—often felt like a constant accounting exercise in which parents kept track of their individual child's achievements: how well they played, how often they got the ball, how many goals or runs or assists they accumulated. I couldn't begin to count the number of times I'd sat on the sidelines of some gym or field listening to parents brag about and comment on their individual child's performance during a game, and I'm sure I had done so, too. But in choirs, directors repeatedly emphasized that achievement in music, especially choral music, is organized around a spirit of collaboration, not competition. Mark Johnson explained that "in the arts, you don't win or lose, you're a winner all the time." He added that there are certainly times when the choir might think that a particular performance could have gone better, but even so "you really walk off the stage every time a winner, and it's something you want to be a part of."

These different emphases—collaboration instead of competition, and group performance instead of individual achievement—also create a different kind of mentoring that older boys can offer to the younger ones in each setting. Of course, some youth sports organizations also work to develop this kind of supportive community dynamic among their players, which is a valuable and commendable undertaking. At the same time, I suspect that sports leagues may be less likely to do so because they aren't self-consciously interested in the project of inclusive masculine identity formation. In that absence, there's plenty of room for boys themselves to bring in their own ideas of how to relate to each other—and the consequences of that aren't always good.

For instance, in the spring before Haydon joined choir, he had tried out for a local youth lacrosse team that enrolled only fifth- and sixth-grade boys. Most of the players who made the team were sixth-graders, which meant that Haydon was one of only two or three fifth-grade boys who had earned a spot on the roster. Not surprisingly, the handful of fifth-graders were slightly smaller and less experienced than the other players, and the older boys found plenty of opportunities to remind them of their lower status.

One day after practice the team's coach looked around the sideline as the boys collected their gear and held up a protective cup, the kind that the boys were required to wear with a jock strap during games.

"Whose is this?" he yelled gruffly. "Who's missing a cup?"

One of the older boys wasted no time capitalizing on the humor of the situation, sidling up to the coach to give himself a role in what came next.

"What size is it, Coach?" he asked.

"I have no idea," the coach answered, tossing the cup onto the ground, to a collapse of giggles from the crowd of boys standing nearby.

A handful of older boys walked over to give it a closer look, after which point their ringleader announced in a loud voice, "It looks like it's an extra-small. So, it must be Haydon's."

The other boys laughed, while poor Haydon protested that it wasn't his. But it didn't matter—the joke had done what it was intended to do: establish a pecking order among the boys on the team in which Haydon, as a younger player, was clearly at the bottom. The older boys couldn't have been more than twelve years old, but they knew enough to know that the way to knock another boy down a few pegs was with a penis joke.

Even if the experiences they acquire in youth sports aren't always positive, boys still recognize the masculine currency that comes with being athletic, and so choir directors often use athletic metaphors to reassure boys that they're doing something masculine, even if that thing is singing. Wes Martin said that he frequently reminds the boys that "there's no glory without the hard yards," a football metaphor meant to underscore how achievement comes only with effort. Bill Adams of the Fort Bend Boys Choir of Texas commented that he and his directorial staff constantly repurpose athletic metaphors to build up the boys' image of themselves, particularly with an eye toward the boys who may not be getting this kind of validation on a sports field: "We tell our boys, you are the first string. There are no second string players. . . . And you're not the last to be picked. You're the first to be picked."

I couldn't help but add silently, to myself, "And hopefully no one will tease you about the size of your penis."

Boys in choirs are scarce and will remain so for the foreseeable future; for most boys, youth athletics is a far more ubiquitous and formative experience than participating in the arts. And yet choirs do attempt to offer some of the same benefits as athletics in a format that potentially teaches boys something different about what it can mean to be masculine. Choirs communicate many of the same values that animate recreational sports—teamwork, discipline, and a sense of identity and belonging. But choirs also couple these values with an open endorsement of emotional expression and collaboration. They also make it clear that there are ways to be a boy that are not oriented around stereotypically masculine characteristics like domination and toughness.

A key component of this vision is the all-male setting in which boy choirs are organized, an approach that many directors see as under potential threat in a cultural context that increasingly eschews discrete forms of gender categorization. Some directors worry that boy choirs will become anachronistic in a more gender-fluid society. Others reassured me that their groups would be or even have been accepting of trans singers—choristers born female who are choosing to live and identify as male in their identity and self-presentation. But regardless of sexual orientation or gender identity assigned at birth, all-male groups like boy choirs are unavoidably invested in the cultural work of constructing men and masculinity.

Directors also believe that boys want to feel like boys and be seen as such by other boys, too. In fact, we learned early on that one of the pieces of repertoire that Haydon would need to learn as a candidate for the KSB Concert Choir is a song called "We Are the Boys," from the 1985 musical *Big River*. "All together now, we are the boys!" the lyrics proclaim, "All together, forever and always!" Other parts of the song's lyrics aren't exactly an anthem to inclusive masculinity—there are references to stealing horses, shooting guns, and forcing girls to dance—something that makes the feminist within me squirm uncomfortably. But by that point we were too far down the road to turn back. And after all, it was only one of about two dozen pieces of music that Haydon would need to learn during his candidacy. The music included an array of classical pieces, folk songs, religious music, and show tunes, and came in a big black binder with Haydon's name on it, the title "Concert Choir Candidate" written underneath. It was a hefty set of requirements, for sure, but in making his way through the songs, Haydon would also inch his way closer to the coveted green jacket.

There was also a role for me to play, as the Candidate binder included a sheet on which each singer was to list the name of the adult who would help them learn their repertoire. Even though they would practice the songs each week in the candidate rehearsals, the amount of music that each boy had to memorize was simply too much to accomplish without some work at home, so we were instructed that each boy needed an adult to shepherd him through this task—perhaps a parent, or a school music teacher, even a friend or neighbor with musical knowledge.

I didn't need to ask Haydon who this would be; we both knew the answer before I wrote my name on the form.

And with that, I became a choir mom.

CHAPTER 3

Unchanged Trebles

Our lives begin in rhythm. The syncopated beats of a mother's heart compose the first soundtrack we'll ever hear—fast when she's hurried, slow when she's sleeping. And babies know the sounds of a mother's voice, since it's the one constant sound they've heard for nine months. The ability to recognize this distinctive intonation points to the persistent human ability to recognize and interpret sound. As one choir director told me, being tone deaf is simply "not a thing"—hearing tone and register is fundamental to recognizing the difference between speaking voices. Birth must feel, to the infant, like a concert's abrupt conclusion with little warning and no hope for an encore. It makes sense that the twentieth-century Austrian psychologist Otto Rank believed that birth was the trauma that inaugurated the human experience.

Outside the cadence of the womb is the distinctive rhythmic accompaniment of motherhood. Discovering a pregnancy means counting life in weeks, to the beat of the otherwise arbitrary signposts that structure maternal care. The sonogram at thirteen weeks, waiting for the first kicks around sixteen, then the longer ultrasound that can identify physical genitalia at twenty. My firstborn arrived early—just past the "full term" mark of 37 weeks—making his appearance almost a month before we were expecting him. Haydon has always been such an extrovert that I like to joke that he must have gotten fed up with the loneliness of being in utero

67

and decided it was time to get out and see what he'd been missing during all those weeks spent in gestational captivity. By the time he was in preschool the rare moments when Haydon wanted to snuggle up in my lap came only when he was sick. The single good thing about the interminable waiting in the pediatrician's office was the feeling of a cuddly, feverish toddler nestled quietly in my arms, his soft curls plastered on a damp forehead beneath my chin.

Haydon's entry into the KSB Concert Choir introduced a new rhythm into our lives that fall, one that alternated between time spent learning his music and time spent in the car, driving to and from rehearsals. Ours was a symbiotic relationship because he needed my help to learn the music and drive him to choir practice, while I acquired hours each week during which he was forced to spend time with me. We sat side by side in the car, both of us facing front, which presented a different way of talking than when we were face-to-face. Often our conversations felt like a call-and-response anthem—of course, I was the one making the initial bid for engagement—but there were occasional precious moments when it approached true counterpoint, our two distinct melodies joined in harmony. Those rare instances when true conversation erupted between us felt so pure, so authentic, that I actually looked forward to the 45-minute drives to and from rehearsal. They offered what I knew were surely waning opportunities to have access to my son and his increasingly adolescent world.

On one particular October morning, however, we were thinking only about how we were running late. Mr. Fisher had declared that every chorister who was in his seat by nine o'clock with his binder of music and a sharpened pencil would be entered into a drawing for a fifty-dollar Visa gift card at the end of rehearsal. To a twelve-year-old, of course, this was a princely sum and a powerful motivator. We had managed to get into the car with the music binder and could still get there on time if we managed to hit all the stop lights just right.

But once we were on the interstate, Haydon discovered that he had forgotten to bring a pencil.

"There's probably one in the car somewhere," I suggested hopefully, knowing that the odds were at least fifty-fifty that a pencil was lurking underneath one of the seats, next to other souvenirs of a harried family life, like candy wrappers and clumps of dog hair.

A full-scale excavation ensued, after which Haydon triumphantly produced a dull nub of a pencil that had lost its eraser from beneath the passenger seat.

"Lucky you!" I said, raising my eyebrows in affirmation.

He didn't answer. Instead, he wanted to look at his phone, but since I'd installed time limits on his device, this distraction didn't last for long. When he'd gone through his 20-minute limit on Clash of Clans, he set the phone aside and performed several minutes of annoyance with me ("but none of my friends have time limits on their phones!") before deciding that sporadic conversation was ultimately better than gazing out the window in complete and utter boredom.

We managed to get to the church about two minutes prior to rehearsal. We were too late to find a spot in the parking lot, so instead I slowed down outside of the enormous sanctuary edifice so that he could get out at the curb.

"Go!" I said, with a smile, as he reached for the door handle. "I'll see you after practice."

He hopped out of the car and was about to shut the door as I hollered after him, "Haydon! The binder!" He turned back, grabbed the binder—the pencil had already been tucked into the interior pocket—and gave me a good-natured smile.

The door slammed shut and I started looking for street parking, joining all the other mothers who were swarming the same three city blocks looking for an available metered spot. After that I would head inside and find a place to work for the next three hours. The irony of all this rushing around was that it also involved a lot of waiting, a frantic push-and-pull rhythm that tended to extremes rather than a steady state of equilibrium.

There was also a nagging awareness that what we were doing here was limited by a schedule that we didn't control, since we had no idea at all when Haydon's voice would start changing. Ironically, all of this hurrying was meant to give Haydon as much time as possible as a trained soprano before his body eventually quit cooperating—in musical terms, the tempo was decidedly *presto* so that we could get to a treble *fermata*, that mythical, lingering moment when a boy soprano's voice is supposedly its most beautiful. Choral directors describe the classic boy soprano sound as a straight, piercing tone with no vibrato or embellishment. As they approach puberty, however, a more three-dimensional quality enters a boy's voice and signals that he is "peaking." For some boys that doesn't happen until fourteen or fifteen, for others it starts as early as ten or eleven.

And boys' voices change substantially earlier now than they did a few hundred years ago. In Bach's day a boy might have been an unchanged treble until his late teens, when the difference between boys with changed and unchanged voices was sometimes called "bearded and unbearded" or "knowing and unknowing."[1] It's little wonder that the expanded larynx that betrays a boy's changed voice is colloquially called an "Adam's apple"—the lingering mark of Eve's betrayal, when she allegedly forced the fruit of the tree of knowledge down her unsuspecting husband's throat. Nowadays the choristers at the eight-hundred-year-old St. Thomas Boys Choir in Leipzig, Germany, where Bach was the choirmaster from 1723 to 1750, may find their soprano career ends as early as age twelve.[2] Demographer Joshua Goldstein estimates that the average age of puberty's onset among boys has dropped each decade by about 2.5 months since the middle of the eighteenth century.[3] If boys generally started to enter puberty around age sixteen in Bach's time, they're now doing so closer to age eleven. Not only does this mean that boys have fewer years to sing as unchanged trebles, but it also means that choirs must work faster to train them in a shorter period of time.

So far, Haydon appeared to be on the later end of this range. He had yet to hit the growth spurt that signaled puberty was in full swing, and although he was slightly taller than the average twelve-year-old, he wasn't yet growing hair on his face or armpits. And as a series of voice checks that fall had confirmed, he could hit any notes from the G below middle C to a C two octaves above, which meant that his vocal range spanned nearly three octaves. He'd even auditioned to be a "Descant" and had earned himself a coveted spot in this section reserved for the boys with the highest voices. Few pieces include notes that stretch this high—most choral music asks sopranos to reach only an A, the outer limit of the upper range of most females—but the boys who were Descants would occasionally sing even higher if a score gave them the opportunity. Never one to shy away from a chance to show off, Haydon relished this ability to hit notes in the treble stratosphere. It might have seemed effeminate to sing that high in the middle school choir, but in a boy choir the tables are turned: the Descants are the stars, the boys with the highest voices the most prized.

This fascination with the sound and range of boys' voices has a long and unsettling history. Unchanged trebles were once considered so precious that boys with promising soprano voices were castrated in Europe during the sixteenth and seventeenth centuries to preserve their timbre into adulthood, producing a class of singers called *castrati* whose voices were quite literally frozen in time. The practice was born partly of perceived necessity since women and girls were prohibited from singing in public; at a purely practical level, castration offered a way to incorporate soprano voices into an ensemble while maintaining the exclusion of women. Some parents also saw it as a necessity, offering their sons for the procedure, especially younger sons who had no inheritance, believing that it would offer them access to musical training and education and, if they were lucky, a lucrative career.[4] In opera halls that lacked contemporary means of vocal amplification, the most successful of the castrati could use the lung and cranial capacity of a man to project the pristine treble voice of a child.[5] In cathedral choirs, the place that these singers were more likely to end up, they simply filled out the treble section.

Castration also produced distinctive physical characteristics—deprived of the body's hormonal rhythms to regulate growth, the castrati were generally taller than average and didn't grow facial hair, placing them in a kind of liminal space between male and female.[6] Castrato roles from this period also illustrate just how much fame and status awaited the handful of castrati who made it to prestigious opera houses. Although castrati were sometimes used to play female characters, the more notable roles written for castrated male singers in the Baroque era were typically princes, military leaders, or kings. Handel's operas often assigned the titular role to a soprano castrato, as in *Giulio Cesare* (Julius Caesar) or *Serse* (Xerxes, King of Persia); Christoph Willibald Gluck did the same in *Orfeo ed Euridice* (Orpheus) and *Paride ed Elena* (Paris). These high voices were considered not feminine but rather an expression of strength and in many cases signaled proximity to the deity, which made the castrati who performed those roles the modern-day equivalent of pop superstars.

Thankfully, the practice of castrating boys to forestall puberty and prolong their soprano voices ended long ago. In fact, today we rarely stop to notice aspects of boyhood that feel open-ended, even androgynous, before they go through puberty. Instead, our culture offers precious few opportunities to celebrate boyhood that aren't inflected with the expectation that boys will become men. Even the quintessential boyhood pastime of Little League baseball gestures at maturity, as coaches and parents eye the team for boys who could be breakout athletes later. Boy choirs are doing something else entirely, focusing attention on the final, fleeting moments before boys will inevitably be ushered into manhood. This happens on a schedule not of their choosing, and whether they find themselves ready for it or not. After all, boys' voices don't just *change*, they *break*. The power of the performance may have more to do with the preciousness we associate with the fleeting nature of boyhood and the loss that comes with leaving childhood behind. This suggests a subtle, somewhat uncomfortable question that we don't always think to consider: Are we really that eager for boys to become men?

I have learned that if you ask a boy choir director whether they think boys' unchanged treble voices sound different than girls', they'll almost always say yes. If you ask a former boy chorister if they think boys' voices sound different than girls', they'll definitely say yes. But if you ask a girl choir director or a mixed-gender choir director the same question, they're more likely to shrug their shoulders or roll their eyes and say something about gender inequality and the disparate resources that are devoted to boys' choral training as compared to girls'. They're also quick to cite studies that show that most listeners, whether trained or untrained musicians, can't tell the difference between all-male and all-female children's ensembles when they're deprived of visual cues.

I decided to put the question to someone who manages to check all those boxes—a former boy chorister who's been a conductor of both same-sex and mixed-gender choirs, Nathan Wadley. We first met in 2019 in a noisy coffee bar near the private Quaker high school where he was working as a coed choir director in Philadelphia. Eight years previous he founded and still currently directs the Philadelphia Girls Choir, the sister organization of the Philadelphia Boys Choir. But prior to either of those jobs, Wadley directed the training choir at the American Boychoir School, which he himself attended as a chorister in the 1980s.

Wadley had found his way to ABS in a manner that was typical of boys during that time: being serendipitously plucked from midwestern obscurity and entering the country's most prestigious boy choir almost overnight. In his case, a music teacher had suggested to Wadley's parents that they might want to take him to hear the American Boychoir when it came through town on tour. Wadley remembers clearly several things about that first interaction with ABS—most importantly, that he had bronchitis and was coughing incessantly. He was also transfixed by the choir's performance. He was determined to hold his breath and wait for the applause break to attend to his hacking cough because he didn't want to do anything that would tarnish the beauty of the performance. Wadley was impressed by the quality of the music—it was unlike anything he had heard before in school or in church—but also by the realization that the performers were boys his own age. As he explained about growing up in the Midwest, "That part of the country is very athletic minded—not that other parts of the country aren't," he added quickly. "But it was very football, baseball, basketball driven, especially for boys. So, to see something different with kids—with boys my age—was pretty revolutionary for me."

That night Wadley ended up participating in an impromptu audition after the performance (bronchitis and all), and the school called a few weeks later to invite him to come for a school visit. He'd never been on a plane before, so the trip to New Jersey with his father was memorable for a lot of reasons. His parents didn't have the resources to afford a boarding school, but with a scholarship, help from his grandparents, and some of the money his parents had started saving for college, they were able to scrape together the resources for him to attend the American Boychoir School for his middle school years. He was eleven years old when his parents, sister, and grandmother left him at the school that would become his home for the next three years. "Watching them drive away was . . ." his voice trailed off, before he added simply, "We've had a lot of conversations about that moment." Years later, Wadley learned that leaving him behind was one of the most difficult moments in his mother's life.

He eventually became a featured soloist with the choir. Of course, solos are always a big deal for singers, but being a soloist with the American Boychoir might mean recording an album with Jessye Norman or singing with the New York Philharmonic in Carnegie Hall. Wadley recalled auditioning for a particular solo during his first fall at ABS—the second movement of *Chichester Psalms*, the three-part choral work by Leonard Bernstein that features a beautiful extended solo for a boy treble that continues throughout the piece. Bernstein's score states clearly that the solo "must not be sung by a woman, but either by a boy or a countertenor."[7] (A countertenor is an adult male singer with a changed voice who uses falsetto to access treble notes.) The entire work is one that sets the Hebrew words of several Psalms, some in their entirety and excerpts of others, to a musical score that is alternately jubilant and mournful, lyrical and dissonant. The solo in the second movement conveys the words of the twenty-third Psalm ("The Lord is my shepherd") in a boy's voice that carries on throughout the piece, first alone with a harp, and eventually with other soprano voices woven against punctuated interludes of tenors and basses, who sing part of Psalm 2, "Why do the nations rage, and the people imagine a vain thing?" Due to its length and difficulty, the solo is probably one of the most significant—and coveted—solos for a boy treble that has been written in the past seventy years. "I think Bernstein was conducting," Wadley said of his *Chichester Psalms* audition, adding that it would have been one of the last appearances the esteemed American conductor would have made before he died in 1990.

However, Wadley wasn't quite ready for a debut that big. At that point, he was still quite new in the choir, and director Jim Litton explained to him that although he had done very well in his audition, the solo would be performed by a slightly older boy who was more seasoned and experienced. Had Wadley been a year older—or if he had joined the choir a year earlier—he might have been ready. And admittedly, he did miss out: not only was Bernstein conducting, but the concert was celebrating both the year of Bernstein's seventieth birthday as well as the forty-fifth anniversary of his debut as conductor of the New York Philharmonic.[8] The elevenyear-old Wadley was disappointed, of course, but quickly channeled any sense of disappointment into his quest to land the next solo; he eventually got one on an album recorded with the Christian recording artist Michael W. Smith.

These memories start to get at some of the things that Wadley thinks differentiate boy choirs and girl choirs at the middle grade ages. The competition for solos that he recalls among the boy choir—a dynamic that was always somewhat central to the group's social fabric—is not something he notices among the girls whom he now directs. Instead, he has observed that girls are often more invested in the social experience of the choir than they are in the music; the boys, on the other hand, are primarily motivated by the music, with friendships a secondary outcome. But I'm generally inclined to be skeptical of conclusions like this that reify gender norms, so I challenged him further for evidence—how did he know this difference was real, for instance?

One example he offered was how singers behave when they're on tour, in which the tour experience for the girls is more anchored in their friendships with each other, while the boys are much more focused on the business of performing. Wadley was quick to qualify his observations by noting that he may relate differently to the boys' experience because there he speaks primarily of his own memories as a chorister, while he's speaking about girls from his experience as the director of the Philadelphia Girls Choir. But his observations align with what I heard repeatedly in conversations with choral directors—that they observe different patterns of social relationships among boy-only and girl-only choral groups. They find that boys are motivated by a vertical relationship with the director of a boy choir, along with a spirit of competition for solos and recognition, while girls are more animated by horizontal relationships with one another. Of course, no one goes so far as to suggest that these behaviors are rooted in biological differences between boys and girls. Most of the directors I talked to acknowledge that these could simply be expressions of the different forms of socialization that boys and girls are exposed to in childhood and adolescence—ones that may be particularly pronounced during the middle school years, when puberty forces children to reckon with questions of gender and its meaning.

But do unchanged treble boys *sound* different than girls, I pressed him. Among the various reasons to separate boys from girls at this age, this was the one I most wanted him to weigh in on. "I will say yes," Wadley hesitated, "but not to the extent most people think." He went on to explain, "I think physiologically, there is something that has yet to be quantified that separates the sound of an unchanged boy's voice from an unchanged girl's voice. However, I think the amount of difference has been overblown. And I think the reason we hear it—because we do hear it—is because girls' voices at that age are not trained in the same way because we know that the [boy's] voice is going to change, and so we put an extreme amount of effort to getting that sound while we have it." He explained that even though girls' voices do change and develop further during puberty, it's only the timbre of the voice that will change, not the range. Boys, on the other hand, have a treble voice that we see as a precious commodity, which brings with it a sense of urgency that invites accelerated forms of training.

In fact, Wadley has been conscious of this in his work with the Philadelphia Girls Choir, deliberately taking the kind of chorister training that he received at ABS and translating it to a girl choir setting—a focused emphasis on tonal and vowel development in the choral sound, for instance. In his view, many community girl choirs encourage a bright, shallow, innocent sound from their young singers. Wadley sees this as part of a larger sociological construct in which our society attaches different meanings to aging for men and women. In his view, we're attracted to vocal maturity in men and immaturity in women; he notes that women will sometimes speak in ways that make them sound younger, while men push their voices deeper to sound older and more masculine. Wadley reasons that these social constructs—gendered expectations about traits that are sexually desirable in adults—also seep into the choral world, and even into the training that children's organizations create for boy choirs and girl choirs, respectively. "There are amazing girl choirs around the country and around the world," he said, "but I think by and large we have this perception that a girl choir or a children's choir is going to sound young and cute and sweet, in a kind of elementary school innocence kind of way."

"But don't we want the same kind of innocence from the boys?" I countered. "No," he responded emphatically, shaking his head. "No, we want a different innocence from the boys. We want purity from the boys, but not innocence. We want a kind of angelic perfection from boys." We both paused for a moment to take this in, and I restated this hypothesis: "So we want innocence from girls, but purity from boys?" Wadley nodded, adding, "And I think that results in the girl choir sound—or a perception of a girl choir sound—as young and airy, kind of unformed." But with boys, he continued, "we want that earth-shattering, emotionally moving experience." In Wadley's view, there's no reason that female voices couldn't accomplish this kind of sound, but he added a final qualification: "I think there probably is a physiological difference. But it's small, and it's not what we think it is. I think you could put a boys' choir and a girls' choir on a stage next to each other that have had the same training and have the same experience of being moved."

It turns out that Wadley's impressions are exactly the ones that are borne out in the research literature. The most in-depth research on sex and vocal development has been conducted by David Howard and Graham Welch, who conclude that the biggest differences in vocal sound are those between adults and children, not boys and girls, at least prior to the age of ten or eleven.[9] In an oft-cited study, Howard and Welch asked expert listeners to distinguish between trained choirs of differing gender composition. One experiment arranged for fifteen choirs with varied gender composition—all-girl, all-boy, and mixed ensembles—to record identical repertoire and then asked a panel of ten trained evaluators to listen to forty-five excerpts of the recordings and report how certain they were of the choir's composition by sex. The results of this study were telling: only one of the all-boy choirs was consistently identified correctly, and two of the girls' choirs were consistently labeled incorrectly as a boys choir. Beyond that, the evaluators' accuracy hovered around 50 percent—in other words, their judgments were no more accurate than a random guess.[10]

Of course, the hormonal changes associated with puberty do affect the bodies of male and female singers differently. Although boys get the lion's share of the attention during these stages, girls' voices change during puberty, too—the changes just aren't as noticeable because they don't result in an entirely different vocal register or a visibly larger larynx. Up to and until about age eleven, girls and boys share the same "head voice" tones, but by age eleven or twelve girls' voices become lighter and breathier due to a gap that temporarily develops in the back of the vocal folds in girls around this age.[11] The innocent sound that Wadley describes is one that can actually be exacerbated by girls' vocal folds during this stage of maturation. Singing at this age can even feel painful for girls—giving the feeling of having a sore throat or hoarseness in the voice—until they pass through the final stage of puberty by ages thirteen to fifteen, during which a more mature sound begins to develop and the breathiness disappears as the vocal folds close.[12] The mature sound of older teenaged girls is also different than that of the boy treble—stronger, more powerful—which means that many choir directors worry that combining younger boys with older girls would almost certainly overpower any distinct sound produced by boys with unchanged voices.[13]

For boys, the vocal folds in the male larynx become longer and wider as the voice becomes lower, a change that is usually completed by the age of twenty.[14] If any differences truly exist between boys and girls, then, we would expect them to appear only among children in the adolescent years—in other words, in the final few years that boys remain unchanged trebles. And indeed this is what Howard and Welch found in another experiment that asked professional evaluators to listen to eighty samples of untrained children singing and then to rate both their impression of the singer's sex as well as their confidence in their evaluation. The evaluators' accuracy increased with the age of the singer and particularly among the boys, suggesting they were less able to detect any difference by sex among younger children but became more accurate in identifying the voices of older boys.[15] Taken as a whole, these findings suggest that it's much easier to discern something special in the voice of an individual boy—a thirteen-year-old soloist at his "peak," for instance—than within an entire choir of mixed-age unchanged trebles.[16]

But achieving this outcome, at least for boys, requires that years of training be invested in a boy's voice prior to the comparatively short window of time before his voice changes and begins to "peak"—an unpredictable period that could last only a few months or perhaps as long as a year. Something about the preciousness of this time, its fleetingness, its precarity, is what conveys the notion of purity that Wadley thinks audiences expect from a boy choir. Boys whose voices have yet to change still show something of the purity of childhood, those last final moments before their beards and their knowing Adam's apples begin to emerge. Time will take them across the abyss. After that there's no turning back.

As that first fall semester continued, Haydon and I made our way through the Candidacy binder together, slowly checking off each piece of repertoire that he dutifully learned and sang for Mr. Fitz. In what seemed like no time at all, we were preparing for the December concert, which involved almost as much pageantry as singing. For the boys who were candidates, part of the choreography involved each boy having an adult stand behind him with their jacket while the boys arranged themselves in a long row that stretched across the front of the church sanctuary. At the dress rehearsal for the concert, the program manager reminded the boys to pick which one adult would hold their jacket and help them put it on when they crossed over from being "candidates" to "jacketed trebles." She explained that there was always some uncertainty around whether or not the jackets would fit the boys, since they're not permitted to try them on before they are declared members of the Concert Choir, but also told us not to worry if the jacket was too big or too small once they put their arms in the sleeves; they would have a chance to exchange it for a different size after the concert, if needed. The boys were also told that when they pick the person who will "jacket" them, it should probably be the person who has done the most to help them accomplish all of the requirements of their candidacy.

As Haydon and I drove home from rehearsal, I asked him if he'd thought about who he wanted to help him put on his jacket, in the same manner that a sixteen-year-old girl might mention the prom to the boy she's already dating. So I was not prepared for what happened next, when he innocently tilted his head as he thought about the question and then said the name of the choir's accompanist.

"It's supposed to be me!" I said immediately, surprised and somewhat wounded.

"Oh," he said, equally surprised. "Then, you."

Of course, I was the one who stood behind Haydon when he got his jacket—it wasn't ever really a question, at least not for me. The other twenty-odd boys who got their jackets that night were almost all accompanied by their mothers, too, although a few were jacketed by a dad or an older brother who was also in the choir. Since the candidates couldn't wear the jackets until they were officially made members of the Concert Choir, they were wearing the long-sleeved V neck sweaters that indicated their status as candidates; Haydon couldn't wait to get his off, partly because it was itchy. Even though the boys' uniforms included a white oxford shirt, the shirt had to be short-sleeved to ensure that no chorister had white cuffs extending at the edge of their jacket sleeves. After all, boys grow a lot over a year; a short-sleeved oxford couldn't betray a jacket sleeve that had suddenly become too short. But it also meant that the long-sleeved wool sweater was particularly itchy on Haydon's naked arms while he sat and waited for the concert to begin.

When the moment came for me to put his jacket on, he took off the green sweater as quickly as possible and slid his arms into the jacket, all smiles and pride. He wasn't sure what to do with the sweater, so he handed it to me in an awkward clump while he and the rest of the newly jacketed trebles bounded back onto the risers to continue the concert. The next bit of the performance was a blur, but he was finally one of the boys in the jackets singing a mixture of Christmas carols, a Hanukkah suite, and an arrangement of "Sleigh Ride" in which it was tradition for the choir's high school seniors, whose voices had all changed, to join the sopranos and sing their part in falsetto. The bearded joined the unbearded for a fleeting, sentimental moment.

The Concert Choir's part in the performance was relatively small. Most of the remainder of the concert showcased the more experienced, older boys: the ones in the Towne Choir, the highest group for unchanged trebles, and the high school singers with changed voices, colloquially called the Grads. That night the two groups were performing the third movement of *Chichester Psalms*—the same work in which Nathan Wadley had hoped to land a solo decades ago, when Bernstein was conducting in the late 1980s. The Towne and Grad choirs would be singing all three movements of the challenging work at their final concert that May.

Mr. Fisher and Mr. Fitz knew that the boys would need many months to nail this work, so it was a good decision to start them learning it in the fall. It's decidedly not music for children—the notes are often dissonant, the rhythms sometimes seem nearly inscrutable, and the lyrics are all in Hebrew. But it was, ironically, initially composed for boys' voices, commissioned in 1965 by cathedral dean Walter Hussey for a yearly festival of choirs from the combined British cathedrals in Chichester, Salisbury, and Winchester, which were composed only of men and boys. Bernstein had initially considered titling the work "Psalms of Youth," before ultimately deciding that the name would misrepresent the work. Explaining the change to Hussey, Bernstein wrote, "'Youth' was a wrong steer; the piece is far too difficult."[17] As the KSB boys made their way through the melodic tapestry of the piece, I momentarily forgot that we were watching children perform. The boys were effectively doing the work of adults in singing this difficult score, and they did it from memory, something that even adult performers in a professional chorus almost never attempt.

After the concert ended, I went backstage to meet up with Haydon and return the borrowed wool sweater to the volunteer who was collecting them. It struck me as curious how the choir consistently referred to "parent volunteers" when it seemed like they were almost always moms; as much as they tried to message otherwise, the labor of women is what powers the boys and, with them, the choir itself. We were the ones who brought the snacks, made sure they learned the music, bought the pants and shirts that fit, and remembered to bring the jacket to the concert. Tonight's accomplishments were supposed to be about the boys, but I couldn't help thinking that they were also partly mine to celebrate. On that point, it's no accident that the jacketing ceremony included an adult; I felt I earned my spot behind him. It's also not surprising that my own son didn't immediately recognize this labor when I asked him who had most helped him pass his Candidacy requirements. This work of mothering is so commonplace, so much a part of childhood that it's often taken for granted and rendered invisible.

Mr. Fisher found me in the sea of people backstage and made a point of asking me if Haydon would consider becoming a candidate for the Towne Choir in the spring. He expected that only one or two of the boys who had just become Concert Choir members would be ready to take this next step, but he was thinking about Haydon's age and about his voice, both of which made Mr. Fisher eager to promote Haydon as quickly as possible. Fisher mentioned that the Towne and Grad Choirs' performance of *Chichester Psalms* in the spring would be at the prestigious Kimmel Center for the Performing Arts in Philadelphia, part of the city's ongoing celebration of Bernstein's hundredth birthday. Would Haydon like to make the leap? It would mean more rehearsal time, of course, but these opportunities wouldn't come around again—at least not while Haydon was an unchanged treble.

I said that we would think about it over the holidays, when we would thankfully have a bit of a break from the driving and running around. But I knew that we would eventually say yes. After all, time was moving on, with each day taking us closer to the moment when his treble voice would disappear. After all, you can't grow up to be a boy soprano.

Except that sometimes, maybe you can.

Not yet forty years old, the countertenor Anthony Roth Costanzo is a luminary of the contemporary opera world. Winner of the Met's National Council auditions in 2009, Costanzo has performed countertenor roles internationally, from Los Angeles to Madrid and in venues ranging from Carnegie Hall to Versailles. As a vocal classification currently enjoying something of a renaissance, countertenors are male singers whose vocal range encompasses that of a typical (female) mezzo-soprano. Also called falsettists, countertenors use only the top portion of the vocal folds to produce a sound that is squarely in the treble range, even though their "chest voice" range would make them a tenor or even a baritone. Costanzo's identity as a countertenor emerged somewhat by happenstance, when he was still a boy soprano, performing the role of Miles in a production of Benjamin Britten's *The Turn of the Screw*. Then thirteen, Costanzo possessed some physical indicators of male puberty—hair on his arms, a faint mustache—which led some of his opera cast members to gently suggest that perhaps his voice had changed without his recognition. Indeed, they were correct: his voice had dropped while Costanzo wasn't paying attention. He had simply continued to sing as a treble, preserving his countertenor range.

Costanzo's experience confirmed what many boy choir directors told me that they had witnessed over the years in their work with boy choristers—that boys who sing through the voice change actually preserve their treble notes even after their vocal folds thicken and elongate to begin producing notes in the bass and baritone range. This is the reason why the boys in the KSB Grad choir could sing the soprano part of "Sleigh Bells" at the December concert—they'd sung through the voice change simply because they were in a boy choir. In this way, the falsetto, or "head voice," is something of a muscle that can be maintained, and boys who sing through the voice change are activating a muscle that all males can access, even if few of them ultimately do so. This is probably why pop stars like Michael Jackson, Justin Bieber, and Justin Timberlake have such outstanding falsetto ranges: they began singing, like all boys do, in their head voice. They just continued doing so even after their chest voice dropped.

I asked Costanzo if there's a metaphor about gender in there, that extends beyond the voice—that all people can access masculine and feminine registers within their bodies, even though we tend to think of puberty as a moment that brings these androgynous opportunities to a sudden end. After all, as a countertenor he routinely performs roles that were written for castrati, whose bodies had been modified to produce the kind of sound that he is able to produce through practice and training. He considered the question for a moment before agreeing, "I guess the analogy or metaphor that I would make is that in the people I know, and within all of us, there is this whole range of gender, and sometimes it requires some physical effort to change the natural setting on some level, or the rhythm that you've fallen into. I guess I do believe that within some constraints, there's a kind of spectrum." For the falsetto, however, there is probably a limited time window during which those muscles need to be activated and developed for an extended falsetto range to be accessible for a biologically male singer, and that window is one that is open throughout childhood but closes in late adolescence. This isn't to say that an older male singer couldn't work diligently and faithfully to learn to sing in falsetto, but accessing the muscle memory and stretching the vocal folds to do so would be much more difficult. Costanzo suspects that there are many more men who could be countertenors, but boys just don't sing high after their voices change due to prevailing social norms that tend to discourage the practice. What he does now as a countertenor was simply what he knew how to do instinctually when he was singing as a boy.

Of course, he's also spent years training as a countertenor, which means focusing on using a smaller portion of his vocal folds to continue singing in his head voice. (Costanzo's chest voice is squarely in the baritone range, although he sometimes assures audiences they don't want to hear him sing in his chest voice.)[18] His training now as a countertenor is also different than that of a tenor or a baritone, but he explained that "it's very similar, if not identical, to what happens with a female voice." The sound itself isn't what's remarkable, however; what strikes audiences is the novel experience of a man performing vocal work that sounds feminine. This is different than performing in drag, Costanzo clarified, which would carry with it a kind of implicit critique or punch line, signaling that this performance is one constrained by the boundaries of time and performance. Costanzo sees this initial "surprise" factor as being only a hook that draws an audience in to a different kind of listening. "Once you get past that—because they're listening in a different way—it becomes about the communication of an emotion, it doesn't become about the construct of gender because that's a hook that disappears instantly. It's like a barrier that you break through and then immediately forget about."

It probably helps that the kind of roles that Costanzo has been performing lately are ones that explicitly take advantage of the countertenor's ability to blur gender boundaries. After 1750, the roles that were once written for castrati started to dry up and disappear from the operatic literature. Two centuries later, around 1950, British composer Benjamin Britten began writing operatic roles for countertenors after being inspired by the Renaissance and Baroque performances of the countertenor Alfred Deller, which led to a resurgence of interest in this form of male vocal performance. If the older castrato roles are generally about the power and status associated with a high voice, these more recent creations tend to write for the countertenor as someone whose gender is amorphous, blended, located in the realm of mystery and the supernatural. The role of Oberon, King of the Fairies in Britten's *A Midsummer Night's Dream* falls into this category, along with the Voice of Apollo in Britten's subsequent *Death in Venice*. Notably, these roles were written for men—not women—singing in a treble range, which further underscores how the power of the performance comes not through the pitch of the voice so much as the novelty of a male performance that blurs the boundaries between male and female.

This newer, more recent emphasis in composition for the countertenor voice is perhaps best illustrated by Philip Glass's *Akhnaten*, written in 1983. Costanzo has now performed the title role five times—twice each in England and with the Metropolitan Opera in New York, as well as once at the Los Angeles Opera. The role is one that emphasizes the sexual ambiguity of a young boy who becomes Pharaoh in 1400 B.C.E. Egypt and whose radical agenda of monotheism leads to his eventual demise and execution. Costanzo has described Akhnaten as the "first trans icon" in an opera that tells the story of a young Pharaoh whose gender was depicted in ways both male and female. The performance also requires Costanzo to appear nude onstage and fully waxed, with successive forms of costuming that signal the character's intertwined maturity and sexual ambiguity.[19] Reviews of his performances in the role, not surprisingly, emphasize both masculine and feminine qualities of Costanzo's performance: The *Washington Post* described him as "a perfect choice" due to his "firm, light voice, which projects power without ever letting the audience forget the underlying vulnerability of his own naked body beneath the robes."[20] The *New York Times* praised Costanzo for singing "with exceptional tenderness while bringing out inflections in the music that hint at the character's isolation and insecurity."[21]

Costanzo is deeply aware that this kind of gender-bending is still somewhat countercultural, a stance that he signals repeatedly in interviews by referencing his dual-career psychologist parents as one reason that he didn't give up his soprano register after his voice changed.[22] He pointed out to me that this kind of singing in falsetto can actually be rendered as masculine and highly sexualized—as in the pop vocals of a singer like Adam Levine, Bruno Mars, or Michael Jackson—but quickly added that "being a countertenor is more extreme than being Michael Jackson because you actually sound like a female opera singer, when already singing opera can be kind of effeminate in someone's mind." He also enumerated how falsettists appear in cultures outside of the West—Kabuki Onnagata opera, for instance, or Hawaiian falsetto singing, known as *leo ki`eki`e*. Similarly, men have long sung in falsetto voice in Black gospel music, particularly in "quartet" style, which writer Anthony Heilbut has described as "the aim of talented boys long before their voices change."[23] The influence of the Black gospel sound on modern-day popular music can be traced directly back to the kind of crooning pioneered by gospel artists like Reverend June Cheeks and the subsequent imitations of popular ensembles like the Temptations and the Four Seasons.[24]

These vocal forms are also traditions that emerged from contexts of exclusion. The castrati were prized as a source of soprano voices in religious and operatic settings that prohibited women from singing in public; Onnagata developed in Japan after women were prohibited from public performance settings in the early seventeenth century.[25] Similarly, Heilbut notes that gospel developed in a religious culture that privileged men and masculinity, in which "religious song and sermon were very early identified with the male sex."[26] These settings are also ones in which singers typically conveyed particular kinds of emotions—the agony of an operatic protagonist who is experiencing loss and pain or the hope of liberation from the suffering experienced by Black Americans enduring systematic racism. Costanzo went so far as to say, "There's something primal about it, for a man to sing in that register. It also straddles the world between singing and screaming, which means that it's an extreme expression of emotion in some way."

I couldn't help but notice that the examples he offered are ones in which male performers express strong emotions in settings that also privilege male power; work that would otherwise come across as highly emotional and feminine is destigmatized for male artists because they're performing in settings that exclude women. Maybe the value of the performance isn't so much the quality of the sound or the artistry of the performance—after all, girls or women could do that, and perhaps even do it better—but rather the fact that male performers are doing something that female performers aren't permitted to do. The countertenor's sound is arresting because we simply don't expect such a feminine sound to emanate from a male body. The tones of a boy choir sound ethereal, in large part, because we listen not only with our ears but also with our eyes and with our socially constructed brains, which register the disconnect between what we hear and what we expect from boys.

At the same time, countertenors like Costanzo remind us that gender and its presentation can't always be forced into neat and tidy boxes that limit its possibilities for expression—and that we lose access to a larger language of meaning when we attempt to do so. In the same way, the performance of a boy soprano highlights the open-ended androgyny that childhood can represent. This is the purity that Nathan Wadley thinks audiences expect from a boy choir performance, the reason that unchanged treble voices are also called "unbroken." It also suggests that something destroys a boy, or at least a part of him, as puberty unfolds; this loss is the price that we pay for maintaining such arbitrary boundaries between what we consider masculine and what we consider feminine. Their natural coexistence in an unchanged treble voice is a rare opportunity to celebrate and appreciate an alternative way of thinking about gender, one that doesn't ask us to perform primarily one or the other.

Leonard Bernstein didn't finish *Chichester Psalms* until May 1965, several months later than Hussey had hoped, since the festival was to be held that July. The correspondence between the two men has all the makings of a comedy of errors, in which the composer is running late, the choir director is increasingly anxious, and the composition turns out to be very different from what was initially promised. The final score, with its elaborate percussion and orchestration, was far more reminiscent of *West Side Story* than anything typically presented in an English Cathedral. Bernstein also sent a question along with the final score in May; would Hussey mind too terribly much if the piece were to have its debut a few weeks earlier, in Carnegie Hall with the New York Philharmonic? This request was clearly a slight, since Hussey had commissioned the work to be premiered at the Chichester festival that summer. But what else could Hussey do besides acquiesce? When he agreed, Bernstein quickly acknowledged his generosity and offered some measure of reassurance, saying that the Chichester premiere would actually be "the *real* premiere," because "it will be a performance according to the original concept of all-male choir, whereas the New York performance will use a mixed chorus, *faute de mieux* [for lack of a better alternative]."[27]

As the summer wore on, Bernstein wrote to inquire how the rehearsals were progressing, particularly how the boys were handling the music. "Can the youngsters manage the rhythms?" he asked. "Are there any questions or problems I can help with?"[28] From what we know of its Chichester premiere, the boys managed to learn their notes successfully. The same could not be said of the orchestra, however. For various reasons, they were late to receive the score, and after witnessing an open rehearsal of the piece, Bernstein was overheard saying to his wife, "All we can do now is pray."[29] In the end, the orchestra struggled but the singers triumphed. Bernstein later said, "The Psalms went off well, in spite of a shockingly small amount of rehearsal. The choirs were a delight! They had everything down pat, but the orchestra was swimming in an open sea. They simply didn't know it. But somehow the glorious acoustics of Chichester Cathedral cushion everything so that even mistakes sound pretty."[30]

Mr. Fisher and Mr. Fitz certainly appreciate glorious acoustics, but they're not ones to count on them to smooth over mistakes in a performance. And that meant that there were plenty of rehearsals devoted to learning the piece that spring. The rehearsals were grueling, for sure, but their ubiquity started to make much of the music feel ubiquitous, too. I began to hear

Haydon unconsciously singing or humming the words to the first movement of *Chichester Psalms*, a distant melody that started operating in the background when he was working on homework or cleaning up his room. I silently reveled in how these melodies were coming to him without any adult coaxing them forth, entirely unbidden from the depths of his subconscious. No one was asking him to sing; it was erupting from inside him. I didn't ever call attention to it, of course; otherwise he would have recognized that he was doing it and made a conscious effort to stop.

In addition to the difficult rhythms, dissonant melodies, and inscrutable Hebrew lyrics, another challenging thing about the piece is its unconventional meter, or time signature. The Western music familiar to most choral audiences is often written in either 3–4 or 4–4 time, which means that each measure of notes includes either three or four beats, with each quarter note getting a single beat. For instance, a song like "Edelweiss" from *The Sound of Music* is written in 3–4 time, and a listener can hear the familiar, waltz-like cadence of three beat segments throughout. A typical march like "The Stars and Stripes Forever" by John Philip Sousa, on the other hand, is written in 4–4 time, with a steady four beats in each measure. The first movement of *Chichester Psalms* completely ignores these conventions, or rather, combines them into a nearly inscrutable meter of 7–4, so that each measure of music contains seven beats. It's as if Bernstein has stitched together the driving, militaristic meter of "The Stars and Stripes Forever" with the lingering cadence of "Edelweiss," leaving the listener unsure of whether each measure is missing a beat or carrying one extra. Because it is uneven, the counting throughout the piece tends to fall into a pattern of one-two, three-four, five-six-seven, with the emphasis in each measure placed on beats one, three, and five. This means that the piece alternates between moods of charging ahead and momentary lingering; there's a liminal space of uncertainty created in the process. The pattern of the missing eighth beat provides something exciting, an absence that "propels the music," as one scholar has written, "spills it into the next bar, one cascading into the next."[31] The unusual meter demands our attention, calls us to focus on what's missing, and how that absence compels us forward.

In addition to learning and memorizing the score to *Chichester Psalms*, Haydon was also working on his music for his Towne Choir candidacy. Since the candidates for Towne Choir had already earned their jackets, the promotion to the Towne Choir would be marked with a single pin: "T" for Towne, which the boys then affix to the lapel of the green jacket. Haydon and the rest of the Towne Choir candidates were set to receive their pins at the Kimmel Center at the final concert, at an opportune moment in the evening's program.

But the day before the concert, which was set to begin at seven o'clock on a Saturday night, we confronted an unexpected wrinkle: severe stomach pains for Haydon that sent us to the pediatrician, who promptly directed us to the ER to rule out appendicitis. After several hours of waiting, the initial lab tests turned out to be inconclusive, which meant we were ultimately transferred from our local hospital emergency room to the Children's Hospital of Philadelphia. We suddenly found ourselves headed back into the city, this time in something that resembled an ambulance, and I noted silently to myself that the last thing we wanted that weekend was yet another trip into downtown Philadelphia. Once there, we spent several more hours waiting for reassurance that Haydon did not, in fact, have an appendix on the verge of rupturing. We ultimately returned home exhausted in the middle of the night, grateful that he didn't need to have emergency surgery but without any clear explanation of the reason for his abdominal distress. I was also thankful that he had most of Saturday to recuperate before he had to be back in Philadelphia for a four o'clock call time prior to the Kimmel Center concert. The instructions for the singers suggested sending a bag dinner for our chorister, but Haydon still didn't have much of an appetite. I viewed that as a telltale sign that he was truly fighting off some kind of illness.

But the show must go on, and so it did. As the concert began, I found my seat in the elegant theater and watched with pride as the boys filed onto the stage, their uniforms clean and straight, their green and black ties cinched tightly around their white collars. There was an extensive program to look forward to, but *Chichester Psalms* was the opening number. I spotted Haydon at the edge of the risers as the piece began with its unforgettable opening bars, "Urah, h'anevel, v'chinor! A-irah Shahar!" His face looked slightly wan, and he wasn't singing with the kind of enthusiasm and gusto that I'd become accustomed to seeing; I noted uneasily to myself that the past twenty-four hours had surely had their effect on him. The first movement went off beautifully, with silence in the appropriate seventh beat and clean and crisp rhythms throughout the jubilant melody.

As the second movement began, my attention shifted to the soloist, a boy a year or so older than Haydon who was a frequent soloist. "Adonai," the solo began, his voice clear and pure as the harp played the lone accompaniment. The sparse instrumentation meant that we could pay attention only to the boy and his voice, and somehow the simplicity of the interplay between the voice and the harp left nothing else to be desired. Bernstein's score dictates that the solo is to be performed "semplice, senza cresc. or dim (non-sentimentally)." In other words, there's no need to gild the lily; the voice of an unchanged treble, by itself, conveys more than enough sentiment. The soloist's vulnerability that night was on full display—there was only his voice and a harp, and the moment that the notes entered the air they became an offering of joy and purity that forced us to be truly present, momentarily forgoing the urge to look back with longing or ahead with trepidation. We were all in the here and now, and it was glorious to behold.

A sudden tap on my shoulder disrupted my brief moment of reverie. I looked behind me to see that the program manager was coaxing me to follow her out of the performance hall. Once outside she explained that Haydon had a terrible stomachache and needed to leave the risers and head backstage. A pang of guilt traveled through my own gut as I realized that I hadn't even noticed that he'd left the group; I'd been entirely focused on the soloist. I quickly followed her through a series of hidden passageways that led us around to the area backstage, where Haydon was sitting by himself on a folding chair, looking pale and so very tired.

"My stomach really hurts again," he explained to me, his eyes brimming up with tears. "Can we go home?"

The concert had only just begun, and leaving now would mean not only that he would not get to finish performing *Chichester Psalms* but that he'd also miss singing the rest of the semester's repertoire and the pinning ceremony through which he would officially become a member of the Towne Choir. But the program manager had thought of that already and held Haydon's shiny "T" pin in her hand already, carefully pinning it on his lapel.

"He's been feeling pretty badly all afternoon," she explained. "I think it's probably best if you take him on home."

I looked at my son, his face so tired, his eyes blinking back tears, and nodded in agreement. We quietly headed out of the backstage area as the applause began—*Chichester Psalms* had just ended, and there were at least another ninety minutes to go in the performance. Haydon didn't get to finish singing the piece he'd worked months to master, to take in the glow of an adoring audience at the Kimmel Center, or to enjoy his pinning ceremony. But at least I could take him home and tuck him into bed; he might be twelve years old already, but he still wanted his mother when he was sick. We walked slowly to the car, which was parked in a garage next door to the performing arts center. Once the doors were open, he untucked his shirt, took off his jacket, belt, tie, and shoes, and tossed them unceremoniously into the back seat, grateful to be rid of the constraints of his dress uniform. He was quiet as we pulled out of the garage and drove toward the interstate, a 45-minute drive stretching out ahead of us in the dark.

"Are you mad at me?" he asked, quietly from the passenger seat.

My heart filled with love for my son as I quickly answered, "No, of course not!"

And it was true: I wasn't mad. I was admittedly disappointed, and I also felt a bit guilty because I was secretly wondering if his stomachache was my fault. After all, he'd spent hours each week learning this music, passing his candidacy requirements, and sitting captive in the car on all those drives to and from. For better or worse, this was the final concert of the season, and the choir wouldn't rehearse again until September. I was sorry that I didn't get to hear the concert that night, but I was already feeling the lightness of knowing that we wouldn't be driving to and from Philadelphia for the next three months. We'd have to hope his voice didn't change over the summer, but if it did, there was nothing we could do about it now.

I reached over and put my hand on his head, feeling his curls in my fingers as I rubbed the left side of his head a few times with my thumb. He leaned his head into my hand, answering my unspoken apology with one of his own.

"I'm not mad," I said again, and he seemed satisfied with this answer.

Once again, we were sitting side by side, staring ahead at the windshield, but this time there was only the highway before us, no traffic to contend with, no rehearsal or call time to make.

And I realized that for the first time in a long time, I wasn't in a hurry.

CHAPTER 4

Don't You Want to See the World?

It was a Thursday night in late August, the week before Haydon would start seventh grade. We were once again in the car, even though fall choir rehearsals wouldn't officially start for a few more weeks. The air of that late summer evening was just cool enough to warrant cracking the windows on the interstate, bringing little breaths of early fall into the car. This time we were returning from Philadelphia after Haydon's start-of-the-year voice check, which preceded the beginning of every boy choir season. Mr. Fitz didn't hear any signs of his voice changing just yet; Haydon would be a Descant for at least that fall, if not for the entire year. We'd also just finished a conversation with Mr. Fisher, who had asked to talk with Haydon personally about whether he would join the choir for its summer tour. Although it was almost a year away, KSB wanted the boys to commit by the early fall so they could secure the plane tickets, plan the concerts and sightseeing ventures, and arrange for the home stays that would house the boys while they were traveling, usually with the families of other boy choirs in the destination cities. That year the tour would be to Poland and Czechoslovakia, with a special focus on sites of Holocaust remembrance. As enrichment opportunities go, this one was pretty rich. And the price tag showed it: for a little under two weeks of traveling, our bill would be more than three thousand dollars.

We were prepared to fork over this cash if Haydon wanted to go on the tour, but so far he wasn't sold on this excursion. Instead, he had his mind on something else with a similar price tag: club lacrosse. Not only was paying for both beyond our reach, the dates overlapped, which meant he would need to choose either one or the other. "Club" or "travel" sports teams are pay-to-play opportunities for kids to join a team where they're promised better coaching and the chance to play with other players at a higher level than the come-as-you-are recreational ("rec") leagues that are offered in many towns and communities. Haydon had been asking to play a club sport for years now. He especially loved lacrosse and thought a club could help him improve as a player; moreover, it would give him something in common with the boys he wanted to hang with in school, who advertised their sports affiliations on T-shirts, hoodies, and ball caps. For these middle school boys, playing a sport at a higher level offered access to an exclusive, masculine club.[1]

The boys were too young to know the definition of what sociologists call social capital, of course, but they'd managed to grasp pretty clearly how it works. In its simplest form, social capital is a resource that exists in the relationships between people, one that can be converted into other kinds of access and advantage.[2] Social capital is the kind of thing that most of us don't think about explicitly in our daily lives but that plays a critical role in how they unfold nonetheless. Social capital explains how people find out about new opportunities, like jobs or educational programs, as well as how they navigate hardships and obstacles. Living in a neighborhood with lots of close friends or being a member of a religious community can translate into significant forms of social support when a family or loved one experiences a crisis, like a medical emergency, job loss, or other unforeseen difficulty. At the heart of social capital is being a member of a social network in which others recognize you as someone worthy of the group's attention and resources.

My son wasn't thinking about things in such complicated terms, of course. As a middle schooler, he just wanted to sit with the cool kids at lunch. (Whenever I try to explain sociological concepts to either of my children, they roll their eyes at me and say that sociology is just using big words to explain what everyone learns in a middle school lunchroom.) And Haydon thought that being a part of a club sports team would signal to other boys that he was a jock, with a place on a club roster shoring up his athletic bona fides. I was sympathetic to his feelings, to some extent—I remember how acutely I felt about belonging, or more accurately a lack of it, when I was his age. But I was more cynical about this goal, especially as an adult who can recognize the abbreviated life span of any benefits associated with being cool during adolescence. The social capital that he imagined he would acquire at school by presenting himself as an athlete seemed to me only a transitory goal, one rooted in the temporary anxieties of being a teenager that would inevitably recede into the background once he was a bit older.

For his part, Mr. Fisher wanted a crack at convincing Haydon, in person, to choose the tour. Mr. Fisher didn't know it, either, but he was advocating for an investment in a different kind of capital—what sociologists would call cultural capital. Cultural capital can mean a range of things, including physical works of culture, like art or music, but it can also mean being knowledgeable about these expressions of "high culture" and at ease in settings where these ways of being and knowing are valued by others.[3] Cultural capital can also be conveyed in the form of institutionalized credentials—like earning a college degree or receiving a prestigious award—as well as the body itself, as when people learn how to look and feel at home in groups that may not make conventions of belonging explicit. We can see this in how some people hold their bodies with ease and confidence around wealthy people at a country club reception, while others might feel innately uncomfortable or out of place in that kind of setting. Cultural capital, like social capital, can be converted into other kinds of resources—being able to comfortably navigate a fancy reception can solidify one's place in an elite social group, for instance, or having a prestigious college degree on one's resume can lead to an otherwise elusive job interview. Cultural capital is made even more valuable by the presumption of its scarcity, what French sociologist Pierre Bourdieu likened to "being able to read in a world of illiterates."[4]

Social capital and cultural capital aren't meant to be conflicting; often, they work in tandem with each other, each with the potential to expand resources through the other. This is one reason that kids who grow up in low-income neighborhoods experience more upward mobility if they attend school with middle- and upper-class peers, whose parents are more likely to have attended college.[5] It's also why kids who grow up in well-resourced homes tend to maintain those resources and advantages in their adult lives. Sociologists who study the influence of social and cultural capital on inequality consistently find that the resources associated with cultural capital—most importantly, an appreciation for the value of education—are conveyed through groups and social connections.

And contemporary research on parenting demonstrates that these advantages don't just happen accidentally—instead, today's parents intentionally seek out the benefits of social and cultural capital on behalf of their children. Sociologist Annette Lareau coined the term "concerted cultivation" to describe the way that middle- and upper-middle-class parents approach the development of children's aptitude in school, sports, and artistic activities.[6] The gardening metaphor is intentional—in this paradigm, children are the flowers and parents are the gardeners, carefully deciding where to plant their offspring and how best to help them bloom. Alongside the advent of the digital world, this is one of the most significant ways that our society has changed in the thirty years that have passed between when I was a child and when I became a parent. Without question, today's kids are growing up in an environment that is structured quite differently and where the stakes of childhood and adolescence feel much higher. The strategy of concerted cultivation may be practiced in individual families, but it is rewarded by institutions—especially schools and colleges—that we believe, rightly or wrongly, lead to success in the capitalist marketplace.[7] Most parents won't use terms like "social capital" or "cultural capital," but (like my son) they understand pretty well how these concepts work in practice. Ensuring that your child is accomplished and connected is one way to help guarantee that their future adult life will bring continued advantage and security—or at least, that's what we hope.

This explains why my time spent in the trenches of suburban parenting often made it feel like every parental decision was fraught with some kind of tenuous uncertainty, as if all this achievement could be wiped away by falling in with "the wrong crowd" at school or picking the wrong extracurricular activity.[8] I felt myself falling into these worries, too—as if the conflict between my son and me was about much more than just whether or not to play club lacrosse or go on the choir tour. I can certainly recognize this as a problem of the highly privileged. But even so, the stakes of the outcome felt like a referendum on something much bigger. What kinds of values and commitments was my son going to embody as he grew up? And how much power did I have to determine that outcome?

For his part, Mr. Fisher had been prepared with a hard sell for the tour. He explained how choir tours give kids the chance to explore the world—to leave the confines of their hometown, to engage audiences in other places, and to stay in the homes of other kids who are members of choirs in other countries. If Haydon went on this tour, he'd be able to sing in cathedrals in Poland and Czechoslovakia, learn about European history, go to art museums, and eat authentic pierogies and sauerkraut. Mr. Fisher had always maintained that there was something special and irreplaceable about going on tour as an unchanged treble. It was partly about how the audiences reacted to you, he explained, but also about seeing things abroad through the eyes of someone who is still a child. "You may not have another chance to go on tour as a treble," Mr. Fisher warned, although this justification didn't land with quite enough force to convince Haydon that this was the year to choose tour. In Haydon's mind, there was a lifetime of other summers when he could go on tour with the choir, but he felt like he was already behind in the race with other boys to become a better athlete. And there's no exchange rate that could convert two weeks of a choir tour into the currency that matters to an almost thirteen-year-old, which mainly has to do with boys at school seeing him as part of the group. In fact, as best as I could tell, Haydon had taken pains to ensure that none of his friends at school knew that he sang in a choir. We left the voice check after agreeing to talk about it more and to decide within the week. After that point, Haydon's spot on the tour roster would be offered to someone else.

As we got into the car and buckled our seat belts, I expected to have an engaged, thoughtful conversation about the pros and cons of each possible decision. But instead, Haydon let loose on Mr. Fisher for not understanding how much sports mattered to him.

"I bet Mr. Fisher was never on any kind of team," he said after slamming the car door. "It's like he was saying that sports are stupid."

"I didn't think that's what he was saying," I protested, taken aback momentarily. It occurred to me briefly that his annoyance with Mr. Fisher might actually be a proxy for some new frustrations with me, but I decided not to dig too much further on that point—at least, not just yet.

Admittedly, I was on Mr. Fisher's side in all of this. In my mind, there was no form of arithmetic that could make six weeks on a scorching lacrosse field worth more than two weeks spent singing in cathedrals across Europe. But thirteen-year-old boys aren't known for their superior reasoning skills, and I knew better than to try explaining to him all the reasons why the long-term cultural benefits of going on the tour should win out. I also couldn't change the realities of social life for an adolescent boy, in which no one at the lunch table wants to hear you talk about your European choir tour.

"It's just that I've just never been able to do a club team," Haydon said, his tone softening from its earlier impatience. "Everyone else has been doing a club since at least second grade," he added. I wanted to correct him on this, to remind him that these activities are incredibly expensive and there are plenty of kids whose family resources don't make this kind of thing possible in the first place. But I stopped myself before I fanned the flames. I had to admit that it did feel like most of the kids we knew were involved in some kind of club sports team. Haydon's best friend from elementary school had already been playing club hockey for two years by the time they met—at the tender age of seven. Ellen's son Sam played club baseball, and many of Haydon's friends from sixth grade played club basketball together on a team that Haydon had tried out for the previous year, without making the cut.

The pressures we were feeling have been documented elsewhere, particularly by researchers who study middle-class families who live in suburbs.[9] By some estimates, as many as 90 percent of kids participate in some kind of organized sports during their childhood.[10] Club sports, in particular, allow a subset of families to invest even further in more specialized, advanced training, with parents of boys investing more than parents of girls.[11] Of course, athletics offer many positive things—a chance to have fun in a game and meet other kids, and an opportunity to learn life lessons, like how to show up on time, work with others, and win and lose with grace. But these benefits increasingly come with a high price, in terms of time, money, and emotional well-being for both kids and their parents. As club sports have become more pervasive and more organized and have recruited children at younger ages, many parents report feeling as if they are in a kind of inescapable arms race that compels them to spend unreasonable amounts of time and money on youth athletics.[12] Plenty of parents would prefer that their kids not become so invested in sports at younger and younger ages, but the effect of all this early training is that it feels more and more necessary, especially in order to be a competitive athlete on a field later on.[13]

This is partly why I felt inclined to reject the opportunistic allure of club lacrosse in favor of the cultural capital that the choir tour promised. Much of parenting is, unfortunately, about helping kids find their way through a ceaseless number of competing values and goals that will inevitably require trade-offs. And as parents, we often approach these decisions in ways that are shaped by our own adult regrets and longings. It's not lost on me that a desire to travel is something that I actually want for myself, now that I'm in my forties and aware of all the opportunities I missed when I was younger. I still rue my decision not to study abroad in college, a choice I made for reasons that now seem incredibly shortsighted: I didn't want to spend three months away from my then-boyfriend. And on top of that, living abroad for a semester seemed . . . well, scary. I didn't regret the decision at the time, but in the intervening years I've recognized that choice for what it was: a mistake. Now I wonder if my life would have been different—by which I mean better—if I had taken that leap and gone abroad like so many of my friends. Would I have navigated my confused and halting years of early adulthood with more confidence? Would I feel more at home now with my worldly and well-traveled colleagues, who seem to have an unlimited supply of entertaining stories from college that involve backpacks and a Eurail pass? I am reminded uncomfortably of the claim attributed to Carl Jung, that "nothing has a stronger influence on their children than the unlived lives of their parents."[14]

I considered expressing some of these thoughts in the car as Haydon and I drove home that night, but I knew it probably wouldn't matter. Now that he was moving closer to adolescence, he seemed less and less inclined to take my advice. But before I could attempt to string any half-baked thoughts into words, Haydon managed to summarize this conflict in a way I didn't anticipate: "I feel like choosing lacrosse is choosing dad. But choosing choir is choosing you."

I was stunned into silence by the way he framed this conflict as one that was ultimately about the parent with whom he was going to identify. I'd been thinking all along that this impasse was about his desire for short-term social capital versus my goal of developing cultural capital in the long term. But this was not how my son saw things. In his view, the cultural capital that I was trying to sell him on—things like singing, the arts, and cross-cultural learning—could be reduced to things that girls do. Likewise, his longing for social capital was about more than just wanting to be part of the group.

He wanted to be one of the boys.

NPR reporter Rob Schmitz is the kind of person whose life has amassed cultural capital in leaps and bounds. You might recognize his name and voice from *Marketplace* on American Public Media or as an occasional host on the NPR daily podcast *Up First*. His NPR bio notes that his reporting has taken him to places like Kazakhstan, Mongolia, and New Zealand; that he spent a decade as a journalist in China, speaks fluent Mandarin and Spanish, published an award-winning book, and has a graduate degree from the Columbia School of Journalism; that his reporting has been singled out for national recognition by his colleagues. But his bio doesn't mention the thing that interested me most about Schmitz: that he grew up as a member of a boy choir in the 1980s.

There's nothing about Schmitz's background to suggest that his current work and accomplishments were ever a foregone conclusion. He grew up in Elk River, Minnesota—about thirty minutes outside of St. Cloud. "Back when I grew up it was actually a beautiful small town," he said, adding that it's now more of an exurb of the Twin Cities, which has changed the town's character in the decades since. Neither of his parents were particularly worldly—at least, not in a way that would have predicted that their oldest son would eventually become an award-winning international journalist. His dad had dropped out of college before joining the military and eventually becoming a pipe fitter, and his mom taught school before having kids and staying home with her three sons. Schmitz wasn't a musical virtuoso by any stretch either, and Elk River wasn't the kind of town where one would expect to find a thriving boy choir. But thanks to the steely determination of an enterprising choir director named Craig "Andy" Anderson, Elk River's Land of Lakes Choirboys managed to draw a robust cohort of boys into rehearsals each week. And there was something else about his choir that was unusual: they had a partnership with the world-renowned Vienna Boys Choir, which meant that they took turns visiting Vienna to stay with their counterparts there, and vice versa.

It didn't surprise me to learn that joining the choir had initially been his mom's idea. Singing wasn't something that Schmitz especially enjoyed, although in retrospect he's able to realize that his current life is one that would hardly have been possible without the cultural capital he acquired through his choir experience. He suspects that his mom was attracted to the travel opportunities that the choir would give him to see the world beyond Elk River. Like Mr. Fisher, Schmitz didn't use the term "cultural capital," but it seemed to be at the heart of what his mom was seeking out on his behalf. "I think she grew up with a bit of wanderlust," he mused, "she read books constantly, and she knew about the outside world," something that was unusual in those days, pre-internet, when seeing the world beyond your hometown came mainly through reading books from a library or watching TV specials. "She knew that this was a choir that toured," Schmitz explained, and "she knew that it would give me opportunities that other kids in the community were not getting." There was also the fact that some of the boys who lived on his street were also in the choir, and his mother had a practical need to keep her sons busy after school. She convinced Schmitz that joining the choir would be another way to tag along with his neighborhood friends. If they weren't going to be on the block to play after school, she reasoned, wouldn't he prefer to go with them to choir rehearsal?

Another reason his mom may have pushed him toward the choir is that it was clear to everyone early on that Schmitz was not going to excel in sports. Unlike my son, who had always been inclined to pursue athletics, Schmitz wasn't lusting after a team jersey in middle school. In fact, he seems to have had as much fear as my son did excitement at the thought of heading onto a rink or a field. "I was too scared to play football. I was too scared to play hockey," he remembered, "I was just sort of scared to get hurt." Schmitz added that he was also on the smaller side as a kid—taller than average, but very skinny, something that made him feel even more vulnerable in the contact sports that were popular with other boys in town. Beyond dabbling in basketball for a short while, due to his height, he remembers that his body had always seemed a poor fit for youth athletics, something that made him acutely aware of falling short when he measured himself against the teenaged boy ideal that he imagined at the time. "I think because I wasn't into sports," he hypothesized, "my mom started to look around for other things that I could do."

Looking at Schmitz now, who at nearly fifty years old is tall and lean and self-assured, it's hard to imagine him being gangly and unathletic as a kid. He's a good example of why middle school is not a moment that can accurately predict what kind of person someone will ultimately become. Schmitz may have been geeky and awkward as a teenager, but his adult life has been marked by adventure, success, and plenty of prestige. He's also a good example of how moms know what they're doing—even if their kids protest otherwise. Schmitz readily admits that he hated being in the choir when he was in middle school: "Oh my God, the practices were two hours every Tuesday and Thursday. It sucked. And then there were the concerts," he added, grimacing. But looking back, he can recognize that being in the Land of Lakes choir did two important things for him: it showed him that there was a world outside of his small Minnesota town and taught him how to navigate that world with confidence. Put simply, the choir offered access to cultural capital that opened doors to other kinds of opportunities: educational attainment, jobs and promotions, and perhaps most importantly being comfortable in a range of settings with a variety of different people.

Schmitz was terribly homesick at the beginning of his first tour, "the most homesick that I've ever been in my life," he said, adding that he remembers crying uncontrollably at the feeling of sadness that came over him once he was in his host's small apartment and getting ready for bed. He had just turned ten years old. To make things worse, his friend and home-stay partner wasn't crying, which meant that Schmitz was simply sitting there while his friend watched him cry—a mortifying experience for a ten-year-old boy. His anguish at missing his family was so palpable that even now, decades later, he can still remember the visceral fear of being so far away from home in a stranger's small apartment. The host arranged for him to call his parents, which helped, and he ultimately completed the tour without any more tears. It would be the first and last time he was ever that homesick.

When I asked him if it was an overreach to attribute some of his life and career choices to his experience in the Land of Lakes Choirboys, he quickly shook his head no. "I think it had a pretty large influence on the arc of where my life took me and the choices I made," he explained. Being in the choir "opened up my mind to possibilities I never would have known had I not experienced them," he said. A big part of this was simply seeing the world beyond his hometown and developing the confidence to feel that he was equipped to belong there, too. Schmitz can also recognize differences between the Elk River boys he knew who were in the choir and the ones who weren't, especially now that their lives have played out in the decades since. "When I look at my peers who weren't in the choir from my hometown, most of them ended up never moving from either Elk River or the Twin Cities," he observed. He's quick to add that this isn't necessarily a bad thing, of course—there's a cost that comes with leaving behind your roots and the family and friends that make up your social network. But at the same time, Schmitz readily acknowledges that his current life would probably never have occurred to him had he not been in a choir that took him far beyond the confines of what was familiar in his childhood.

Most importantly, it was the tours that made the difference for Schmitz, especially the Land of Lakes Choirboys' partnership with the Vienna Boys Choir, which infused the group with a particular kind of prestige. The uniforms that the Land of Lakes boys wore even mimicked the Vienna Boys Choir's trademark sailor suits. Schmitz remembers these uniforms with amusement, since they involved wearing a "dickie"—a fake shirt collar that the boys wore underneath their sailor tops, and which led to an endless string of jokes among the boys that were variations on the theme of "where's your dickie?" Schmitz recalls that the youngest boys in the training choir wore a red dickie, while the boys in the touring choir had a red and blue striped version that signified their senior status. So even as much as he resented the time spent in rehearsals, he was thrilled beyond measure when he was promoted to the touring choir and got to wear a new dickie. "I remember feeling elated," he laughed. "Because suddenly I knew I was going to go on tour; I was going to leave Minnesota; and I was going to see things."

The partnership with the Vienna Boys Choir meant that each choir took turns visiting the other, staying in the homes of the respective choir boys during the tour. Schmitz doesn't recall much about his first trip to Europe, except for seeing mountains and hating what they ate for breakfast in Vienna. "I came from the land of Cocoa Puffs and Lucky Charms," he joked, momentarily channeling the culinary mindset of a ten-year-old from the 1980s. "Suddenly you're eating this tiny piece of bread that's hard as a rock. And then you're given jam and margarine, or something like that. And that's your breakfast." The tea tasted so bad that he almost vomited trying to drink it until he figured out that it was palatable if he added heaping spoonfuls of sugar—something that amused his host family to no end. Even if Schmitz doesn't remember anything more about his visit to Vienna—he was only ten years old, after all—he can still describe the two Vienna choir boys who came and stayed with his family in Elk River during their U.S. visit a few years later. "They were just like me," he said. "And they spoke English really well"—something that astounded him and his brothers at the time. He also remembers that they took the boys snowmobiling across the frozen lake near their house—something they weren't supposed to do, but which the boys convinced his dad to permit.

The home stays also gave the choir's director a reason to explicitly coach the boys about how to behave politely. When the choir was getting ready to go on tour, Anderson would typically devote three or four of the choir's weekly practices to how to act in the home of a host family, including things like how to address adults (always "sir" or "ma'am," Schmitz remembered) and generally how to "impress grownups with our behavior." It's not that Schmitz didn't learn these things at home, necessarily, but rather that learning them in the choir gave him a larger community of peers in which these behaviors were known and recognized. This was also a place where social capital and cultural capital were aligned—the social graces that Anderson was seeking to impart to the boys were ways of communicating a kind of status and appropriateness that was embedded in the group context of being a Land of Lakes chorister.

Later, in high school, it also helped distinguish the former choir boys from the rest of the town, particularly in a public school system that pulled in kids from the surrounding area, which included rural communities and trailer parks. Bullying was also common in the high school, especially for boys who weren't athletes—it was the football, hockey, and basketball players who "sort of ruled the school," Schmitz remembered. These were the boys who had power, at least in his mind, which was why most boys aspired to be jocks. "If you weren't a jock, you know, you were just basically surviving," he recalled. "But the thing is, when you saw other choir boys at school, it was sort of this code. You knew each other. You knew that these were civil kids. That you didn't need to have your guard up."

Hearing Schmitz talk about his teenaged angst made me slightly more sympathetic to my own son's adolescent worries. It also illustrated the enduring power of the masculine culture that permeates American adolescence—nearly three decades had passed since Rob Schmitz left Elk River, Minnesota, and yet the memory of his high school's social stratification system seemed etched just as powerfully upon his memory as the homesickness of his first home stay on tour. And Schmitz was not the first man I'd talked with who could recall so keenly the social consequences of *not* being a jock in high school—with memories of bullying, or feeling like a second-class citizen in a social order that privileges the boys with athletic prowess.

So perhaps it should have come as surprise that Haydon interpreted the "choir or lacrosse" conflict as one that was about gender, and how he was going to fit into the social networks that structured his daily life in middle and high school. At a fundamental level, staying in choir would mean doing something feminine, which his mom values, while focusing on lacrosse would mean doing something affiliated with the masculine identity that he associates with his dad—and which definitely had more currency in the middle school lunchroom. I could have pointed out to him that these things don't matter in the long term, but that's not exactly true. Rob Schmitz still remembered what it was like to not be athletic in high school, even years later and in spite of everything that he had accomplished professionally as an adult. At the same time, he admitted that being in the choir and participating in the tours were a fundamental piece of his life's puzzle. Without those experiences, it's hard to see how his life would have unfolded in the same way. And although Schmitz can recognize the benefits of the experience in retrospect, he didn't especially understand it at the time.

That's the part of Schmitz's story that made me uneasy as I thought about these inflection points in my own meandering road as a parent. What if his mother hadn't cajoled him into choir, and eventually into the tour? Would he still be bringing us the news on NPR? What would he have done instead? Would he be as happy in his life as he is right now?

For those fortunate enough to not be worrying about providing our kids with their basic needs, it's tempting to channel our extra anxiety into other, adjacent worries inspired by the concerted cultivation paradigm—are we providing them with enough nurture and reassurance? Academic challenge and academic support? Extracurricular learning? Discipline and structure? The privilege of parenting in an environment of relative abundance can paradoxically create a dark and twisted fantasy that would give parents—and especially mothers, who do more of the hands-on work of raising children—an outsized vision of our influence and importance.[15] I'd seen this firsthand with my own friends and social networks, where even the smallest decision could feel like it carried seismic and world-changing significance. Which car seat had the best safety rating? What was the best way to motivate a child to embrace early reading? Which piano instructor had the best reputation in town?

My own suburban milieu—nestled between a major American city on one side and an Ivy League college town on the other—undoubtedly made for a very different environment than the mostly working-class Minnesota small town in which Rob Schmitz grew up. By virtue of geography alone my kids were growing up in a more culturally enriched and socially advantaged context—not to mention the ways in which our global society has become more connected over the past thirty years, thanks to the internet and social media. Even so, there's something about a story like Rob Schmitz's that speaks to the idea that seemingly small, chance interactions like a mother cajoling her son into a local boy choir can have seismic influences on that child's future life.

What's ironic about contemporary parenthood is that regardless of the wealth of information and resources that parents can acquire, there's no guarantee that we can convince our kids to use them in the way that we would like. We can find a good piano teacher, but getting our child to practice their weekly music lesson is another matter entirely. We can take a four-year-old to the public library but that doesn't mean they're going to take an interest in learning to read before they start kindergarten. And perhaps the most worrying thing of all is that no amount of resource investment can protect a child from risk or harm. Even the highest rated car seat might fail to save a life in the event of a serious accident. The paradox of abundance in the face of this powerlessness may be one reason that these everyday decisions can feel like they carry outsized significance.

I didn't really think that Haydon would be like Rob Schmitz, and one day draw a solid line between being a boy chorister and the professional ambitions he would later explore. But I did believe that where he chose to put his time and energy mattered, partly because these two activities would seem to place him in very different relationships to the larger world. A frequent criticism of club sports is that they too often put well-resourced kids into contact with kids and families whose race and income level mirror their own.[16] As Anne Helen Petersen wrote in a widely read piece with the polemical title "Against Kids' Sports" in 2021, "Like elite college and playdates, professionalized kids sports are an apparatus for bourgeois kids to be with other bourgeois kids, to extract them from their (potentially) less class-siloed public schools, and for people who are not bourgeois to learn how to pantomime it."[17] In contrast, a choir tour was potentially about showing young people the vast and humbling expanse of the world. Like Rob Schmitz experienced, it could mean making friends across countries, even languages, and seeing your own life differently in response.

Of course, boy choirs do still wield a sense of prestige—and perhaps none more so than the world-renowned Vienna Boys Choir. It's now been many years since the choir had a partnership with the Land of Lakes Choirboys, and the Vienna Boys Choir gave up homestays in favor of hotel rooms long ago, too. But the Vienna Boys Choir is still touring—and in fact, the choir isn't one choir but rather four different, equally trained and talented choirs that take turns traveling to sing for audiences around the world. The group's name is a bit misleading, because not all the boys are from Vienna. In fact, they're not even all from Austria. The VBC starts with an elementary day school in Vienna, which enrolls boys and girls young as six years old. The auditions for these children are not that different from the ones that kids do for community choirs in the United States—the school is mainly looking for kids with a good ear and a sense of rhythm, and of course a desire to sing.[18] But choristers start boarding at the school when they reach the fourth grade, and by that point boys audition from all over the world—France, China, Japan, Romania—to live at the boarding school and sing in the choir. By ages ten to fourteen, the equivalent of fifth through eighth grades in the United States, the boys are part of one of the four touring choirs, with international tours that can last as long as eight to ten weeks—a commitment and itinerary that makes a community boy choir tour look like true child's play.

I wanted to find out how those boys felt about singing in the choir, given that their tours bring both prestige and an all-consuming level of commitment. One of the VBC's choirmasters, Oliver Stech, explained to me that the tours are one of the most compelling things about being in the VBC. "They can see the whole world," he said. "Get to know different cultures, they can try different foods, visit the country and of course, give a lot of concerts." He added that they simultaneously acquired a first-rate musical education and that the costs to their families were minimal. Although there are modest fees associated with attending the elementary school and, later, the high school for singers who have aged out of the touring choir, the boys who tour pay only a nominal sum each month to cover the cost of vocal lessons. While they're on tour, they generate revenue from the concerts, and that covers the costs of the travel, food, and lodging for the ten weeks that they're away from Vienna.

I asked him if the boys ever had to be cajoled into all of this, thinking of Rob Schmitz's mother back in the 1980s as well as my own current attempt to convince my son just how much he would enjoy the chance to sing his way across Europe. Stech's answer surprised me. "I think nowadays, it's really the boys who want to be here. If a boy doesn't want to be a member of the Vienna Boys Choir, he wouldn't stay here." In fact, Stech thinks the pressure campaign today works in precisely the opposite direction—it's the boys who must convince their parents to let them join the choir. "We have to motivate the parents to let the boys stay in our institution and go on to boarding school," he said, especially because this means that they are living away from their families during the week. Like with other choir boarding schools, the boys in the VBC are allowed to go home on the weekends and spend one weeknight at home, if they want to. "In almost every case it's the boy's motivation to go here," Stech said, "and sometimes they really need to convince their parents." Parents, in his view, are thinking mainly about the things that *they'll* miss out on rather than what their child might gain by going on tour.

I was struck by this radically different portrait of childhood achievement, one that's almost unrecognizable from the concerted cultivation model of parenting that my friends and I seem to be following. For the boys in the world's most elite children's choir, their excellence and commitment emerges from a child's true love of singing rather than an adult's instrumental goals. And this shows in the kind of maturity that the boys themselves acquire on tour. The demands of an extended international tour mean that the boys have to learn how to be independent and self-reliant. "They have to pack their things on their own," Stech observed, adding that while the chaperones help, the boys are generally responsible for themselves. "They have to make sure they have their things on the bus," he enumerated, and "don't forget anything at the hotel.... Of course, we tell them everything on tour, 'Be there at nine o'clock, pack your things, wear your uniform, take your hat, take your gloves, etc.'" he said. But even with all these instructions, the boys are the ones who have to carry out these responsibilities, which means that they learn to manage their life on tour without their parents.

Of course, these benefits probably matter little to the choristers. After all, they're not inclined to be thinking about much of anything that's long term. Stech noted with amusement that sometimes the things that the choristers most enjoy about a tour are the things that kids would enjoy anywhere—a trip to the arcade or an eighties-themed roller-skating rink. These experiences, which they enjoy alongside their friends, are sometimes more memorable than seeing landmarks like the Statue of Liberty or the Golden Gate Bridge.

"Do they realize what they're able to experience in the moment?" I asked Stech, unsure of how he would answer. This question gets to the heart of the parenting challenge that I've yet to find my way through—navigating the razor-thin margin between compelling children to do things that will benefit them in the long term while also respecting the desires that they articulate in the present. Stech pondered this for a moment before describing one of their recent U.S. appearances as a way of answering my question. "When we had our concert in Carnegie Hall," he explained—a concert that drew two thousand people at one of the most prestigious venues in the United States—"I feel like I'm the king of the world for an hour," he laughed. "Sometimes I think the boys are also feeling that," he said. "I tell them, you know, there's so many people who would love to sing [here], to be there once in a lifetime, and you have this opportunity." But the kids don't always recognize this, he admitted, because part of what it means to be a child is to live in the moment. "I'm sure that every choir boy from my choir really enjoyed the experience at Carnegie Hall," he said. "But then maybe they just get on the bus and drive to the hotel. And before long they're thinking to themselves, 'And let's see, burger and fries,'" he laughed. "I think this is just because they're kids and they have different priorities or a different way of perceiving their life. Sometimes I feel that the boys just need a few years to let it sink in," he shrugged. "And then they really know what they experienced."

Along with an unchanged treble voice, this is ideally one of the fleeting gifts of childhood—the ability to be in the moment, unbothered by long-term goals or worries (except for the ones that we parents give them, of course). Kids aren't generally thinking about the instrumental value of their choices; they are more inclined to want to be with their friends and have fun. But adults have the benefit and the burden of knowing that decisions made in the short term can have significant ramifications for the future. In fact, when I think about it this way I realize that Haydon may have much more in common with the choristers in the Vienna Boys Choir than I recognized. Like them, he was advocating to a parent to be able to follow his own lead—it's just that he wanted to play lacrosse instead of sing. He was trying to convince me to let him follow his short-term passions, which prioritize a sense of belonging in the group that mattered to him and of course the enjoyment of playing a game he loves with friends. Parents can see the long-term horizon in which both social and cultural capital may be important, but we can't always reverse engineer the things that our kids will want to be committed to along the way. I'm invested in the boy choir experience because I believe that the long-term benefits are worth a little arm-twisting—things like the musical training and the inclusive masculinity and (if only my son would agree with me!) the chance to acquire cultural capital by touring Europe this summer. There may have been additional reasons that Haydon thought choosing choir would be like choosing me. He could tell that I wanted to be in the driver's seat for a bit longer. Perhaps I wasn't that different from the parents who felt so compelled to keep their kids involved in club sports.

In the end, he chose lacrosse.

I was disappointed, of course, but mostly succeeded in keeping my feelings to myself, silently fuming at his father (somehow this was his fault!) while I bit my tongue and paid the lacrosse club fees. I wrote the dates for the summer tournaments on the calendar and resigned myself to a summer spent driving across multiple states to sit on a folding chair in a desolate landscape of overfertilized grass fields next to forlorn rows of porta-potties. I could have tried to make friends with some of the other parents—perhaps expand my own social network, which is mostly full of overeducated colleagues who, like me, weren't particularly athletic in high school. But I chose instead to keep my distance, silently judging their elitist intentions, imagining them hoping their sons' lacrosse skills would guarantee them a spot in a highly selective East Coast college so that this next generation, too, could secure their rightful place in the white male hegemony. From my safe distance of removed judgment I reminded myself that at least my son was still in a boy choir, after all, and had other interests besides a sport with a complicated history of exclusion and violence.

On closer examination, of course, they weren't the ones deluding themselves. The boy choir tradition that I had so proudly allied myself with is one that is similarly rife with injustice and exclusion. Even if I was right that singing in a boy choir would help protect my son from learning the "wrong" kinds of masculinity, boy choirs do mostly engage boys who already have multiple advantages—most importantly, parents who can pay the tuition and have the freedom and flexibility to drive them to rehearsals whenever it's required. And this tradition also has its roots in a history of exclusion that is inflected with particularly white, Western influences. Not to mention the part about excluding girls and women. And what about kids who identify as transgender? What do single-gender choirs have to offer them?

I was about to learn that there are boy choirs that are turning a new page in this age-old story, finding new ways to identify and develop talent among boys who don't have access to these opportunities through school or well-resourced parents—mostly boys who aren't white or Asian. They're cultivating both cultural and social capital, but attempting to rewrite the very rules of social exclusion in the process, by reshaping both who gets to sing as well as the music they perform.

CHAPTER 5

Draw the Circle Wide

My cousin Susanna is a high school choral director, and after I'd told her about Haydon's newfound singing career, she'd been following it with interest and encouragement. I'd texted her earlier that spring to tell her that I was working on a book about boys and singing, asking if I could interview her for the project. Susanna was eager for the assignment. She comes from a very musical family—her parents are opera singers, and her brother is a professional violinist—and she grew up embedded in the vibrant world of the performing arts in San Francisco. And for the past twelve years she's been directing high school choirs in California—first at a school in North Stockton and more recently at a school in a Sacramento suburb. I knew from our past conversations that these two schools were very different in demographics: the school in North Stockton was a Title I school, with a large representation of Asian and Hispanic students with immigrant parents who didn't yet speak English. In North Stockton, more than three-quarters of students were eligible for free or reduced lunch, there was no IB curriculum, and the school offered just ten AP courses, only one of which was in science and none in the arts or a non-English language. The suburban Sacramento school, in contrast, is majority white and situated adjacent to an affluent lakeside community where many former basketball players for the Sacramento Kings own homes. Less than a quarter of students at the Sacramento school were eligible for free or reduced lunch, and the school offered both an IB diploma program and twenty AP courses that span the arts, languages, and sciences.[1] Outside of school, these kids were doing all kinds of enrichment activities—sports, mathletes, coding camp, you name it.

I'd expected Susana to tell me that the choral program in the North Stockton school was anemic compared to the Sacramento school, given the resource disparity between them. Public schools are "privilege-dependent organizations" whose resources, opportunities for enrichment, and perceived social status are largely determined by the socioeconomic status of the neighborhoods attached to them.[2] And the arts, themselves, are often perceived as an optional enhancement less deserving of scarce public resources; American public schools have long viewed arts education as peripheral to the core academic program—a "tender-hearted" diversion from the "hard-headed" requirements of reading, math, and science.[3] And we also know that students growing up in the most resource-deprived schools are most likely to miss out on high-quality arts programs, either because of inadequate funding, a perception that low-income schools should prioritize STEM curriculum that promises more economic mobility, or both. These inequities are pervasive and widespread: more than 3.6 million students in the United States do not have access to any music curriculum in their public schools, and over 2 million have no access to any forms of arts education.[4]

But what Susanna told me was a slightly different story, at least when it came to the kids who were in choir. These two schools were a world apart in terms of socioeconomic inequality, but the way that gender was represented in her choirs was markedly different. In North Stockton she had a choir that was reliably half boys, half girls, which generally represented the gender breakdown at the school. She never had a problem recruiting boys in North Stockton; in fact, it wasn't something that she even thought about there. But when she moved to Sacramento, she was shocked at what she found. "My first semester at the new school," she says, "I had a choir of thirty and I had three boys."

She doesn't credit any one factor for this discrepancy; now that she's been teaching in Sacramento for several years she has a more nuanced understanding of the differences between these two districts. For one thing, in the suburban school the kids have many more options for course electives, which means that choir competes with students' other interests, and appealing electives like computer science or engineering would often win out in a school where students feel pressure to demonstrate academic achievement, particularly in STEM fields. The Sacramento kids are also more involved in athletics; over 60 percent of students were on an athletic team in the 2022–2023 school year. Susanna points out that this requires both money and free time—things that the kids in North Stockton often didn't have to spare. After school they often went to work, either to their own part-time jobs or home to take care of their younger siblings.

But this doesn't fully explain why the boys in North Stockton would have been more interested in choir to start with. Perhaps the students in North Stockton were just more likely to participate in choir because of the relative lack of opportunities offered at their high school. For young people growing up outside of the resource- and time-intensive infrastructure of kids' enrichment activities, any school opportunity might look more appealing because students are choosing among fewer options, both at school and outside of it. But Susanna has a more interesting theory to offer—most importantly, that these boys came from cultural traditions that encouraged male singing. Many were very active in religious communities where they frequently sang in church, for instance. Moreover, they saw other, older boys and men singing in these settings, which probably further emphasized the message that singing and masculinity aren't necessarily in conflict. And aside from these sociocultural explanations, there was another reason that the choir in North Stockton was thriving with an equal representation of boys and girls. It was just fun.

On one hand, perhaps it shouldn't have mattered that Susanna had only three boys in her new choir when she started teaching outside of Sacramento. After centuries of gender-based exclusion, what difference should it make if there are more girls than boys? For Susanna, the challenge was mostly just practical: she didn't know how to pick repertoire for the group. It wasn't an all-treble choir, after all, and those three boys needed something to sing that was in their vocal range. At the same time, three boys just weren't enough to cover the lower-voice parts required in most SATB (soprano, alto, tenor, bass) music, which represents the majority of choral repertoire. And this is especially true of the more interesting, complicated music—just three low voices isn't enough to fill out the lower voice parts.

Susanna initially tried moving some of the girls with lower voices around so that they could sing some of the tenor parts—most of the vocal range of a (typically male) tenor and a (typically female) alto overlap, save for the notes on the outer margins of each. "Wouldn't that be a solution for the tenors, at least?" I asked. Susanna explained that while it's true that a good bit of this vocal range overlaps, asking altos to sing tenor misses the physical differences of vocal resonance that tend to be associated with male and female vocal ranges. "It's about where the voices are strong," she said, which means that "an alto in the low range doesn't have as much power as a tenor in the high range." In other words, a female singer may be able to produce the sounds in the upper range of a tenor, but the notes aren't coming from the strongest register of her chest voice. Likewise, the power of the upper range of the male tenor packs more punch than the same notes sung by a female vocalist.

Susanna was careful to emphasize that she also believed that a strong vocal choral program could include only one vocal range; after all, many all-boys or all-girls schools can and do have outstanding choirs. But she does think that having low voices in a high school choir helps to build a program that can sing a broad range of repertoire. So, she set about finding ways to increase the male representation in the chorus. First, she set up twice weekly choral rehearsals that students could attend outside of the formal schedule during a special intervention period that the school had set aside each day for students to seek tutoring, catch up on homework, or pursue extracurriculars. She also held separate rehearsals for girls and boys, but without mentioning gender by name—these were "Treble Tuesdays" and "Baritone Thursdays," the latter of which included the handful of boys who were already in chorus. She also worked on recruiting other boys she knew who were in band or who were friends of current choristers with the goal of creating a culture of male singing at the school. She pointed out that the school is in a more politically conservative district and that she noticed immediately that this school had more of an "air of machismo" about it. What this meant in practice was simple: boys often saw singing as not masculine.

"So how do you counter that machismo when you're with this group of just boys?" I asked.

"I mean, in a way I kind of lean into it," she said. "I don't say that it's only for men or it's only for boys," she clarified, adding that she has welcomed more than one trans singer into her choir in Sacramento. "But I think I lean in a little bit to the machismo sort of thing" by recognizing that "boys have a little bit more energy and they need to exert. And so, we just make it really high energy." The sports metaphor is useful here, she thinks, likening an all-male choir rehearsal to a fast-paced sports drill where you "go go go" until the endorphins start flowing. Athletics are a big part of students' social lives in suburban Sacramento, which means that the kids who started joining choir, especially the boys, were interested in learning the national anthem so that they could sing at the school's football and basketball games.

Susanna is not the first choir director to see a connection with sports as a way to fill out the risers in choir with more low voices. Christine Bass, a retired high school chorus teacher and creator of the choral resource "Where the Boys Are"—a video for choir directors who want advice on how to recruit boys—figured out early on that one way to get more boys in choir was to go after the jocks.[5] In other words, if you want to make singing cool for boys, then the first step is to recruit the boys who are already at the top of the high school masculine hierarchy. Fans of the TV show *Glee* will recognize the familiar storyline of football players navigating their jock identity alongside singing.

It took a few years, but Susanna's choir is now almost half boys and half girls—or put differently, half "low" voices and half "high" voices. By 2024, she even had enough low voices to create a dedicated class for their rehearsal. She likes having the flexibility to sing more repertoire, but even more than that Susanna is proud that the chorus offers a place for young people to come together and find a common identity. Some of those boys are jocks who have plenty of social capital already, but others are students for whom navigating the social dimensions of high school is challenging. "It's students who need a home, a community," she said. She also thinks it's a place to start dismantling some of the more destructive stereotypes associated with masculinity—after all, a thriving tenor and bass section challenges the insidious idea that boys who sing aren't sufficiently masculine. And ironically, despite the high-energy way that Susanna runs her rehearsals, she finds that the boys often most enjoy the music that is more lyrical, the songs with more expressive texts, not the more stereotypically masculine repertoire.

But her story also tells us something bigger. After all, the problem that she encountered in the suburban school is one borne of a certain kind of privilege. The kids at her school, mostly white, are embedded in a particular social context—one that prizes athletics and the machismo of jock culture that can often accompany it. Therefore, getting boys to sing required Susanna to lean in to that traditional masculine culture—making choir rehearsals more like a sports practice, for instance, and squeezing practices into a more flexible class period so that they wouldn't conflict with kids' athletic activities after school. When she was at the school in North Stockton, she didn't need that many tricks in her bag, perhaps in part because those boys had already been able to integrate singing into an understanding of masculinity that was, in other ways, still fairly conservative. And at a practical level those kids weren't involved in recreational sports, since their after-school responsibilities often included practical concerns like work. Still, there is no getting around the fact that the kids in North Stockton were receiving an education that, by almost any metric, was inferior compared to that of kids in the Sacramento suburbs.

Overcoming inequalities that are manifest in social institutions, like schools and neighborhoods, is something that many directors of contemporary boy choirs are thinking about intentionally. Most are quick to mention how scholarships are available for boys whose parents can't afford the tuition. And in many ways, this is the intervention that seems most natural from an upper-middle-class perspective—find individual boys who have vocal talent and interest and remove any financial obstacles that would keep them from participating. From the vantage point of Lareau's "concerted cultivation" form of parenting, this is a one-by-one strategy for helping kids whose family resources wouldn't otherwise give them access to the childhood achievement industrial complex.

But there's another way of thinking about access that looks at these discrepancies and suggests that the individual give-a-kid-a-scholarship model isn't quite the answer—or at least, not on its own. After all, boys must know about an opportunity before they can take advantage of it. With this goal in mind, some boy choir directors are working to broaden low-income kids' access to the performing arts by offering choral opportunities to entire communities. They would look at the low-income kids in Susanna's first school and see implicit strengths and promise just waiting to be harnessed rather than problems of access that need to be overcome individually. They're refashioning the linear progression of childhood achievement into something that looks more like a circle. In the words of a well-known choral anthem, they want to draw the circle wide.[6]

But there are also limits to these visions of inclusion. Exclusion predicated on socioeconomic status functions quite differently from barriers constructed around gender. Resources might enable participation for lower-income choristers who are Black or Hispanic, while a different kind of work is required to welcome gender-nonconforming kids into a spot in a children's choir that has historically determined membership by biological sex. My conversations with boy choir directors suggest that despite their desire to cultivate a more inclusive form of masculinity, these spaces often maintain fairly conservative expectations for how choristers present their gender due to the value that they place on physical conformity in performance settings. In the same way that Susanna invoked subtle "machismo" cues to encourage boys to join her school choir, boy choirs rely on explicit masculine signaling to provide a kind of protective shield for behaviors that could otherwise be read as gender-nonconforming. This suggests that the more expansive masculinity that boys-only choirs seek to develop in young singers may be more about attitudes and emotional expression than gendered forms of physical presentation.

Like schools, boy choirs are privilege-dependent organizations powered largely by the contributions of well-resourced parents. This was abundantly clear to Jeremy Tucker when he became the artistic director of the Raleigh Boychoir in 2014. "When I first came in, I realized that this organization really served a majority of kindergarten through eighth grade boys from a certain bracket of income level," he recalled. This was exacerbated by the location of the choir's rehearsal space—the choir owned a building in a multimillion-dollar residential neighborhood in Raleigh, North Carolina, which wasn't easily accessible by public transportation. So one of his goals when he first took the job was to make the choir more inclusive, which meant recruiting from a broader socioeconomic background as well as underserved populations. In his mind, this meant being "really intentional about race to make sure that our boys look like our community." Part of this required changing the choir's physical presence in the city and revising the composition of its board, which had mostly included parents when Tucker arrived. Over his tenure, the board's composition has shifted to include more business leaders from the community, and the board eventually decided to sell the property in the upscale Raleigh neighborhood and move to a more accessible, downtown location. Now the choir has rehearsal space at an Episcopal church on the city bus routes that charges them a "crazy cheap" rent that Tucker anticipates will allow the choir to move away from the fourteen-hundred-dollar annual tuition and toward a sliding scale model.

Tucker is a white male, but he quickly added that he grew up in a family that would not have had the resources to enable his participation in a group like the one he was directing when we spoke in 2024—and he said that he probably wouldn't have wanted to join the choir that he found at the beginning of his tenure as artistic director. "It was a very specific genre and a specific sound and repertoire and mission," he explained, which was performing mostly very traditional, formal Christian music. While he admired the focus, as an organization that received grants from the City of Raleigh and its United Arts Council, he knew that they needed to be more representative of the community. Tucker has now broadened the kind of repertoire that the boys perform—something that has ruffled more than a few feathers. Tucker recounted that parents were some of the most challenging stakeholders to convince that "quality and excellence and standards can apply to any style or genre of music. It doesn't necessarily have to be dead white men. We know that good skills and technique can be applied across all genres of music."

The biggest shift, however, has been in how parents are encouraged to think about their sons' participation in the choir. Tucker thinks that ten years ago parents generally felt that having their sons in the Raleigh Boychoir was a sign of status; they would "think of this group as an academically gifted or advanced group." Keeping the boys in the choir, then, sometimes felt a bit punitive, and driven primarily by parents' own needs. (I shifted uncomfortably in my seat as he said this, recognizing something of myself in those parents' motivations.) As Tucker saw it, "The prestige and the reputation of the Raleigh Boychoir was something that drove the parents to have the boys in it, but I don't think it drove the boys, if you want my honest opinion." Now that the choir has moved locations and is working to attract a wider range of singers, he's aiming to frame the motivation for joining the choir as one that's about being part of something in the community that's bigger than what any one boy could accomplish on his own. Tucker wants the boys to think of themselves not as outstanding individual singers but as a group that serves as ambassadors and servants of the city.

The changes that directors like Tucker are instituting feel innovative in our current context, but they represent a return to some of the organizational strategies that characterized many of the country's prominent city boy choirs at their founding. Groups like the Cincinnati Boychoir and the Philadelphia Boys Choir, as noted in chapter 2, actually began in the city's schools as "all city" ensembles that drew singers from all of the city's public elementary schools. Not surprisingly, partnerships with public schools (alongside private school and homeschool families) are a key component of Tucker's vision for building a more diverse and representative choir. The long-term vision is what Tucker calls a "satellite-based program" where the choir would develop a relationship with a cluster of schools for a period of time that would involve a short-term after-school enrichment program. At its conclusion, boys who were especially interested in singing could proceed to join the choir and the organization would work with the district to eliminate any transportation barriers.

Other directors are also experimenting with school partnerships to expand both their numbers and representation. Daniel Bates, director of the Florida Singing Sons, piloted a new recruitment initiative in 2021 that was designed to find new singers and enhance the choir's diversity of representation. Like many choirs, the Singing Sons are based in a city (Fort Lauderdale) even though the boys in the choir, particularly the older boys, have generally overrepresented the suburbs. In contrast, the public schools that are closest to the group's rehearsal space in the city are Title I schools, with a high percentage of low-income kids and families. Bates approached the music directors of those schools with a proposition: any boy who was recommended for the Singing Sons by a school music teacher and who successfully auditioned for the training choir would receive a scholarship to participate (the tuition for the year had typically been set at a hundred dollars per month). The scholarship program had at least two benefits—first, it led to a growth in singer representation from Fort Lauderdale schools, and second, it destigmatized what it meant to receive a scholarship because it was offered to all boys who entered this way, regardless of financial need.

It is also changing the choir's demographics. In the first, pilot year of the program the Singing Sons had eleven boys who entered the choir through the school-based nomination program, almost all of whom were persons of color. In the second year, that number grew to sixteen. What's more, the eleven boys from the first year stayed on, which means that within two years Bates had added almost thirty boys to the choir, most of whom were Black or Hispanic. By the end of the third year, in the spring of 2023, Bates estimated that half of the choir was Hispanic—a level of diversity that exceeds the racial diversity of Fort Lauderdale as a whole, where approximately 60 percent of residents are non-Hispanic whites.

I was curious about what would happen when these boys from lower-income families moved up through the ranks of the choir—after all, the choir is currently balancing the books through the tuition paid by the older boys, most of whom had been in the choir since they were trebles and whose parents were able to pay the tuition, which works out to about a thousand dollars a year, excluding the cost of tours. What Bates and the choir's board decided was to ask the newer families—both those who needed the financial assistance and those that didn't—to pay a modest sum of twenty-five dollars per month for their second year in choir. The additional singers who had been added to the choir were helping to make up for the difference in revenue, and Bates added that they already provided some of the older boys with tuition assistance through a special grant that had been earmarked for scholarships. In those cases, Bates said that they offer a discount of 40 percent, which brings the monthly tuition down to sixty dollars. "And as soon as I've done that, for parents, it's like a light," he said. "They literally light up, because they're like, 'Oh, my God, you're able to help us that much!'" He added that no one has yet asked for more assistance than that, but that if they did, "We would find a way to make it work."

This model does require a shift in how the choir is funded—away from parents' tuition and more toward grants and sponsorships. The downside of this is that Bates has had to work toward hiring staff dedicated to fund development or outreach, and his position as artistic director of the Singing Sons is only part-time; his main, full-time job is as a voice teacher at a local private school, where he works mainly with high school students. He does get money from state and county public arts funds, and those funds have steadily increased (in 2021, Bates estimated that they got almost $30,000 from Broward County, a figure that had grown to $49,000 by 2024). Some particularly committed individuals have been intermittent funders, but keeping those donors engaged requires time—things like sending them videos of kids singing and finding other ways to communicate how their gifts make an impact. These are the sorts of things that an executive director or another staff person devoted to development might do, but without an infusion of resources at the beginning Bates admits that it's hard to prime the pump. This means that most of the bills are still being paid by parents—the parents who have resources, that is—and that this model of recruitment necessarily needs to include kids who aren't from Title I elementary schools, too. The robust response that Bates has observed through the school-based recruitment system is not financially sustainable in the long term without an accompanying shift to a different funding model.

"How do the parents feel about the changing racial and socioeconomic composition of the choir?" I asked him. Bates acknowledged that the choir has changed a lot over the past several years. In fact, he says, "It used to be known as a rich white boys club." But now he thinks that the diversity of the choir is a draw for everyone—meaning most of the parents and most of his board. Furthermore, Bates reports that the parents in his group haven't resented this discrepancy—at least, not yet. Instead, he thinks the twin growth in numbers and increase in diversity have made parents even more committed to the organization. "People have really commented on that [the increase in racial and socioeconomic diversity]," he said, "I'm getting more parent recommendations than ever." And despite the marketing that he's been doing through schools, he said that "the most prevalent thing that gets people to us is parents," something that wasn't happening when he first became artistic director several years previously. "When I started, nobody was recommending anybody to the group. And now, we get it a lot." Admittedly, there are members of the board who are worried about the financial sustainability of a model that lets people in for free (or close to it), but the growth that the elementary school initiative has generated has also created new momentum and excitement that's contagious.

Although the Singing Sons' model of free tuition for boys recommended by their elementary schools is unusual, most directors whom I spoke with did assure me that no boy who wanted to sing in their choir would be turned away due to an inability to pay tuition.[7] So finding ways to incorporate boys from lower-income families shouldn't, in theory, present a financial challenge for a choir's regular-year programming, if there's a solid core of tuition-paying boys each year. And Bates is also learning how to be entrepreneurial. For instance, this year he had a small group of boys perform in the Miami Opera's production of *Tosca*, for which the group got paid just enough for Bates to hire a sixteen-person orchestra and two professional singers to perform Faure's *Requiem* with the entire choir.

Where the funding challenges come, however, are with opportunities to tour with the group—sometimes to other domestic locations, but often to international ones. Daniel Bates wonders if he might eventually move in a direction that prioritizes fund-raising for the cost of the tours to ensure that no boy misses out on a tour for lack of funds. Few choirs currently do this, however, perhaps because it's so easy by comparison to offer a boy a spot in the choir without charging incremental costs. Jason Holmes of the Cincinnati Boychoir is fond of saying, "What's one more chair?" at rehearsal when there's an opportunity to incorporate a boy without the family resources to cover tuition. But when it comes to making flight reservations for a tour, Holmes says wryly, "United is not going to let us say, what's one more boy?"

Resources still imply who can participate in extracurricular activities like community boy choirs. Dismantling the individual achievement model is made more difficult by the simple reality that most people who pay for these programs are parents and they're doing so largely because they want their own, individual child to have a particular kind of experience. Jeremy Tucker's observation that the Raleigh Boychoir initially seemed to be functioning primarily as an enrichment experience was one that was shaped at least in some part by the group's financial model. Being a member of the Raleigh Boychoir meant that you had parents who could pay for it.

It also meant that you had to be a boy, although this is another boundary that Tucker and other directors have been challenging. Two years after Tucker and I first spoke, his organization had undergone a significant change and reorganization: they now include girls. These changes were motivated by a couple of interrelated factors—desires to offer comparable choral opportunities for girls but also to maintain the distinctive vocal training that, in Tucker's opinion, is critical for boys. On this point, Tucker himself has changed his thinking in the eight years that he's been in the director role, partly as a result of listening to public school music teachers talk about what they thought students needed during puberty. Tucker's full-time job is as the director of arts education for the Wake County Public Schools. "We listened to the teachers," he says, and the teachers repeatedly emphasized that the voice changes that kids, especially boys, experience during adolescence meant that "there needed to be an ensemble that had high standards, but also was safe for snap, crackle, and pop [the unpredictability of the male changing voice]." At the same time, "We also listened to our teachers and the alumni, especially in the community, who wanted the opportunity to collaborate with the parallel voice types in middle and high school." At the start of the 2022–2023 school year, the

Raleigh Boychoir was reconstituted as the Raleigh Youth Choir, with six different ensembles for young singers to choose from. The youngest groups (through fourth grade) combine boys and girls. After that, the ensembles split into different choirs for fifth to eighth grade and for ninth to twelfth grade. These groups are nominally intended for boys and girls, but their names don't imply any particular gender identity. The group for fifth to eighth grade boys is called the Capital Choir, for instance, while the comparable group for girls is called the Mosaic Choir. The high school boys are the Sibley Singers, named for the Raleigh Boychoir longtime director Tom Sibley, while the high school girls are called the Page Singers, after the founder of a well-known women's choir in town, Fran Page.

Tucker is still working toward the goal of making the choir more representative of the city of Raleigh. Diversifying the board, which now includes more racial diversity and more members from the community, has been the first step. They also halved tuition—from one hundred to fifty dollars monthly—in an attempt to make the choir more accessible to lower-income families. What's interesting is that Tucker's experience suggests that diversifying the choir's sociodemographic composition was less controversial that erasing the gender boundary—a change that he admits some parents and alumni considered a diminishing of the group's long-standing identity as a boys-only choir. I asked Tucker what he thinks explains this; after all, the shift to include girls has also come on the heels of other changes that intended to make the choir appealing to boys who fell outside of the white, mostly Christian, relatively affluent subculture that had previously been overrepresented in the ensemble. Tucker answered the question by returning to the description of his changing board of directors, which had previously been composed almost entirely of choristers' parents; as he put it, the board was mostly "parents sitting around saying 'What are we going to do for our sons?'"

This gets at what Tucker thinks is really behind the consternation that some parents and alums voiced at the group's decision to incorporate girls. "There's lots of subsets of parents," he stated, before summarizing his interpretation of one particular subset this way: "I think parents that are very involved in their sons' extracurriculars want to make sure that the opportunities remain the same or increase, and that they don't want to feel like opportunities are taken away." I asked him what kind of opportunities he's referring to—the quality of the program itself or the specific performance opportunities? Tucker said that he thinks highly involved parents care about both things, but that in his opinion parents are more concerned about performance opportunities that might involve their son—for instance, the chance to sing solos or be part of a small ensemble that would perform with the local symphony or opera—that are historically considered high-level experiences.

"It sounds like they were more upset by bringing girls into the organization than they were about the socioeconomic integration," I responded. "What do you think that's about?"

"I think it's a fear of losing opportunity and privilege," Tucker said plainly, though I wasn't initially convinced by this. So I followed up with what seemed the obvious next question: Wouldn't that privilege also be threatened by racial and socioeconomic diversity?

Tucker explained that he sees these two different forms of diversity and inclusion operating a little bit differently. In his view, "If you are a privileged white family, bringing in racial diversity at times does not threaten your privilege." On this point he offered the example of parents of a talented singer who have the resources to pay for private vocal coaching, adding that those parents probably aren't threatened by "those that can't afford those opportunities." If anything, the presence of lower-income singers of color might just reinforce the white families' privilege since they could still find additional ways to further develop their boys' vocal talents.

But girls? This is where some parents of boys can get uncomfortable. Tucker is quick to emphasize that the boys-only opportunities for singers didn't go away with the reorganization; those opportunities are just recontextualized in a broader organization that seeks to offer comparable opportunities for girls, including single-gender singing groups for both boys and girls after age ten. But a few parents still experienced the incorporation of girls as a move that threatened the prestige of the boy choir tradition. Of course, Tucker is practiced at explaining why this is not the case. He said that the reorganization was about preserving high standards and outstanding opportunities for youth while also creating a "safe space" for both boys and girls. "So that means that the treble boy choir is still here," he said, but "it's just not at the top of the pyramid anymore. It's one part of the circle."

These controversies about adding parallel opportunities for girls aren't the same as questions about including trans or gender-nonbinary singers, but they are related. In both cases, the core issue is about whether a child's gender should limit the range of opportunities that they can access. And given the larger cultural conversation underway about trans and nonbinary children and youth, the politics of gender representation are top of mind for today's choir directors, especially directors of boys-only choirs. They're finding themselves suddenly straddling cultural fault lines, often uneasy about how to defend the exclusive training of male voices without aligning themselves with the kind of anti-trans discourse that has recently become a rallying cry on the political right.

In many ways, these debates exist in a realm that is largely theoretical. Of the dozens of boy choir directors that I interviewed, only one had actually been asked to incorporate a trans boy into their choir and reported that the chorister had a typical and in many ways unremarkable experience as a member of the choir. But many of the directors were ready with an answer as to what they and their choir *would* do, and most stated that they would be open to including a trans boy singer in their choir, although it was hard to know for sure how their governing boards would respond until they encountered a test case. Others mentioned former singers (born male) who had later completed a gender transition, or families who had inquired about the choir's policy around trans singers (born female) only to ultimately decide not to pursue membership. Contrary to what the often-alarmist discourse and state-level legislation about gender-affirming medical care would suggest, trans kids and teens represent a very small percentage of the youth population. It's true that the portion of teenagers who presently identify as transgender points to a generational uptick in embracing nontraditional forms of gender expression. But even so, the portion of youth ages thirteen to seventeen who identify as trans is only 1.4 percent, compared to 0.5 percent of the adult population, which suggests that these are highly isolated events that are being made to represent much bigger threats in a kind of moral panic.[8] And it's safe to say that most of that 1.4 percent of trans teens aren't looking to join boy choirs, regardless of their biological sex or chosen gender identity.

But the broader politics of gender inclusion now mean that the notion of any choir determining membership based on biological sex is increasingly controversial, something illustrated by recent changes in the organization of the American Choral Directors Association, which is the leading professional group for musicians who lead choral singers in a variety of settings, including church, school, and community choirs. Craig Denison, a professor of music education and choral music at Indiana University of Pennsylvania, learned this in a somewhat painful fashion when the ACDA decided that it would no longer support an official resource group for boy choir directors. Denison had served as a conductor of both the American Boychoir and Florida's Singing Sons (he preceded Daniel Bates by several years) and had held the position of national chair of repertoire and resource in boys-only choirs for the ACDA for many years, essentially making him the country's foremost official expert on boys' voices and choral singing. Shortly before I first spoke with Denison in 2021, a reorganization within the organization had subsumed boy choirs under the larger heading of choirs for children and youth, which meant that the ACDA effectively determined that boy choir directors did not need any resources or training that could be differentiated from children's choirs more generally.

Denison spoke diplomatically about this change, which was effectively a restructuring that eliminated his position in the ACDA. While many of his colleagues were upset about the ACDA's decision, Denison himself understood the reasons for it; as he said to me, "I think boy choir status as a separate repertoire and research was rightly considered elitist and reflective of hegemonic structures that had been in ACDA since its inception." Even so, he's committed to ensuring that there are still ways for directors of boy choirs to explore the aspects of their work that are part of a distinctive social and musical tradition. In Denison's view, ensembles that are structured by gender have particular kinds of social meaning—for girls to sing together means something different than boys to sing together, and both of these kinds of choirs are different from a children's choir that combines both boys and girls. But single-sex choirs, especially boy choirs, raise more interest primarily because of the presumed uniqueness of the voice as it relates to the singers' biological sex and the fleeting period of time in which boys can sing as sopranos.

A key decision point for boy choirs will be how to incorporate trans boys into all-male ensembles that have, to this point, been able to presume biological sex as a satisfactory condition for membership. Denison believes that boy choirs should accept as members any child who wants to live and identify as a boy, regardless of the sex assigned at their birth: "My feeling is that students and choristers get to say who they are," he said, "and if they want to be in a boy choir, and they're identifying as male, that there is a place for them. And if I was still a boy choir director, I would be very clearly stating that to my board." But he realizes that not every choir director will see things quite this way and that even those who do will need to help board members and other choristers' families see how this stance doesn't undermine their choirs' identity. "Boy choir directors are going to have to make a strong ethical and moral stand," he said, adding that "I know that there are boy choir directors who would not be accepting trans males."

These debates about the degree to which biological sex and gender identity should be conditions of membership in choirs have much in common with similar conversations about trans athletes participating in sports, which tend to center around protecting the hard-won opportunities and access that women have gained in sports. Choirs for boys present an interesting counterexample since the accelerated training of a boy choir is one that is predicated upon the narrow time window afforded to a boy's treble voice. When it comes to the ability to sing treble notes in the head voice range, boys are in a storied race against time that children born female aren't. The biological argument for separating male voices at these ages—that boys need accelerated training to ensure that they can sing at their "peak" just prior to the voice change—doesn't apply in quite the same way to children who identify socially as boys but were born female.

Yet the social aspects of being in a boy choir and allowing a child to be engaged in the intentional social construction of maleness might certainly be an appealing goal for a trans male singer. Parents of trans children and teenagers repeatedly emphasize the role of organizations and institutions in constructing a young person's chosen gender identity—after all, one of the things that makes a gender identity real is how it is accepted and affirmed by social organizations, particularly those that make biological sex a condition of participation, like sports.[9] But Wes Martin, of the All-American Boys Chorus, noted that a boy choir's position of being a place for expressing somewhat feminine impulses in boyhood might make it less likely to be a place of interest for a young person who was looking to embody and articulate a clear gender transition. "My gut feeling," he hypothesized, "is that a trans girl is probably going to want to do either something much more feminine, or if it was a girl, transitioning to be a boy, something much more masculine, like more of a sporting undertaking or something. . . . We kind of occupy the middle ground there."

The boy choir directors who did indicate that they had considered this possibility and developed a stance of openness toward trans singers emphasized how individualized their response has been or would be. Mark Johnson, who directs the Minnesota Boychoir, explained that if there were a chorister who wanted to join his choir whose gender identity wasn't as a cisgender male, his response would be one of openness and acceptance: "If [boy choir] is your thing, and you want to be a part of it, we'll figure that out." For him, the bottom line is that if a singer wants to make music as part of a boy choir, and "be yourself as well as part of that community," then the opportunity should follow. For directors who see their work as being about developing young people as much as their voices, the opportunity to help a child assigned female at birth find a sense of identity and belonging as a boy in their choir fits seamlessly into their vision of their work and purpose.

This piece of wanting to live and identify as a boy is key. Ironically, the fragility of masculinity means that it may be easier for choir directors to imagine incorporating a trans boy in their ranks than a gender-nonconforming male singer who wanted to practice forms of dress and grooming that are more typical of females. The uniforms for a boy choir are typically still traditionally masculine—shirts and ties, slacks and jackets. And even these uniforms may be slowly disappearing—when the Raleigh Boychoir became the Raleigh Youth Choir, the uniforms for all of the singers shifted to all-black, for both boys and girls. Still other regulations govern gendered aspects of physical appearance. One director, who asked that his choir not be identified in sharing this story, recalled a boy who had been in his choir who routinely chose to dress in girls' clothing at rehearsals. The boy's style of dress during the week wasn't a problem, exactly, but when it was time for the group to perform, the chorister wanted to wear nail polish. This choir wears a very traditional uniform (a blazer with slacks) and even allows boys to wear long hair down for a performance but drew the line at nail polish, reasoning that boys *not* wearing nail polish was simply part of a look that was intended to ensure that no particular singer stood out more than any other. The aspirational circle drawn by inclusive forms of masculinity still bars some people from entry.[10]

Other directors emphasize that the acceptance of trans boys is simply a place where the institutions must change, and these directors are able to put that sense of threat and risk into a larger perspective—particularly those who are situated in more progressive political and cultural contexts. Kent Jue, who directs the Ragazzi Boys' Chorus in Silicon Valley, told me that trans boy choristers are a frequent source of conversation among his colleagues in the area (the Bay Area, as a hospitable incubator for both wealth and artistic expression, has several active boy choirs that attract different choristers based on their location, among other things). Jue said that "the internal policy that we have right now is that—and we have discussed it—that we want to maintain the musical quality of the sound that we think we're trying to produce." This is easier for treble boys, Jue acknowledged, than for the older boys in the changed-voice ensembles. Even though he has an idea of what an unchanged treble voice sounds like, he admitted that even among boys, there's a range of vocal qualities that complicates the vision of one solitary boy choir sound. "Is that vision just tied into some gender specific norm that will be outdated?" he asked himself out loud. "I don't know. But I personally am open enough to explore the issue." Julian Ackerly of the Tucson Boys Chorus echoed these sentiments. Although, like Jue, his choir hasn't yet encountered a trans boy who wants to audition, he expects that this request is inevitable. As he explained, "We know that [transgenderism] is a part of life, and that has been a part of life forever, but it's just been more acknowledged and accommodated now. And we want to be on the problem-solving edge of that."

When it comes to creating a more equitable future, boy choirs do have an opportunity to be on the leading edge of change, even if doing so has the potential to destabilize or even threaten the long-term prospects of these choirs. Choirs can play a role in creating access and inclusion for trans singers as well as creating more racial and socioeconomic diversity. But the solutions to these problems are quite different, something that exposes the radically different origins of these two examples of inequality. Gender identity questions are somewhat different from the issues surrounding race and socioeconomic inequality, in that they can be addressed more immediately through policy changes at the organizational level. The current conversations around gender identity mean that these questions are front and center in the minds of choral directors as well as parents who might be advocating for the inclusion of their own, gender-nonconforming individual child.

Socioeconomic diversity will be a much more difficult and ongoing struggle, given the deeply embedded social and historical reasons for racial inequality in the United States. Directors like Jeremy Tucker and Daniel Bates show how innovative, grassroots partnerships with schools and communities can begin to shift a group's representation, but it is slow-going, painstaking work that requires resources from sources other than parents who are paying tuition.

In contrast, the relative ease with which choral directors anticipate incorporating trans singers points to key elements of ongoing conservatism in these organizations. Admittedly, most of this speculation is still hypothetical, but the relatively traditional forms of dress and grooming endorsed by many boy choirs means that trans boys could blend in relatively easily since these spaces demand that singers conform to traditional forms of masculine self-presentation. These conversations also reveal the limits of the inclusive masculinity that boy choir directors promote: these ideas about masculinity are more about encouraging emotional expression and attitudes of respect and civility than they are about unmaking masculinity altogether. The importance attached to boys looking like boys in performance settings affirms a long-standing conclusion of social science research on masculinity: it's easier to perform acts that read as "masculine" when one presents a male body.[11] It also underscores the persistent discomfort associated with more feminine forms of male self-presentation and thus the fragility that accompanies masculinity as a category.

But why are these more visible forms of gender transgressions so threatening? The next chapter continues to explore these questions, particularly as they relate to adolescent male homosexuality.

CHAPTER 6

Closets

"I told the boys that they don't want to see my other Freddie Mercury outfit," Mr. Fisher joked to the audience, igniting a ripple of knowing laughter that traveled throughout the packed sanctuary. Mr. Fisher was wearing a black leather jacket over a KSB T-shirt and jeans, having intentionally dressed down for that night's unusual spring concert. The uniform for an evening that included mostly a cappella music had been billed as "a ca-casual," which meant that the boys could skip the pleated black dress pants, oxford shirt, and ties in favor of jeans with a T-shirt underneath their dark green blazers. Haydon and I had already argued about the uniform, which I insisted required a plain white T-shirt, only to have arrived and discovered that the boys were actually free to wear any T-shirt they wanted. Haydon glowered at me when he saw his friends wearing far more interesting T-shirts, realizing that he'd missed an opportunity to show some sliver of individuality in an environment that usually required total conformity. Instead, he was stuck wearing the most boring T-shirt imaginable while the other boys got to advertise a favorite superhero or their club sports teams inside of their regulation green jackets. But it was too late to do anything about that now, and the show would go on. And the show that followed did not disappoint those of us in the audience, to whom Mr. Fisher was now joking about his leather jacket. The reference to his "other Freddie Mercury outfit," even though he claimed to have threatened the boys with wearing it, was really meant as a knowing exchange between him and the adults in the audience: that what we were about to see, like Mr. Fisher himself, is openly gay.

The concert was a joint fundraiser for Commonwealth Youthchoirs, the organization that governed both the Keystone State Boychoir and its sister choir, Pennsylvania Girlchoir (or PG for short). Combining the two choirs for the fundraiser created a larger audience, and it also allowed for a longer concert program with less rehearsal time since they could work on repertoire separately even though they would perform some of the big numbers together. The kids had learned this music only recently, which meant that it was still coming together, especially for the younger boys who make up the soprano section in KSB. It's useful that the high school girls in PG had already mastered the music, since they're older and less likely to be goofing around at rehearsals. These two advantages meant they could help carry the soprano melodies for the boys who didn't yet fully know their notes. Including the girls usually sparks concerns about how the stronger, more resonant sounds of the mature soprano voice will overshadow the timbre of the unchanged treble sound among the boys, but tonight that would probably be a good thing.

Just as the boys got to skip their formal uniform for this concert, the girls left behind their velvet, floor-length gowns in favor of jeans, a white oxford shirt, and the green and gold ties that the boys typically wore with their formal uniforms. In fact, the KSB parents had been instructed to bring our boys' ties to rehearsal the previous day to lend them to the girls; some parents worried about how they would get their boys' ties back later, especially since we were required to pay for this portion of the uniform ourselves. The night had been billed as "Bach and Rock," and the advertising was accurate, as there's nothing on the program that fell in between those two extremes. The high schoolers who were in the elite Anonymous 16 ensemble first performed a Bach cantata, but after that the program took a very different turn, with a tribute to the rock band Queen. The different choral ensembles that fall under the CY umbrella had each prepared different songs for the performance—a cheerful coed rendition of "Crazy Little Thing Called Love" was followed by a spirited performance of "Another One Bites the Dust," during which the singers threaded their way through the congregation, clapping their hands above their heads, encouraging the audience to join them. After that, the high school girls sang a light and lyrical version of "You're My Best Friend," which was followed by a pulsing, rhythmic arrangement of "We Will Rock You" led by the high school boys. A smaller group of boys with treble voices sang a slow, searching arrangement of "Under Pressure," while a group of high schoolers, both boys and girls, sang a melancholy arrangement of "Somebody to Love," which ended with the singers partnering off in different couplings—some of the pairings were boys with girls, but just as many were among same-sex singers. One boy even jumped into another's arms at the end, in a caricature of a jitterbug move.

Toward the end of the night the two choirs came together for the night's biggest number: a rendition of "Bohemian Rhapsody" that involved both choirs and was accompanied by a small set band made up of choristers who also happened to play the drums, electric bass, and electric guitar. There was planned choreography—at one point the choir jumped up and down waving their arms, invoking "Wayne's World"–inspired head banging—and a surprise move when a soloist rose up on the sanctuary's organ bench and then turned backward to trust-fall into the arms of the choristers below. It occurred to me that the only thing that could have possibly made this presentation more dramatic would have been a smoke machine, but I couldn't imagine the church would have given that the green light.

That 2019 concert was notable for lots of reasons—the music first and foremost among them. Not many choir programs include both a Bach cantata and "Bohemian Rhapsody," for starters. "Bohemian Rhapsody" is also a song that is typically interpreted as narrating Queen singer Freddie Mercury's struggle to accept his homosexuality, even if the meaning of the lyrics eluded many of the young choristers singing them. But what's more, everyone who was assembled there—parents, performers, the directors, and especially the audience—was invited to set aside many of the typical rules that govern expressions of gender, particularly in our everyday lives. After all, we spent an evening together where girls dressed like boys, boys sang like girls, and together they performed music written by a rock star who made gender-bending a staple of his own performances. Much of this felt revolutionary, even subversive.

For boys like the ones in KSB, feminizing performances like these aren't always welcome. Even though performance itself can provide a kind of protective shield that allows for gender-bending play, performances can also remind us of all the ways that gender and sexuality represent carefully constructed presentations for an audience of others. This is part of what makes these performances potentially subversive; in the classic words of Judith Butler, gender is "a construction that regularly conceals its genesis."[1] In other words, gender can seem fixed and immutable primarily because our day-to-day performances of it are so successful. But this also means that formal performances, like the kind that happen in front of an actual audience, can poke holes in this façade, with transgressions that remind us of all the ways that gender itself is a tenuous social creation.

Mr. Fisher's joke about his "other Freddie Mercury outfit" could also be seen as somewhat transgressive, although this remark functions somewhat differently: to reassure the audience, not unsettle it. His joke hinted at a realm of privacy—gesturing toward Mr. Fisher's home, his closet, and perhaps a harlequin-themed spandex onesie that might be hanging there, waiting to make an appearance at a more appropriate opportunity that does not involve the choristers. It also makes a passing but public acknowledgment of Mr. Fisher's own sexual orientation. Although it's not something that he discusses with the singers, most of the parents know that Mr. Fisher is married to a man. His remarks also offer an explicit endorsement of homosexuality, which seems fitting given the theme of the evening, but he also accomplishes this within the confines of a joke that hints that his private affairs are a source of humor, not salaciousness. But this doesn't ultimately matter because he's acknowledged the (gay) elephant in the room, and we're all reassured that the things we need to know are out in the open. His acknowledgment of his identity redraws the boundaries between what is private and what is public, confirming to us that he understands the difference. For gay men like Mr. Fisher, this kind of openness would have surely seemed unimaginable a generation ago, particularly in a setting that involved children. But publicly acknowledging his sexual orientation, and his understanding of appropriate boundaries when working with children, is fundamental to his role as a boy choir director today.

This reassurance about boundaries matters to parents. For too long, secrecy around sex and sexual abuse has been part of the boy choir legacy, and parents are right to worry about keeping their sons safe from the kind of sexual abuse that occurred at the American Boychoir School decades ago. The very structure of a boy choir creates risks that demand preemptive attention—boys who go on tour, for instance, are often lodged in home stays in which they share sleeping quarters with other choristers. ABS was also a residential boarding school, which meant that boys as young as eight or nine were consistently in the company of adults without their parents' supervision. Additionally, many of the directors whom I interviewed confided to me that they think parents worry that abuse is somehow endemic to organizations that feminize boys and disproportionately attract gay men to positions of leadership, like the Catholic Church. (Women, on the other hand, tend to get a pass here—the notion that women are more naturally nurturers means that they have more freedom to interact with adolescent boys without suspicion.)[2] Something about a boy choir—in which boys are regularly engaged in the performance of something that we would otherwise consider "feminine"—suggests that there might be a danger of same-sex misconduct, whether molestation by choir directors or unwanted sexual attention from other boys. Either way, the implication is that boy choirs are places where gay men and boys may be overrepresented and that something about this means that boys are at risk.

But what exactly are they at risk of—being molested or being made into homosexuals? Being sexually abused by an adult or being hit on by other same-age peers? And how well are today's boy choirs finding ways to have conversations about these difficult subjects? On one hand, tracing how these fears, both real and imagined, are being addressed by contemporary choirs shows how far we've come toward embracing a more open acceptance of homosexuality, something that sociologist Eric Anderson promises will help to cultivate inclusive masculinity. Only when boys and men stop seeing homosexuality as a threat, he argues, can they develop close emotional bonds with each other and begin to dismantle the power of hegemonic masculinity. Considering how stigmatized homosexuality was a generation ago, it's remarkable that a man like Steve Fisher can joke about his homosexual identity in front of a packed house. No one in the audience that night seemed uncomfortable having their son in a group led by an openly gay man—something that would have been unthinkable when Fisher himself was a boy.

At the same time, this acceptance has limits. While I live in a place that doesn't formally curtail this kind of talk, states like Florida, Louisiana, Alabama, and Indiana have recently passed laws that constrain the ability of public school teachers to discuss topics like homosexuality and gender fluidity with students. And even in communities that might see themselves as relatively open and accepting of homosexuality, choral directors seem much more comfortable instructing boys about how to recognize and report abuse at the hands of an adult than they do in offering guidance or information about potential same-sex exploration among boys who are peers. Though they may not feel compelled to cultivate a thoroughly masculine, compulsively heterosexual ethos, current boy choir directors still find these conversations challenging, given that having them requires an explicit acknowledgment of homosexuality in the first place. Therein lies at least part of the problem.

Moving forward means first taking an honest look at the past, and when it comes to boy choirs and sex, there are plenty of skeletons in the closet. Devastating accounts of male choir directors or other staff molesting boy choristers have appeared repeatedly in recent decades, across different kinds of organizations. In response, today's boy choirs typically have a "two adults in the room" policy that mandates that no adult is ever alone with a child in a private setting. This kind of monitoring requires a heavy investment of staff resources (two paid staff are always at a rehearsal), volunteers (parents, mostly moms, who are also present during a rehearsal or a voice check), or both. But even so, stories of abuse have surfaced as recently as 2019, when a staff member of the St. John's Boys' Choir in Collegeville, Minnesota, faced allegations of sharing sexually explicit communications and photographs with a chorister.[3] Unfortunately, a "two adults in the room" policy can't prohibit sexual misconduct by cell phone.

One of the first nationally publicized cases of pervasive sexual abuse in a boy choir surfaced in the mid-1990s, when Brown University law professor Ross Cheit became an early face of the "recovered memory" movement, recalling as an adult previously buried memories of sexual abuse at the hands of a counselor during his time as a chorister with the San Francisco Boys Chorus. The investigations that followed found at least twelve other survivors who had been molested by the same man.[4] The Harlem Boys Choir was similarly beset by scandal in the early 2000s, when a chorister's allegations of ongoing abuse from a choir staff member were reportedly dismissed by the choir's founder and director, Walter Turnbull. The alleged abuser was eventually sentenced to prison and the choir folded under a storm of controversy, mounting debts, and Turnbull's sudden death in 2007.[5] But most egregious are the stories of the boys who were abused at the American Boychoir School, chronicled by Diana Schemo's investigation for the *New York Times* in 2002.[6] The sexual abuse that happened at the American Boychoir School (then still known as the Columbus Boychoir) between the late 1960s and early 1980s was pervasive—one observer has characterized the school during that period as a "rollicking madhouse of pedophilia."[7]

The most extensive accounting of this abuse appears in a suit filed in 2001 by John Hardwicke Jr. against ABS. The claim described sexual abuse experienced by Hardwicke and other plaintiffs at the hands of Donald Hanson, the school's music director, along with the school's then-headmaster, Anthony Battaglia, a teacher's aide (Raymond Wycoff, who later committed suicide), the school cook, and one of Hanson's friends.[8] Another survivor of the abuse at ABS, Harvard lawyer Lawrence Lessig, allowed his story to be told in an in-depth interview with John Heilemann, published in *New York Magazine* in 2005. Lessig and Hardwicke did not overlap during their years at ABS—Hardwicke graduated shortly before Lessig arrived in 1972—but their stories became connected when Lessig agreed to help represent Hardwicke in his legal quest to sue the school for damages. In Heilemann's account, Lessig was reluctant to get involved in the suit at first—he wasn't a trial lawyer, and his expertise was in internet law—but more importantly, the plea for help from Hardwicke asked him to open a chapter of his past that he thought was closed. All these years later, Lessig hadn't even told his parents about the abuse; representing Hardwicke would require him to bring all of those aspects of a buried past into the stark light of day.

The details of Hardwicke's experience, on the other hand, became part of a larger public conversation about sexual abuse of boys in all-male institutions, like the Roman Catholic Church and the Boy Scouts of America. Like so many of the boys who attended ABS, John Hardwicke's journey to the school was initiated by chance and happenstance. As he explained to me in an interview in early 2022, attending the school wasn't even his idea in the first place. He was headed to sixth grade at a public school in

Baltimore when his father joined a new law firm where one of the partner's sons was attending the choir school, then called the Columbus Boychoir School. Hardwicke's father had always loved classical music and relished the idea of giving his son the musical experience that the choir school promised to provide. Hardwicke was already learning piano and enjoyed the classical records that his father liked to play when he was home from the office on weekends. Hardwicke started by attending the school's summer camp, just as my son would do almost fifty years later, and enjoyed it enough to enroll in the school as a boarding student the following year. Hardwicke recalls that his mother had misgivings—adding that "she made that very clear in subtle ways"—but his father's enthusiasm prevailed.

Most of Hardwicke's abuse allegations center around Hanson, the good-looking, charismatic, Canadian concert pianist who drove a Jaguar. John Hardwicke met Hanson in 1970, during Hardwicke's second year at the school, when he was in seventh grade.[9] The first time that Hanson molested Hardwicke, it happened in Hardwicke's own home, after Hanson drove him to his parents' house in Maryland and stayed overnight.[10] In Hardwicke's account, Hanson was a skilled perpetrator who found ways to suggest to the thirteen-year-old boy that his father knew about and therefore condoned the abuse. The next day Hanson molested him in the backseat of a car, while Hardwicke's parents were driving.[11] Back at the school, the abuse escalated further. Hanson would call Hardwick out of class for sex—sometimes multiple times a day—showing him child pornography, using his body for masturbation, or urinating on him in the shower.[12]

With stories like these covered by national news media, parents are right to question whether their children will be safe from sexual violence when they participate in these activities. Admittedly, this concern came up when we chose to enroll Haydon in the ABS summer camp, not that we ultimately handled it very well. The school's history with sexual abuse was something that his father and I had discussed briefly when we considered enrolling him. I felt reasonably reassured by the school's "two adults in a room" policy and figured that an organization that had reckoned with previous allegations of sexual abuse was likely a safer place than one that believed, perhaps inaccurately, that nothing of that nature had ever occurred in its past. My husband, on the other hand, remained worried. For him, the fear that something untoward could happen during that week remained, a nagging fear that lingered on in the back of his mind. The fear that his son could become a victim of sexual abuse, and that this could potentially happen on his watch, was nearly more than he could endure—his job as a protector was paramount in his mind. Of course, I would have never put one of my children in a situation where I thought they could be sexually abused, but somehow I was more willing to give the benefit of the doubt to an organization that promised background checks of its staff and a two-adults-in-the-room policy. But his dad and I never found time to have a reasoned, planned discussion about this, which meant that Haydon became the subject of an awkward, meandering conversation intended as a crash course in avoiding pedophiles in the thirty minutes that transpired between leaving our house and dropping him off at the ABS Summer Experience camp in Princeton.

"Haydon, I want you to promise me that you will scream and run away if anyone tries to touch you," my husband said abruptly from the driver's seat.

"What?!" I said, stunned. I knew that Haydon was already worried enough about how the week would unfold, whether he would enjoy the music, and what the other boys would be like.

"If anyone tries to touch me?" Haydon reiterated, confused.

I felt it had somehow fallen to me to smooth over this awkward conversation, so I did my best to salvage this lesson. "I think what Dad means is that anytime you're away from home overnight it's important to remember that your body is private and that no one is allowed to touch it except for you." I was trying desperately to recall what I'd gleaned from an episode of the *Oprah Winfrey Show* years ago about how to have age-appropriate conversations with kids about sex. I could remember having those conversations with my kids when they were younger, of course, but this was a very different ball game. The best way to navigate a situation in which one's husband is suddenly warning your child about meeting pedophiles at choir camp was not one for which Oprah had issued standard guidance.

"This is a school where a lot of boys were touched inappropriately by a choir director," he said, undeterred in his mission to provide a thoroughly adequate warning. "If anyone—and I mean, anyone—makes you uncomfortable then you are to call us right away."

"I'm not sure if I want to do this," Haydon said slowly, his voice full of trepidation.

"We wouldn't enroll you in this camp if we didn't think you would be safe here," I said, glaring sideways at my husband from the passenger seat of the car. "Besides, all those people are gone now. It happened a long time ago, and the school has changed a lot since then." By then, we were about five minutes away from arriving at the drop-off point.

"You promise they're all gone?" Haydon asked after a few seconds of silence, looking for one more moment of reassurance.

"Yes, they're all gone now. This is a safe place," I said, signaling an end to a particularly awkward and poorly thought-out exchange.

His father, on the other hand, sighed deeply. "At least you have a phone."

Don Hanson resigned from ABS in 1982, after one boy finally shared the choir director's crimes with his parents, who then reported them to the school and demanded action. The years that followed were something of a rebuilding period, one goal of which was to demonstrate that the school was a safe place for its choristers—a big part of which meant reassuring parents that the school was a well-run place where homosexual activity of any kind was nonexistent. Craig Denison, who served as an assistant choir director at ABS in the 1990s, recalls the phrase "in loco parentis" being a significant touchpoint for the staff, describing the way that the school saw its responsibility to the boys in their care. The structure attempted to mimic some aspects of a family, with "house parents" who were responsible for looking after smaller groups of choristers in their day-to-day life—eating, personal hygiene, manners, and so on. Within this framework, the rhythms of daily life were highly organized—the boys were awakened at six fifteen, after which they had three minutes to shower before they were expected to make their beds and tidy their sleeping spaces. By seven o'clock they were in a double line, dressed in their uniforms, waiting to enter the dining hall for breakfast.

In many ways, this structure was the apotheosis of traditional masculinity—an almost military-like set of disciplined rituals. One former chorister, whom I'll call Brent because he didn't want to use his real name, is an ABS alum now in his forties who attended the school in the 1990s and found it a "sanctuary for not being a guy's guy." Brent wasn't a particularly masculine adolescent, and by the time he was a preteen he was aware that he was attracted to boys. Even though he wasn't formally out to his parents, the other students at ABS were aware that he was interested in boys by the sixth or seventh grade. However, Brent was quick to add that he also experienced the school in a very "heterosexist" way, meaning that "it was very interested in not being gay." For instance, in Brent's view the militarization of the aesthetics and the group's visual image had an ulterior motive. "I'm thinking even just around this notion of the military school," he said, "like, why we're wearing our little peacoats and we're standing in double lines, and we walk everywhere in this military formation. All of that precision and discipline was, I think, partly to offset this idea [of being gay]. I don't think anyone would have said or wanted to say that this was a feminine activity." Brent added that the school's alumni association was another place where heterosexuality was self-consciously on display, refusing to acknowledge adult alums who were gay and partnered with men, instead assuming that all of their alums were married men who would attend ABS reunions with their wives. "The wives would go, and they would have drinks downtown or be at their hotel or out shopping or doing whatever the wives do. And the men are in the room where it happens.... It was a very straight culture."

Heterosexuality was also conveyed in some of the choir's performances—for instance, Brent recalled that one of the choir's standard performances on tour included a medley of opera love songs, during which they would select a female member of the audience to come onto the stage and be serenaded by all of the boys, who would eventually present her with a small plastic flower during the song. Similarly, their performances also included occasional choreography, including a jitterbug performed with acrobatic swing dancing, in which the couples were generally composed of "the smallest kid in the choir and the largest kid in the choir." Brent explained that while he didn't quite consider it "a gender-transgressive joke," there was something about this performance that was trading on a shared assumption that all the boys in the choir were straight. Otherwise, this performance of dancing the jitterbug, which dramatizes "an extremely sexual mating ritual," Brent pointed out, in which "this girl is opening her legs across someone and then sliding through them," would have conveyed actual homosexual desire. Thinking back to both of these performances, Brent reasoned that the choir's approach was "either we're going to name the narrative, which is that there's this love narrative between the boys and some woman or girl," as in the serenading-with-the-plastic-rose performance, "or we're going to totally erase it, and then it's just a set of movements of people, you know, doing this thing" as in the all-male swing dancing performance. He concluded, chuckling, "that's the one that we always joke about, in retrospect."

The school's default heterosexual culture was also underscored by a policy that prohibited same-sex contact among students, even though this wasn't enshrined in writing until later. Instead, Brent recalled hearing the head of school instruct the choristers that "what you do behind closed doors is your business," a statement that could have meant a range of things—perhaps that private masturbation was acceptable or that something that happened between two willing boys in a dorm room wasn't of any concern. Brent, who was sexually active with other consenting boys at the school while he was at ABS, interpreted this to mean that boys who wanted to engage with each other sexually should do so in private. At least that's what he thought it meant until he was called to see the head of school one day to account for a report of sexual activity that had traveled to his office. After hearing about a particular experience with another student, the head of school told Brent, "I have to call your parents about this. And you are in trouble now." Brent was scared, mortified, and most of all confused, remembering that "internally, all I knew to say—and I did not even know how to say this out loud at the time—was like, 'But you said to do it behind closed doors. And I did. So I don't understand.'" What might have been meant as a generalized tolerance for homosexuality was easily misunderstood as permission in the mind of a fourteen-year-old.

In Brent's case, the discovery of his sexual encounter with another student led to a conversation with his actual parents, which still tops the list of his most excruciating life experiences. His parents were summoned to the school for a meeting, after which they took him home for the weekend and had a conversation with him about what had happened, something that they had clearly been instructed to do by the school. Not that he remembers any of it; in Brent's words, "I one hundred percent went to another planet while it was happening." He only remembers that his father concluded the talk by saying, "Do you understand why what you did was wrong?" Brent admittedly had no idea why he was in trouble, but he knew that the only way to end the conversation was to say yes. He was ultimately permitted to return to school and stay in the dorms for the final few months of his eighth-grade year, but he was warned that any further sexual experiences with other students would result in expulsion. Even now, thirty years later, Brent hasn't revisited this incident with his parents.

At some point in subsequent years, the school adopted a formal written policy that declared zero tolerance for any sexual contact between any students, whether consensual or not. The penalty was immediate expulsion for any students who were found to have engaged in same-sex activity.

An ABS school handbook from this era explicitly includes language about respect for chorister's bodies under a heading titled "Honor Code and Discipline." Here, students were instructed to respect their own body and the neatness of their appearance and furthermore to "never touch anyone in a way that makes him or her feel uncomfortable and never let anyone else touch you in that same way." The policy continued, clarifying that sexual activity was never permitted for choristers, even if the touching was something both people were comfortable with. And because the only choristers at the school would be male, the policy effectively prohibited only homosexual activity (emphasis original): "At the same time, you should be aware that **sexual activity of any kind is not permitted at school, on tour, while staying with billets, or when sleeping off campus with host families**. Sexual experimentation, even between willing participants, is not allowed. **Such activity will be viewed as a serious breach of the Honor Code**. The consequence for engaging in such activity will lead to expulsion." The policy concluded by explaining that the focus and engagement required of choristers at a residential boarding school cannot be achieved "if there is disorder in our community or if we lose trust in one another." The explanatory narrative continued, "In a residential middle school community, sexual activity, even between willing participants, too often results in secrecy, painful emotions (such as shame or a sense of violation) and broken friendships." Choristers were therefore admonished to tell an adult if they experienced any touching or other physical contact that induced discomfort.

Taken at face value, the policy was intended to establish bright, clear lines that reassured students and their parents that no chorister at the school would ever be faced with a sexual overture, either from a teacher or other adult or from another student. But the overriding assumption was that same-sex activity was primarily an abusive experience and that only secondarily might it be a pleasurable, consensual one. The policy implied that middle school students were simply not ready to experience or act upon sexual feelings or activities, "even among willing participants." The practical consequences were troubling, as they effectively required that boys who were gay remain closeted at school. Brent observed that "it created a whole underground culture of threats, bribery, and blackmailing. Like, 'If I know this thing about you, I can get you kicked out.'" Therefore, by moving homosexual exploration into an illicit realm of secrecy, the policy created a culture that may have actually facilitated more of the sexual intimidation and coercion, at least among students, that it was meant to curtail.

Moreover, Brent viewed this policy as one that grew out the school's larger, institutional discomfort with homosexuality in general, explaining that "I think you have two questions coming from parents, which are like, is this going to turn my child gay, or is my child going to get touched?" Brent observed that these two concerns became conflated considering the school's history with sexual abuse. "That sexual abuse was always boy on boy or male on male sexual abuse," he explained, adding, "I am not familiar with any cases of a female teacher sexually abusing a student (who would have obviously been male)." Brent saw the school's child protection policy as a blunt, homophobic attempt to manage all forms of risk: "If *this* [same-sex experimentation between students] doesn't happen, then *that* [sexual abuse by an adult] can't happen ... you know, just strip the whole thing of same-sex desire, making no distinction between faculty or two consenting or experimenting students with one another."

Of course, if a policy declares that no sex of any kind is ever permitted, then that also means that there's no need to help students understand and adopt a framework for navigating consent. Eliding these details was partly intentional. "We had a wide variety of parents and parenting styles that we had to act as surrogate parents for," Craig Denison remembers. "So we would skew toward the most conservative approach simply by default." In other words, at that time there wasn't any attempt to discuss consent because the staff knew that some boys' parents would not have endorsed a policy that framed homosexuality as acceptable, even normal. Of course, this didn't mean that sexual exploration between students didn't happen in the 1990s. It did, and sometimes boys were confused and upset afterward, unsure of what they had participated in and what it meant about their sexuality. On one hand, Brent views this as "normal, understandable—or expectable—sexual experimentation," observing that putting "a bunch of middle school aged boys who are coming into their bodies and learning about their own bodies" together can simply lead to sexual encounters borne of curiosity and proximity, not necessarily homosexual identity. But given that the school was trying to accommodate many different parental styles and moral viewpoints, they chose the path of silence when it came to giving guidance about how consensual experiences might be understood, which led to more confusion, secrecy, and shame.

Faltering under growing criticisms in the years that followed, the formal policy was eventually removed, a reform that Brent and other gay alums cheered as a shift away from institutionalized discrimination against same-sex relationships. After all, Brent pointed out, middle school students are not usually expelled for heterosexual activity. Kissing and other forms of sexual exploration are generally considered normal parts of adolescent development. As an adult, he can recognize the ways in which it might be helpful for a residential school for boys between the ages of eight and fourteen to have some kind of policy that placed sexuality in a clear, thoughtful, and age-appropriate framework. Instead, the policy framed *all* sexual experiences as something to be feared and avoided; as a result, the motivations of protecting boys from sexual abuse and deterring boys from sexual exploration were largely conflated. Brent therefore suspects that the real motivation for the policy was to reassure parents that their sons wouldn't become gay because of attending ABS. "That is what we're actually saving you from," he observed. "That's the child that's actually part of child protection. It's not for the kid themselves. It's not for you and your own body. It's for your parents."

Admittedly, it's difficult to know whether what one boy considered sexual exploration among willing participants wasn't experienced as harassment or assault by another student—Schemo's investigation for the *New*

York Times, for instance, found that alums from the early 1990s "estimated that 1 of every 5 students was caught in sexually predatory relationships with other students." At least one lawsuit, filed in 1999, alleged that a student had been sexually abused by a classmate whose record of misconduct should have been met with appropriate supervision and intervention on the part of the school.[13] A school for boys between the ages of eight and fourteen—a range that presents a vast discrepancy in terms of awareness, agency, and sexual development—would undoubtedly encounter problems in parsing what could reasonably count as consent between peers. And as Craig Denison observed, the school was attempting to do a complicated, idiosyncratic mix of things simultaneously—be a school, a dormitory, and a professional arts organization, all for boys under the age of fifteen. But in the absence of clear guidance to students trying to understand this new landscape of developing bodies and sexual feelings, the boys were left to themselves to try to figure out the appropriate boundaries—sometimes with disastrous consequences.

Almost thirty years have passed since Brent was called into the head of school's office at ABS. And as organizations that consciously embrace a more inclusive, progressive form of masculinity, today's boy choirs do look different from these organizations of the past. They also have an opportunity to potentially help boys navigate these dimensions of puberty with more support and guidance than was available to Brent and his classmates. But what would a better institutional approach to talking about sex and sexuality look like in our current era? And how might that help boys negotiate appropriate sexual relationships while also protecting them from abuse?

Some of the most comprehensive research about sexual ethics and sexual assault comes from the work of social scientists Jennifer Hirsch and Shamus Khan, whose ethnographic study of students at Columbia University uncovered the ways that today's young people are navigating sex and relationships—and often doing so badly, in spite of the required student orientation events that emphasize the importance of consent and the risks of mixing sex and alcohol. The young people in their study report that their parents and other adults often haven't talked with them about the conditions that make for ethical, consensual, satisfying intimate relationships. And any sex education taught by their schools or religious organizations tended to cover the things that could go wrong—pregnancy, disease, rape—rather than the things that can make sex feel right.[14] These missed opportunities are gaping oversights in the way that we tend to talk with young people, especially boys and men, about sexual practices. And a tendency to assume that a boy is straight until demonstrated otherwise means that even fewer conversations happen about potential same-sex relationships or experimentation.

My conversations with boy choir directors from around the country suggest that they are much more likely to talk openly with boys and their parents about how to recognize and report abuse at the hands of an adult than they are about navigating same-sex experimentation among consenting peers. And to some extent, this makes sense. Organizations like these are responsible for protecting the boys in their care from sexual abuse, and they know that parents will want to be reassured of their diligence. But parents may not want a choir director advising their sons about same-sex activity with peers, even though the opportunity for peer-to-peer sexual contact comes up in a pronounced way among the choirs that routinely tour and therefore lodge boys either in hotels or with home stays arranged in conjunction with a local boy choir in the city of their destination. The directors whom I posed this question to assured me that they would never place boys from a large age range in the same hotel room—say, an eight-year-old with a fourteen-year-old—but add that they would also prefer not to think about what might be happening between two consenting seventeen-year-old boys who are sharing a hotel room on a tour.

Of course, there are some exceptions. One remarkably candid director explained in depth how he talks about sex with boys on the choir's tours, which often last as long as two weeks. By day twelve, he said he informs the chaperones that "tomorrow the lap dances are going to start, and you need to be ready to tell the boys that they may not sit on each other's laps." In his opinion, after spending so many days together in a setting that encourages close bonds, the boys start to become more physically connected with each other, which sometimes means that the boys start to sit on each other's laps when they get on the subway to travel to a performing or sightseeing destination. In his view, this isn't necessarily "a sexual thing," but he does consider it "a physical thing" that the boys themselves wouldn't necessarily even notice or be able to articulate. But considering what he sees as "the disaster at the American Boychoir," he observed that "any time you put boys together, you are at risk of things. I mean, boys experiment sexually, and it has nothing to do with orientation. It's access, and I know all that and I understand all that. But I don't want it on my watch, you know?" I asked him if he thought that the warning about lap dances would need to happen in an all-girl tour situation, and he replied that it probably *would* be allowed for girls to sit on each other's laps on tour, but that for the sake of parity he doesn't allow that among the girls from the group's sister choir either. Basically, the motto for this organization is that nothing involving one's lap should be happening on tour, whether you're a boy or a girl.

He continued, explaining that the choristers often respond to these rules by asking why they're not allowed to sit on each other's laps. "It's sweet to see," he said of the boys' innocence in not understanding the reason for these rules. "You know, they're just trying to figure it out, and they don't know what's going on, you know, in their bodies and their minds, and they don't half the time even know what they're doing." But mindful of all the sexual activity that could happen on a tour, when boys are often staying with host families and sharing rooms with each other, he also gives what he calls "the penis speech," particularly focused on the middle school boys. This means telling them that while "penises are great things, they help bring life and they have all sorts of functions, and they're awesome," there is a time and place for talking about them and using them—and this doesn't include choir. "So anytime you're at choir," he explains, "and anytime you're on tour, you shouldn't be talking about your penis. And nobody should see it. And certainly, nobody should touch it. I just say it." I asked him how the boys typically respond to this speech, and he replied that he tends to think that they appreciate it and find it empowering to be addressed about things that make them feel like adults and be spoken to like men. The other interesting thing he's noticed in these conversations is that sometimes a boy who's on the younger end of the age spectrum will start to giggle during this talk, and boys who are slightly older will tell them to shush. From his perspective, one of the most valuable aspects of "the penis speech" is that the older boys—who generally receive the talk with an air of seriousness and interest—show the younger boys, through their demeanor, that this is a topic that is important.

Of course, plenty of boy choir directors sidestep questions about same-sex exploration entirely, particularly those in more conservative parts of the country. Ken Berg, director of the Birmingham Boy Choir, has developed a list of "Life Rules" that he shares with the boys, most of which are either about appropriate etiquette during rehearsals ("If it's not yours, don't touch it, and if it's not your note, don't sing it") or general character development ("You can choose your actions, but you cannot choose the consequences of those actions"). But rule 3 is "always make sure your wife and your girlfriend are the same person"—a humorous attempt to communicate and cultivate in boys a sense of moral sexual behavior. Berg said that the youngest boys always laugh at that rule, while boys begin to appreciate the meaning of this rule as they grow up and begin dating. To this point, he told me how a former chorister recently sent him a picture from his wedding with a note that said proudly, "Mr. Ken, I can now tell you that my wife and my girlfriend are the same person." I responded to this by asking, "Do you assume there are no boys in your group who identify as gay who might have a boyfriend or a husband?" Berg demurred in his answer, saying, "Remember, I'm just teaching eight-year-olds, eight- to eighteen-year-olds, so that's never been an issue for us." When I followed up by noting that some boys in high school might certainly know that they were gay, Berg responded, "Maybe. I don't know," shrugging his shoulders across the Zoom screen, adding that perhaps they could internalize the message of this rule as a general endorsement of fidelity. "But really, that's never just crossed my mind," he said. "I've never had to deal with that issue."

Too many examples point to the downside of not "dealing with that issue"—namely, acknowledging that boys can and do engage in sexual exploration with other boys and that these experiences could be either welcome or unwelcome, consensual or coercive, just as heterosexual experiences so often unfold in settings rife with confusion, misunderstanding, and even violence. This is particularly true of sexual interactions between young people who are just beginning to acknowledge their sexuality, often in a framework where few, if any, guidelines have been issued by their parents or by the institutions that structure and scaffold their experiences of maturation. All of us—and especially parents—need to move past our discomfort so that we can talk openly with boys about same-sex experimentation so that they can recognize relationships and encounters that are appropriate and consensual, whether in heterosexual or homosexual contexts. The work of diminishing homophobia—what Anderson sees as a crucial step to creating a more inclusive masculinity—won't happen accidentally. And incremental progress does not mean that we've arrived at the desired destination.

There are no easy answers about how to move on from the epidemic of sexual abuse that occurred at ABS or about what role, if any, contemporary community boy choirs might effectively play in promoting some kind of healing within the tradition. My research brought me into contact with many people who'd had some connection with ABS over the past thirty years—as former choristers or former staff members—and they mostly dispute the notion that the entire boy choir tradition should be permanently marred by the events of the 1970s and 1980s at ABS. However, they are deeply divided in their feelings about whether the school and the people associated with it when it finally closed in 2017 should have paid the price for the sexual abuse that devastated the lives of people like John Hardwicke. Some pointed out that the boys and even some of the staff members at the school at the time of its closure hadn't even been born when this abuse unfolded. The school that was struggling to survive in the twenty-first century, along with its staff, its students, and others who cherished an ongoing connection to the institution, were the ones who bore the burden of the school's closing, while the one person who most deserved to be brought to justice and held accountable, Don Hanson, was never prosecuted.

Many of the ABS alums whom I interviewed were quick to deflect any questions about the school's history of abuse, reiterating that their experience wasn't marred in any way by these crimes; to the contrary, their years at ABS made them who they were in ways that couldn't have been replicated in a different setting. Nathan Wadley, who was both a chorister and a school employee for a short time after college, said, "I've been asked a lot about all the scandal stuff, but it's something that I feel ill equipped to talk about." He's quick to add that he had an experience that was positively formative and untainted by these events. Others suggested that the abuse that happened at ABS was not reason enough for the school to have closed: "If you think of what good that school did for men, young boys becoming men," one alum said, "I think it far outweighs the negative situations." In his view, sexual abuse is a risk in any institution where young people are convened under the care of adults who have power over them, citing examples like Olympic teams, universities, and college football programs.

But others see things quite differently. One former chorister who worked at the school during its final years recalls that the school's legacy of abuse was a frequent topic of conversation among his friends during the tenure of his employment. In this person's view (he did not want to be identified by name), "when [abuse] happens over and over again, and it's confirmed and public, there's not really a way to move forward. No one's ever going to forget or forgive that." Even though none of the individuals who had played any part in facilitating, denying, or covering up the sexual abuse that happened at ABS were still employed there by the time he arrived, the fact that the school had the same name and legal organization was, for him, an obstacle. "I just feel like if you have the opportunity to start with a clean slate and dissolve whatever it was that harbored those incidents, then it's a maybe a good step." Out of respect to the people, like Hardwicke, whose lives were irreparably harmed by the abuse, the school had to close: "Nobody can apologize and make it right."

John Hardwicke's life has never been made right; he gave up on that hope many years ago. His journey after leaving ABS was one marked by fits and starts as he simultaneously tried to live out the life that his father had envisioned for him (law school, politics) while also harboring the secret shame and guilt of being a survivor of sexual trauma. The closest he came to fulfilling his father's ambitions was a short stint spent working as a congressional staffer right after college; he and his wife Terri, whom he met at Catholic University, have mostly worked together in graphic design and freelance public relations.[15] In spite of his marriage to a woman, he struggled for years with his sexual orientation—Hanson had told him repeatedly that he was homosexual—and he says that for a while he had a series of anonymous extramarital sexual encounters with men.[16] A skilled therapist eventually helped him begin to sort out the pieces, and Hardwicke finally told his father about the abuse in 1999, at which point his father helped Hardwicke arrange for a meeting with John Ellis, then the president of ABS.[17] Hardwicke's plan, to that point, hadn't involved a lawsuit. "My intention was to have them apologize," he told John Heilemann, "I was trying to have somebody say, 'It's not your fault.'"[18]

When no apology came, Hardwicke's father helped him find a lawyer and initiate legal action in 2000. The school's initial settlement offer—

$200,000—felt closer to an insult than the apology Hardwicke initially wanted. Instead, Hardwicke started contacting other former ABS students and seeking other survivors who were willing to come forward. The list of other boys—now men—who revealed that they, too, had suffered abuse at the hands of the choirmaster began to grow.[19] Hardwicke built a small army of survivors, each of them having spent a lifetime coping with the abuse and secrecy in different ways, but united in their conviction to tell the truth. Schemo's 2002 *New York Times* piece along with a *Nightline* story that broke simultaneously were both sourced by Hardwicke and the other survivors he'd managed to locate. Not surprisingly, the school suffered as the scandal became national news. Public outcry also accompanied the school's initial statement to Hardwicke, in which the school's lawyers suggested that Hardwicke himself was negligent for not reporting the abuse at the time.[20]

It would take nearly five years of legal wrangling for Hardwicke's case to move forward, partly because New Jersey law at the time granted immunity to charitable organizations from damages caused by negligence, a provision that protected both the choir school and Roman Catholic churches that were now the target of multiplying lawsuits alleging sexual abuse decades previously. But it was the intervening forty years that were interminable—a lifetime that Hardwicke and others had waited for an apology from the school, many of them carrying the shame of abuse in secret, having never told another soul before Hardwicke contacted them. The decision by a New Jersey state court that determined that charitable organizations like ABS were not protected from sexual abuse lawsuits was a victory, but one tinged throughout with untold quantities of bitterness and suffering.

But Hardwicke would have precious little time to celebrate. Less than week after the New Jersey Supreme Court ruled that the suit could go forward, he suffered a debilitating stroke that left him hospitalized for two months. It took another year for him to be able to regain his speech, and even now Hardwicke is quick to warn people that he has difficulty following and engaging in a linear conversation. "It was one of my really good skills," Hardwicke laughed to me when we spoke in 2022, ruefully referring to his former ability to be a lively conversationalist. Partly because of the stroke, and partly because journeys to recovery after sexual abuse are never linear, Hardwicke doesn't have a clear narrative framework for explaining his healing once the trial concluded. He did eventually receive a settlement that allowed him to manage various financial needs in the years that followed—he and Terri added on to their house, put their daughter through college, and "bought lots of furniture and artwork." When I asked him how the settlement might have affected his emotional experience as a survivor of sexual abuse, he observed that the journey of healing from his stroke overlapped with his journey post-trial, which makes it difficult to fully untangle the two; both involve attempts, however incomplete, to return to a state of wholeness even as the wounds of a grave and irreparable injury remain.

One part of his journey that Hardwicke does recount more fully has to do with reconstructing his relationship with his father. Hardwick reflected that his father "was actually kind of responsible because he sent me to this school in a bizarre way, but that's not really the case because he didn't know I was going to get sexually abused." Especially given the ways that Hanson found to suggest to Hardwicke that his father condoned the abuse, Hardwicke lived for years with this sense of betrayal, even though he knows now that his father was completely unaware. Hardwicke's ruminations strike me as a particularly powerful version of the thoughts that most of us might have as we reflect on the aspects of our parents and their parenting that we can recognize, in hindsight, as inadequate or misguided. Parents make all kinds of decisions not knowing what the outcome will be—and even some of the worst ones are decisions made out of love, or at least out of well-meaning aspirations on behalf of a child. Hardwicke's father couldn't have known that his son's life would be wounded beyond repair by going to a choir school, but surely his own life was wounded just the same by eventually learning what his son had endured there. One part of the healing that Hardwicke experienced was simply knowing that his dad, who by the time we spoke had died a decade previously, was proud of him. "My dad said what I accomplished in New Jersey was a wonderful, wonderful thing to have done. And that means so much."

It's important to notice how Hardwicke's journey from injury to recovery both begins and ends with a parent. When Hardwicke first told me his story, I was surprised at how easily I could empathize with his father and his desire to give his son the kind of musical education that he believed would benefit him, developing an interest that they shared but that his father could only daydream about, having been long past the point in his life when any chance of becoming an accomplished musician was a real possibility. It's also notable that both Hardwicke and Larry Lessig didn't tell their parents about the abuse they experienced at ABS until they were well into adulthood. I can only imagine how shattered I would be as a mother to learn decades later that my child had experienced something so devastating but declined to tell me about it at the time. I don't know what would be worse—knowing that my child had endured that kind of abuse in secret or learning that they hadn't felt that they could confide in me about it at the time.

In the end, Hardwicke's father and I aren't all that different. I also sent my son off to ABS for a week of summer camp, not knowing for sure what he would encounter there. True, I knew about the two-adults-in-a-room policy and reassured my anxious husband about this protection, reasoning that institutions with a history of sexual abuse were perhaps *more* protected now than those that hadn't yet acknowledged the hidden violence buried in their secret pasts. But of course there was no real assurance that he would be safe there; parents don't ever have assurance that their children will be safe *anywhere*. Classmates can become assailants when they bring firearms to school, and sexual predators can masquerade as trusted teachers or charismatic mentors. One of the hardest parts of being a parent is surrendering some portion of our imagined power to the parts of life that are full of vulnerability and risk. We can seek to mitigate those dangers as much as possible, but eventually children grow up, leave home, and make their own way. Our protection can feel impervious within our own homes, but living a full life means allowing a child to venture forth into a world that involves danger—a world in which children become adolescents and adolescents become adults who will make their own choices in a world full of risk.

CHAPTER 7

A Ceremony of Discipline

After Don Hanson's dark and devastating tenure at the American Boychoir School, Jim Litton helped usher in what most consider the school's golden age. The kindhearted Westminster Choir College graduate served as the director at ABS from the mid-1980s until 2001, presiding over the choir's most financially and artistically successful era. Despite the prestige he garnered in the role—including induction as a fellow into the Royal School of Church Music in the 1980s, only one of three Americans to have received the honor at the time—his method of working with children focused on encouraging them to develop and strive for their own sake, not his. As one alum recalled, "He never punished, he would just incentivize, because everybody wanted to be a part of this experience. And everybody wanted to be a part of the experience of being led by him." Litton's career had something of a pied piper theme running through it; he told me himself that some of the most useful preparation he had for his position with ABS came from directing informal choirs of neighborhood children in the West Virginia home of his childhood.

I interviewed numerous men who attended ABS during Litton's tenure, and without exception they speak of him with affection and admiration. One alum told me, "There are people who will run through walls for him"; another said, "As far as I'm concerned, that man is a saint. The way he led the choir was never by shame. Never, never once." Many kept in touch with him over the years, something that Litton considered every bit as memorable as the choir's performance work: "Obviously I'm proud of what they were able to do in their tours and all," he told me. "But I'm basically proud that they developed into great gentlemen." When Litton passed away in 2023, I attended his funeral in Princeton and watched a packed sanctuary of those boys, now men, sing in memory of their former mentor.

When I had interviewed Litton a few years prior, he had just moved into a New Jersey retirement home, a few years after his wife died of Alzheimer's. Then eighty-five, his memory was at times uneven, and he was better at recalling particular people and stories than stitching together events in linear time. We mostly talked about his memories from his time at ABS—recording an album with Jessye Norman, for instance, and various memorable and humorous mishaps that befell the boys on their international tours. Toward the end of our time together I asked him, "What if you could go back in time and conduct one program. What repertoire would you want to conduct again?"

He paused for a moment. "That's a hard question."

Even so, less than ten seconds passed before he had an answer:

"I think the one that would work best is Britten's *Ceremony of Carols*." He paused for a moment, smiling at the memory. "The kids always said, 'When are we going to sing it again, we want to sing the *Ceremony of Carols*!' And of course, it was written for boys, with the harp and all that. And the kids loved it and they were intrigued with the harp and the harpists always gave them a lot of attention." He went on to describe how the piece came to be, explaining that it was written by Benjamin Britten in the middle of the Second World War when he was returning to England from an extended residency in the United States. He and his partner, the tenor Peter Pears, were confined to an ocean liner during their trip home, and writing *Ceremony of Carols* was how Britten passed the time on that difficult and unpleasant voyage.

Litton got a bit lost in his soliloquy as he described the journey and his affection for the piece, but then he suddenly paused and said, "Do you know that piece at all?"

I smiled in recognition, thinking about the fact that my own son was currently rehearsing *Ceremony of Carols* and was not in the least bit excited about the harp and to the best of my knowledge had never once asked when it would be possible to sing it again.

The truth of it was that after two years in KSB, my son's interest and investment in the choir were starting to wane. It was increasingly difficult to get him into the car to drive to rehearsals, and his resentment at being "forced" (his word) to spend so much time with this activity was a source of tension between us. In addition, his father and I had decided to separate, which meant that the predictable rhythms of our home life had been upended, creating new challenges that required constant adaptation. It wasn't a particularly contentious parting—ours was a marriage that had been struggling for years, and the decision to end it brought relief, not conflict, at least for the adults. But even the most amicable divorce upends the life of children, and mine were certainly blindsided by the news that their family was being restructured. I'd reached out to Mr. Fisher to let him know about these difficulties, and he was understanding, even willing to cut Haydon a bit more slack than usual if it would keep him in the choir for the year. He also added that he'd seen other families endure divorce while their boys were in the choir and that sometimes having the steady rhythm of the commitment to choir could become a reassuring touchpoint during a period of transition.

For my part, I was determined that Haydon was going to continue singing, and I thought that the discipline of learning a piece like *Ceremony of Carols* was going to be quite good for him, regardless of whether he would enjoy it or not. This kind of interventionist parenting seems commonplace in my social milieu, where we take it for granted that a deep investment in kids' extracurricular activities is an essential part of childhood and adolescence. Given the young age at which these endeavors begin, parents often take the lead—enrolling kids in soccer, dance, or piano lessons, hoping that at least one of these ventures will reveal a spark that eventually develops into a self-sustaining, blazing passion that they can nurture independently. The point isn't so much to develop a virtuoso musician or athlete but rather to raise a child who can be responsible for their own life and achievements when they leave home. In most cases, kids have time to dabble around before deciding to focus more extensively on the things that really interest them—the child who started violin at age eight might wait until their teenaged years to decide to prioritize their commitment to the high school orchestra. But boy choirs are different because a boy's treble voice is accessible only *before* the period of adolescence during which kids begin to own and develop their interests independently. There's simply not time to let twelve-year-old boys wait and see if a treble choir is something they want to prioritize; by the time they're old enough to decide for themselves, they'll be tenors and basses.

For my son and me, the question of staying in the boy choir had started to feel like a test of my will as a parent over and against his rights for self-determination, given that he was increasingly articulating his desire to quit. From my vantage point, his beautiful soprano voice was a fleeting gift, and it was in his best interest that I help him develop it, whether he fully appreciated the opportunity or not. After all, Lareau confirms that part of being a contemporary parent—or at least what middle-class people *believe* makes a good parent—involves compelling children to do things that they simply do not want to do. *Finish your homework. Practice the piano. Put the iPad away. No more candy.* By this logic, there are things we might force kids to do that they don't appreciate at the time, but for which they will thank us later. Music is no exception: one boy choir director I spoke with reflected on his own extended time as a chorister: "I wanted to quit, but my mom made me stay." He went on to add that most of his adult friends who are former choristers would have said the same—his anecdotal estimate is that 80 percent of the men he knows who were in choirs when they were boys did so at the behest of a parent, almost always a mom.

When I think about my own childhood in the seventies and eighties, I know I asked to quit piano lessons on more than one occasion and can clearly remember my mom telling me that I would thank her later for demanding my persistence. Even so, my parents' commitment to my musical interests came mostly in the form of financing and transportation. Beyond my mother's refusal to let me quit early on, I can't recall much in the way of my parents' involvement in these pursuits, which eventually evolved to include piano, the oboe, and a stint as a percussionist in the high school marching band. We seemed to have an implicit, if unspoken, agreement—I had shown interest in an activity, so they were happy to support it. At the same time, they didn't perceive it to be their responsibility to offer me a buffet of activities to sample, one by one, to discover where I might have a secret, hidden gift that would eventually lead me to excel. As a case in point, I never participated in any kind of athletics, a fact that continues to astound both of my children given the ubiquity of youth sports in our suburban community. I like to joke that I might have been good at tennis or track, if only my parents had gotten the memo that girls could play sports, too. My parents' explanation for this oversight is simple: I never asked.

The world that my children and their peers are experiencing, of course, is radically different. Many aspects of childhood now feel like a training ground for the kind of adult achievements that we associate with success in the future world of work. In her study of the extracurricular pursuits of families with younger children, sociologist Hilary Levey Friedman documents the way that many parents view childhood as a competitive practice ground for the "tournament of life" in which college admission is the ultimate contest.[1] Elementary-aged kids can't yet appreciate the long-term benefits of these activities, and so parents often develop incentives for their short-term compliance—one mom in Friedman's study gave her child "points" for different achievements that her daughter can cash in for treats, like video game time. (Interestingly, when asked what this mother hopes for her daughter, she tells Friedman, "I want her to be happy and balanced and not neurotic like me, obviously.") I recognize much of myself in this mother's self-diagnosed neurosis. Using video games as an incentive was a strategy that I employed frequently—the constant allure of screen time made it a powerful incentive for chores and homework as well as a viable threat of sanction for misbehavior. A psychotherapist I know believes that the appeal of video games comes from kids' abiding desire to play, while adults need to see a purpose in things. As a result, we adults manage to turn everything into work. Put another way, kids aren't born capitalists; they learn it by watching us.

Set within this context, it's no accident that the skills of discipline and self-restraint that boy choirs promise to develop in their choristers are values that appeal to middle-class parents who worry whether their kids will be sufficiently prepared for the self-denial, persistence, and hard work demanded by adulthood. And yet, we are also frequently cautioned about the downsides of this kind of childhood, which is associated with higher rates of anxiety and depression among kids whose highly structured, micromanaged upbringings deprive them of opportunities to experience boredom, make mistakes, and find their own motivations through trial and error.[2] But even these critiques of "helicopter parenting" proceed from the same basic premise: somehow our kids' future well-being, both financial and emotional, is entirely dependent upon how well we parent. Our cultural anxiety about these tensions—a childhood that has evolved into a highly regimented training ground for capitalism on one hand, and a corresponding preoccupation with kids' emotional well-being on the other—means that our actual decisions within the family can vacillate widely between these two extremes, depending upon which worry we choose to indulge at any point in time. The same boy choir director who said that his mother was the reason he stayed in a choir during his youth believes that today's parents are much more likely to let their kids make choices for themselves, even if they're the ones who lured their children into an activity in the first place. "You don't understand the benefit [of being in a boy choir] until you've done it," he observes. Boys may not realize what they're giving up when they quit, and parents who are unwilling to endure a sustained conflict with an unhappy teenager are now more willing to give in and let their sons do as they please.

In my own case, I felt sure that the solution would be to keep my son involved in the choir long enough for him to realize that he wanted to continue to invest in it for himself—to transition from external motivation (pressure from me, rewards for compliance) to a more sustainable intrinsic motivation, that kind of appreciation that comes from loving something for its own sake. If he could just recognize a love of singing within himself, it would be sufficient to sustain a commitment and follow-through that he would embrace on his own. More than one boy choir director, including Jim Litton, told me that their philosophy on this subject was pretty simple: just make sure that most of the rehearsal was spent with the boys singing, rather than listening to the director talk. The rest would follow.

―――

Even for choristers who are highly invested, learning a piece like Benjamin Britten's *Ceremony of Carols* is no easy task for children. Despite these challenges, *Ceremony* still looms large in the holiday programs of American boy choirs. It is to boy choirs what the *Nutcracker* is to ballet—a staple for audiences that crave the quintessential boy choir experience around Christmas, even though the Middle English words bear little resemblance to any other holiday carols and are almost certainly unintelligible to the young singers who are performing them. It's a challenging work that embodies the ideal-type repertoire for boy choirs: it's British, it's Christmas, it's ethereal. The suite includes twelve short pieces of old English poetry, set to harp accompaniment, and bookended on both ends with a simple, plainsong processional and recessional. It's also fleeting—some of the twelve movements last barely more than sixty seconds, with the entire composition clocking in at just over twenty minutes long. The name is somewhat misleading, as it's not quite clear what's ceremonial about the suite, and the carols are original compositions, without any familiar echoes of other popular Christmas tunes.

Litton's story of how Britten came to write the piece was mostly correct, although as is often the case in origin stories, the truth is more complicated than the legend. In fact, *Ceremony of Carols* was the outcome of a series of random coincidences that befell Britten as he prepared to leave the United States after an extended wartime residency that had threatened his reputation as a British patriot. The texts of the composition came from a book of poems he happened to find in a Canadian bookstore during a short stop that preceded the journey across the Atlantic, and the harp accompaniment for the piece was inspired by a technical manual that Britten was carrying in preparation for an expected commission of a harp concerto that was never published. Most importantly, however, the composition marks a turning point in Britten's career, as it was one of the last works that Britten created before his composing career shifted into more mature and critically acclaimed subject matter. The origin story of *Ceremony of Carols* offers a window into Benjamin Britten's own artistic adolescence, the last few months before he began taking the kind of independent, creative risks that would make him, by many accounts, the most significant English composer of the twentieth century.

Britten had come to America in 1939 at the age of twenty-five, encouraged to follow his friends Christopher Isherwood and W. H. Auden after receiving poor reviews of a piano concerto, along with a sense that the political situation in Europe was deteriorating as war loomed between Britain and Germany.[3] Auden and Isherwood were openly gay, and Auden in particular seemed to believe that an extended stay in the States would give him an opportunity to mentor Britten into accepting his own same-sex orientation.[4] Britten traveled to the States with his friend and London flatmate Peter Pears, although at some point along the Atlantic journey, or (more likely) shortly after their arrival in the summer of 1939, the two men became lovers.[5] Britten and Pears, a tenor and vocal performer, would become lifelong partners and frequent collaborators in vocal and operatic work.

Auden and Britten, on the other hand, had a complicated friendship that had deteriorated markedly by the time Britten and Pears made ready for that return trip to England in March 1942—a decision motivated by homesickness as well as growing criticism back home of the young artists' avoidance of military service.[6] Most of all, Britten seemed to be losing patience with Auden's overbearing mentoring and unsolicited advice about his sexual life. In contrast to Auden's well-known promiscuity, Britten's romantic interests had stayed loyal to his partner Peter Pears, save for occasional infatuations with underage boys—which Britten's biographers insist remained chaste.[7] He boarded the Swedish freighter bound for England on which he would write *Ceremony of Carols* with a few haphazard writings, among them the harp manual for the concerto he would never compose, and the text to a poem by Auden that would eventually become *Hymn to St. Cecilia*. Auden's poem was also accompanied by a lengthy letter, in which the poet lectured Britten about finding the right balance between discipline and creativity, framing Britten's sexual interests as a symptom of repressed debauchery: "Goodness and Beauty are the results of a perfect balance between Order and Chaos, Bohemianism and Bourgeois Convention," Auden wrote. "Every artist except the supreme masters has a bias one way or the other.... For middle-class Englishmen like you and me, the danger is of course the second. Your attraction to thin-as-a-board juveniles, i.e. to the sexless and innocent, is a symptom of this." Auden's pedantic lecturing continued: "Wherever you go you are and probably always will be surrounded by people who adore you, nurse you, and praise everything you do.... Up to a certain point this is fine for you, but beware. You see, Bengy dear, you are always tempted to make things too easy for yourself in this way, i.e. to build yourself a warm nest of love (of course, when you get it, you find it a little stifling) by playing the lovable talented little boy."[8] Britten's response to Auden has been lost, but Auden's subsequent reply indicated that Britten took offense to its contents, and any subsequent trail of the men's friendship grew cold.[9]

Auden's reference to Britten's attraction to "thin-as-a-board juveniles" is uncomfortable, especially since the composer wrote *Ceremony*—a work that would eventually specify that it should be performed by boy sopranos—shortly after reading it. Auden may have been referring to a particular incident that had preceded Britten's departure, when Britten claimed that he had "fallen in love" with a teenaged boy named Bobby Rothman, whose father had met Britten through the Suffolk Friends of Music Symphony Orchestra, which had offered the cash-strapped composer a job that paid ten dollars per rehearsal.[10] This chance meeting seemed to have developed into a close friendship between Britten and the family, even leading Britten to temporarily declare that he wanted to abandon music altogether and manage the Rothman family's hardware store.[11] David Rothman reported that his son was quite fond of Britten in return, and Britten's biographer Humphrey Carpenter concludes that when "faced with the prospect of leaving the boy and crossing the Atlantic with Pears, [Britten] seems to have longed to abandon every commitment, musical and personal, and settle down in Bobby's household."[12] Britten would later set a group of English folk songs to music, including the song "The Trees They Grow So High," which was dedicated to Bobby Rothman and includes the lyrics "O father, dearest father, you've done to me great wrong / You've tied me to a boy when you know he is too young."[13] In his book about the English boy choir tradition, Martin Ashley posits that Britten wrote so much for boys' voices because he wanted to either be a thirteen-year-old boy or at least be in their company.[14]

Themes of pedophilia would eventually become a thread running throughout Britten's mature work. In fact, his first successful opera, *Peter Grimes*, which was written shortly after he returned to England from the

United States, adapts the work of nineteenth-century poet George Crabbe to tell the story of a violent fisherman whose young male apprentices die under suspicious circumstances; the titular character's latent homosexuality and implied pedophilia was a gloss that Britten and Montagu Slater, who wrote the libretto, added to the original poem.[15] Similarly, the subsequent Britten opera *The Turn of the Screw* adapts a Henry James novella about a governess who battles with ghosts of departed servants who persist in their malice toward the family's children, particularly the young boy Miles.[16] Interestingly, *The Turn of the Screw* also invokes the same reference to a "ceremony of innocence" from William Butler Yeats's classic poem "The Second Coming," which Humphrey Carpenter posits may have also inspired the title for *Ceremony of Carols* in the lines "Mere anarchy is loosed upon the world / The blood-dimmed tide is loosed, and everywhere / The ceremony of innocence is drowned." Carpenter argues that "*A Ceremony of Carols* is indeed a ceremony of innocence, a musical representation of life before the fall."[17]

Even if Britten's friendship with Auden did not endure, Auden's advice to him before he left the United States must have been spot-on: the work Britten would begin to produce did explicitly take up the darker themes of violence and malice that eschew the bourgeois conventions of which Auden warned. Although *Ceremony* celebrates innocence and childhood, it's best understood as the end of a chapter in Britten's personal and professional history that marks a transition to more adult themes: Its title echoes the unsettling lines from the famous Yeats poem; it was written shortly after Auden had challenged Britten to abandon a childish fascination with innocence; when Britten was leaving a teenaged boy with whom he had become infatuated; and when he was about to write his first successful opera, *Peter Grimes*, which is about a man who is understood to have murdered two male teenagers and whose crimes imply pederasty. *Ceremony* marks a turning point in Britten's career—at the conclusion of his own artistic adolescence betwixt and between the poles of innocence and maturity, these two impulses wrestling within the composer himself as he journeyed across the sea.

Though it happened the better part of a century ago, key pieces of this story resonate with my own confused musings about the dilemmas of modern parenthood. And I suspect that other parents can identify with the contradictions of infantilizing children into compliance—what Auden called "playing the lovable talented little boy"—on one hand, while searching anxiously for signs of their own maturing initiative on the other. If Auden's diagnosis was correct, then Britten wrote *Ceremony* when he was still caught up in a childish need to please others that was hampering his ability to recognize his own identity, motivation, and artistic potential. As my own battle of wills with my son continued, I could sense a similar reckoning on our shared horizon. So I was curious about what ABS alums remembered about their own motivation as singers and whether or not those motivations changed as they got older. Do they remember singing of their own volition, or were they doing it to please someone else? And in retrospect, what did they think about spending so much of their fleeting childhood in this unusually structured setting?

For the most part, the former ABS choristers I interviewed dismissed any concern that they were performing primarily to conform to the will of adults; as one alum explained, "There's a little bit of a contract here where the children have expressed their interest, and if you left it to the children to figure out how to sing and what to sing and whatever, then that's when you have the fourth grade Christmas concert and it sounds like, you know, whatever it sounds like." He continued, "I think we all had a very clear understanding that what we were doing was professional because we were receiving professional training, and that there was a way to do it. There was a work ethic, and you work hard, and you work a lot, and you practice, and you receive feedback. Like, 'no, that wasn't good. We're going to do it again.'" He went on to describe Litton's style of interaction as one that rarely, if ever, felt confrontational: "I can tell you I've seen him frustrated. I can tell you I've seen him disappointed. I don't—I can't—really recall him being angry."

But these former choristers also remember how a desire to please their director enriched their own motivations, too. Another chorister from the same time period remembered, "Once in a while [Jim Litton] would raise his voice and then you would take it very seriously. But because the product that he was putting out in terms of the quality of the choir was so good, the kids recognized it right away. And there was this almost father-like figure where everyone was searching for his approval. And his approval was giving you sort of an accolade or putting you in the touring choir or bringing you to a recording gig in New York." Litton himself explained to me that he always thought the trick was to help the boys learn to love the music itself, so that the work of making music together was simply fun.

Tellingly, American Boychoir School alum Matthew Karczewski narrated his memories of ABS, and his interactions with Litton, in terms of *Ceremony of Carols* itself, with recollections that illustrate the tension between external and internal sources of motivation that so often define the transition from childhood to adulthood. Karczewski recalls hearing one movement from *Ceremony* as a fourth grader, when he was a recruit to the school in the mid-1980s, called the Balulalow. The Balulalow looms large in the overall work—as the fifth movement in *Ceremony of Carols*, it is offered as a lullaby for the baby Jesus, with a hauntingly beautiful melody sung by a soloist whose technique and musicianship are showcased in a particularly exposed manner at the end of the piece. The performance stuck with Karczewski, providing motivation and inspiration to continue his own progression in the choir: "The fourth graders would watch the concert choir in the main hall on Friday afternoons," he reflected, remembering the first time that he heard the Balulalow, which immediately captured his attention. "In my mind at that point in the fall, I'm like, I'm going to be a head boy and I'm going to sing that solo. I just thought it was cool the way that the singers, the older kids, stepped out."

Karczewski's journey through ABS would be marked by fits and starts. Although most boys at the school were boarders, Karczewski lived nearby and attended as a day student. His home life was chaotic, and at times that chaos played out in his interactions with adults at the school. Perhaps for these reasons, his recollections of his years at ABS emphasized more struggle than that of other choristers whom I interviewed. What he perceived as an inflexible discipline structure—for instance, a rigid bell schedule, rules about walking in lines throughout the campus, the overwhelming expectation of conformity—seemed to invite challenge at every step from a boy who, in his words, "didn't want to be a robot." Even so, by seventh grade Karczewski was being trained as a soloist along with two other boys. The soloist training became competitive, especially when Karczewski realized what solo was at stake—the Balulalow from *Ceremony of Carols*. He continued, "I was like, all right. This is my journey. This is my story, you know?" Karczewski was determined to fulfill the dream that he'd established years before, when he was one of the younger kids watching the older boys sing a coveted solo to an admiring crowd.

But seventh grade continued to be a tough year, and the disruptive aspects of his home made it difficult to keep up with his schoolwork, which meant that he would sometimes use small amounts of free time before morning rehearsal at school to finish his homework assignments. Once or twice he tried to skip rehearsal, which led to a confrontation with Litton. Karczewski described this exchange as follows: "He was like, 'You are responsible for your talent. This comes first. You get [your homework] done when you need to, but you need to be responsible for your talent.' And so, I had a lot of conversations with him that year about humility. I was humbled a lot, you know, by him trying to teach me something more than just this sort of competitiveness that was kind of coming out of me." Karczewski explained further that he was struggling to handle the breath control needed for the end of the Balulalow, which requires the soloist to hold a high note for an extended period of several seconds. He said that Litton would "give me this look when I was getting it wrong—and nothing when you were getting it right. It was like, 'This is where you should be. That's the standard.'" As much as Karczewski desperately wanted to sing the coveted solo, he found himself anxious and unsure about his vocal technique when he was asked to perform. Feelings of confusion and resentment began to take root. "I came in here with no musical training before I started at the school," Karczewski thought to himself, and in his mind he blamed the school and its voice teachers for any shortcomings he experienced when performing. "I was like, 'I don't know what technique is. Isn't that your job?'"

Karczewski's recollections of this struggle felt uncomfortably familiar to me as a parent—this contest between the will of a child and the discipline of adults, and between the promise of natural talent and the dedicated, intentional practice that brings talent to fruition. In his retelling he was a cocky kid who broke the rules and wanted exceptions to be made for him because, in his view, he was a particularly talented singer. Another version of the story could highlight the vulnerability of a thirteen-year-old boy from a difficult home situation who was looking for adult attention and external discipline that would compensate for what was missing at home. Either way, he wasn't quite ready or able to do what was asked of him—he never got the Balulalow solo that he'd set his sights on years earlier. Even now, decades later, Karczewski isn't quite sure whether he should blame himself or his teachers for falling short. When I asked him to explain what he thought Jim meant by warning him that he "had to be responsible for his talent," Karczewski described it this way: "I get the feeling that he was saying that at a certain point, you're going to have to own this talent. You're going to have to be responsible for it because you're not going to have these things around you to keep it going. Right now, you have this whole system of people and you know, directors and administrators and teachers that are helping you with this talent. At some point you're going to have to own it—or put it down and do something else."

Karczewski's words were on my mind a few weeks later when I drove my son and another chorister to choir rehearsal in early December for a two-hour session devoted entirely to *Ceremony*, which they would be performing for the first time a few days later at a small Pennsylvania town about an hour west of Philadelphia. Our neighbor and carpool partner chatted excitedly as we started the drive, saying things like "Did you know that the harpist is going to be there tonight?" and "My mom says that we can have pizza when I get home from rehearsal, even though it's going to be really late." Haydon was mostly silent, except for the moment when he gave me a sideways, mostly accusatory glance and said, "Why can't *we* get pizza?" The drive seemed endless as we fought our way through the traffic on the dark, rainy night. When we finally arrived, the first thing Haydon said was, "Can we leave early?"

Admittedly, I knew that the boys would be standing for most of the two hours ahead, repeating the same harmonies over and over again until Mr. Fisher was satisfied. Parents were usually able to wander into the wood-paneled sanctuary during rehearsal to listen as they pleased, but tonight the doors were shut with an implicit "please keep out" vibe. So I settled myself onto the floor outside, my back against the exterior sanctuary wall, as the rehearsal ensured. I wondered if Haydon was still singing first soprano—there had been some discussion the previous week about pulling him down into the alto section, now that his voice was starting to show signs of dropping. At fourteen, his days as a treble were numbered, but he was still able to hit most of the high notes throughout the piece—though not nearly as effortlessly as he had two years prior, when he first joined the choir. The other thought that came to my mind as I leaned against the wall was exactly how well-trained these boys had become. It was a Wednesday night, they were wearing sweatpants and sneakers, but even through the wall they sounded like professionals.

When the rehearsal finally ended, I joined the ranks of other exhausted parents and quickly collared the boys and ushered them to the parking lot, hoping to beat the rush as we started yet another journey home. I expected Haydon to exit the sanctuary glaring, but his buoyant mood and suddenly pleasant disposition took me completely by surprise.

"Well, you're in a better mood," I said as we headed toward our car. "What changed?"

He shrugged it off. "I don't know. I guess we just had a really good rehearsal."

I was reminded of one thing that Matthew Karczewski had told me a few weeks earlier: "This is the thing we learned from Jim: some of the best music you're ever going to make, no one's going to hear it. It's going to be in this room, in this rehearsal, and you have to be okay with that. The goal is not out there. The goal is in here. It's the joy in doing that."

Three days later, on a cold December morning, we started our *Ceremony of Carols* road trip for the choir's first performance of the season. It began the way that many choir events did for my son: with him complaining about the uniform. After what seemed like endless nagging on my part, he finally emerged from the house and ambled slowly toward the car, shirt untucked and hair unbrushed. His dirty white sneakers looked out of place with his black slacks, but he was at least carrying his dress shoes in one hand and his belt in the other. His jacket hung unevenly on his shoulders.

As he got into the car he said, "I wouldn't mind this so much if the clothes weren't so uncomfortable."

I surveyed his expanding frame, and it registered on me that he was going to need new pants this year. I'm not sure why I hadn't anticipated this before—he'd already outgrown most of the joggers he wore to school during the week; perhaps I'd been hoping that the concert pants would get us through at least one more season. But now it was clear that the pants were about an inch too short and wouldn't button unless he was willing to permit the waistband to dig into his groin. Given that we had about eight hours ahead of us, wearing the pants unbuttoned seemed a wiser choice, at least for now.

The church was a little over an hour away. Haydon nestled into his headphones and closed his eyes—not sleeping so much as escaping from my desire for conversation. We had most of the Pennsylvania Turnpike to ourselves that Sunday morning and eventually wound our way through a cluster of small towns before finding the Catholic church where we would spend most of the day. The church campus included a central sanctuary built in the mid-sixties in a contemporary style and a separate fellowship building that looked like a gymnasium. In between the two buildings was a vast parking lot, speckled with cars and punctuated by little cracks in the asphalt where rows of grass attempted to find sunshine.

Choir volunteers greeted us after we got out of our car, ushering us into the fellowship building, which turned out to be a huge gymnasium filled with people and an abundant hot breakfast. The boys were thrilled, quickly taking off their jackets and using them to claim folding chairs alongside their friends before they jumped into the hot food line. The menu included scrambled eggs, bacon, sausage, scrapple, waffles with fruit and whipped cream, orange juice, and lots of hot chocolate.

Parishioners watched the boys with curiosity and interest. I couldn't say that the choristers were on their best behavior, and the formal attire complicated things by highlighting the disjuncture between their pressed dress clothes and their friendly roughhousing. I watched my own son cautiously, waiting to intervene the moment his behavior started to deteriorate. His current appearance didn't help—his pants unbuttoned and his hair wild and overgrown, with coarse, brown curls exploding out of his head. I'd given up suggesting haircuts months ago, reasoning that hair was not the place to stake yet another battle. There were so many other battles to fight—at that very moment, in fact, Haydon was carrying his belt in both hands, the very belt that should have been used to cover up his unbuttoned waistband, and had folded the belt in half so that he could pull swiftly on the two ends so as to make a loud slapping noise in the faces of other boys.

As the clock ticked past eleven o'clock we migrated to the sanctuary, which gave the boys time to rehearse and prepare for the three-o'clock concert. I realized uneasily that this meant we would be spending the next

A CEREMONY OF DISCIPLINE

four hours engaged in various forms of waiting. The boys realized this too, as Mr. Fisher assigned each one of them a pew and explained that that pew would be their home for the next few hours. He encouraged them to take a nap if they wanted to while their section wasn't rehearsing and reiterated that there was to be absolutely no talking. At some point, another parent volunteer approached me to say me that Haydon's shirt did not meet the dress code regulations because it didn't have buttons at the collar. She extracted another shirt from the bowels of a duffel bag and said that he could go and change in the men's room where, given that the boys just ate the breakfast of a lifetime an hour prior, there was already a long line. Haydon did not receive this news well, and after changing into the new shirt immediately began to complain that it did not smell clean and itched his neck. I felt torn between wanting to reiterate the party line about wearing the regulation uniform—some version of "just suck it up, kid"—and feeling true sympathy for his discomfort. Now he had to endure both pants that were too small *and* an itchy shirt.

The ensuing hours ticked by. The harpist arrived at one o'clock, which provided some novelty and allowed the boys to begin rehearsing different sections of the work. I silently noted that, unlike Jim Litton's recollections, this particular harpist did not seem interested in paying the boys any special attention. Instead, they continued struggling to keep themselves from talking at every opportunity. At several points boys had to be reordered in line so as to separate the ones who were being particularly disruptive. Surprisingly, it wasn't the youngest boys who were the problem—boys as young as nine or ten managed that interminable rehearsal without any difficulty—it was the older boys who at fourteen or even fifteen were still in the treble choir, waiting for hair to grow on their upper lips and for their Adam's apples to drop. It must be difficult, I thought to myself, to be one of the smallest boys at school, still stuck in the treble choir while their lucky friends were visited by puberty on time and as scheduled.

By two-forty, which seemed to come only after an eternity of waiting, the parking lot had begun to fill. Amazingly, people who were just at church a few hours previously still wanted to come back in the afternoon to hear the choir sing. And sure enough, by three o'clock the church was almost full—old people, young people, families with kids. At last the boys filed onto the risers in their ordered lines, and the sanctuary settled into expectant silence.

The concert began with a short introduction to *Ceremony of Carols*, in which Mr. Fisher explained that this work by Benjamin Britten was the most famous work ever written for a boy choir. "Each movement is like a little polished stone that lasts only a couple of minutes," he said. "As soon as you recognize what it is, it's over." I wondered to myself if Benjamin Britten ever imagined that this work would be performed like this, in a contemporary Catholic sanctuary in rural Pennsylvania, performed by boys overstuffed on pancakes, some of whom were wearing pants that didn't fit and most of whom were surely exhausted. The good thing about the British chorister's uniform of cassock and surplice must be that it doesn't involve a belt and could only get too short, never too tight. Mr. Fisher continued his instructions to the audience, explaining that the convention with this piece was to withhold applause between each of the movements and concluded with his usual announcement about turning off cell phones and being in the moment: "Celebrate this sound, which is fleeting, which is ephemeral, because you may not hear it next year."

The boys began with the upbeat "Wolcom Yole," but the previous five hours had worn on them—we had been there since ten o'clock, after all—and the performance betrayed that exhaustion. Yet despite their fatigue, the boys bounced to the beat, a movement barely perceptible because the visual specter of the group kept the audience from noticing any one singer's slight imperfections. Next came "There Is No Rose," with a sublime melody that seemed to reach to the very ceiling of the aging building. Mr. Fisher carefully mouthed the order of the final succession of words, all sung in unison on middle C: "Alleluia, Res Miranda, Pares Forma, Gaudeamus, Transeamus." Soon it was time for the solo in "That Yonge Child," and the boy who came to the microphone was so small that I

A CEREMONY OF DISCIPLINE

assumed he was barely more than nine years old. He wasn't sure exactly how close to get to the microphone, and he settled on a spot that was perhaps a bit too far, and so it didn't pick up his voice as much as needed. But this, of course, was preferable to the opposite problem—being too close and suffering a screeching reverb. The captivating Balulalow came next, and the soloist did it justice. One got the feeling that the audience wanted to clap but remembered Mr. Fisher's instructions and thought better of it.

The next piece should have been "As Dew in Aprille" but they skipped it; perhaps it wasn't quite ready for prime time, even here with a friendly audience. Instead, "This Little Babe" followed, with the boys all trying to find their spot in the complicated round that always feels, itself, like some kind of frantic, searching contest. Then came the harp interlude, which is longer than any other piece in the entire composition. It's always beautiful, pulling in cryptic phrases of melodies from the other pieces in the suite. Watching a harpist perform is an experience in and of itself—she knows how to find the unmarked strings and her arms never appear to get tired. I remembered, suddenly, an email that Mr. Fisher had written to me two years prior, after one of the first holiday concerts in which Haydon had participated. That year, the older trebles in the choir had also performed *A Ceremony of Carols*, while Haydon sat with the younger boys who listened as audience members. The note read, "During the harp interlude in *Ceremony*, I happened to be seated in front of Haydon, and he was blissing out. (Perhaps not share that with him, don't want to embarrass him.) But it was a wonderful thing to witness. This is what you hope for— that they "get it" at this age. (Though surely, looking back, they will get it, the incredible music they're experiencing.)" I watched my son then, standing at the top of the risers, and he was doing anything but blissing out. He was mostly scratching his neck in the itchy, loaner shirt, and I could see that at the border where his unruly curls met the white shirt with the proper button-down collar there was a ring of crimson. He cast a miserable sideways glance to where I was sitting in the audience, hoping that I could see his suffering. He looked down at his shoes, back to me, and then back at Mr. Fisher with a performance of resolve meant only for me to notice.

This was the final blow that unleashed in full the uneasy feeling that I had been trying to suppress for most of that long and difficult day: that perhaps this ceremony of discipline was not really in my child's best interest. Of course, I'd rationalized this activity by telling myself that he did enjoy this, once, that he was very talented, and that every minute spent in choir rehearsal was a minute *not* spent in front of a screen, which seemed to be the primary alternative temptation. He was learning to read and interpret music in a structured way, becoming acquainted with notable classical compositions. But I also had to be honest that there was another, countervailing explanation of these events: that I have been too overbearing by nudging my child into something that primarily I enjoy, that activates my own sense of what is worthy and valuable, and that this was no longer a connection that forged us together as musicians but a disagreement that created distance between us, as I insisted and he resisted.

And then, of course, there was the neutral, descriptive narrative that emphasized that whether or not my child truly enjoyed being in a boy choir, there was no denying that we had spent most of the day in various forms of waiting (driving, sitting, standing, lying on a church pew), that his clothes were uncomfortable, and that he was singing music written by a composer who may have been a pedophile or who had, at best, serious boundary issues when it came to adolescent boys. I considered all these different narratives and found that, in most of them, I didn't end up feeling so great about my mothering.

The final piece in *A Ceremony of Carols* is "Deo Gracias," and it's easy to tell that it's the finale. The mood of the piece is markedly different, setting the words of an anonymous fifteenth-century poem to music: "Adam lay ybounden / Bounden in a bond / Four thousand winter / Thought he not too long." The piece ends with the refrain "Deo gracias" sung several times in a row, and in between each one of these refrains the harp issues a commanding, aggressive glissando that accelerates and announces the downbeat of each new measure. It's a powerful effect, and by the end of the piece the harp accompaniment reaches a near frenzy. At this point, the suite was over, and the audience realized they were allowed to applaud, and of course they did so eagerly. The soloists bowed, the choir bowed—they had been taught to do so with such uniformity and gravitas that they looked as if they were being manipulated by strings and a giant puppeteer—and the applause continued. Only twenty minutes had passed, and the boys would sing for another hour—other Christmas songs, a Hanukkah suite featuring one of the choristers on the clarinet, show tunes from *Oliver*. The audience seemed particularly to enjoy the connection between "Food, Glorious Food" and a public thank-you for the morning's hot breakfast: "If you want to know how to motivate boys, you have to first recognize that it starts with their stomachs," Mr. Fisher joked.

As we approached the end of the program, Mr. Fisher gave his usual speech about how our culture often doesn't celebrate boys' singing. He explained that this choir was the travel soccer team of singing, saying to the audience, "Let's celebrate them right now!" to which they responded with another enormous round of applause. Finally, Mr. Fisher announced that the concert would conclude with a South African folk song, sung in rounds that the audience could also sing, with the boys' help. That day it was "Sthandwa Sam," a song of forgiveness. As many times as I'd heard the song, and sung it as an audience member, I still wasn't sure what or who was being forgiven. Interpersonal slights? Apartheid? Overanxious parents with control issues? The boys spread themselves throughout the congregation, and soon the sanctuary was full of people, young and old, singing the Zulu lyrics and performing a set of hand motions that accompany the words, which translated mean roughly, "My sweetheart, I'm sorry, tears are flowing." The words seemed appropriate for my own state of mind as an interminable day finally came to an end.

With that, the concert was over. The boys were exhausted, but the appreciative audience seemed to infuse them with a bit more energy as they started to leave the building. I waved goodbye to Mr. Fisher, who noticed Haydon's white shirttail hanging out beneath his jacket. "You need to tuck that in," he called after us. I didn't have the energy to speak up—to defend Haydon, really—and explain that his shirttail was hanging out because he couldn't button his pants. And anyway, I wasn't sure that would have helped his case. Either way, I'd failed to provide the regulation uniform and make sure that my fourteen-year-old's last-year pants would still button. It was another reason to confirm that my mothering fell short.

Our car was freezing, but the heat started to come through a few minutes after we got on the road. Whether my son was simply tired or truly furious at me for putting him through this interminable experience, I couldn't be sure. But he was not in a good mood—no sudden change of heart as was the case with the rehearsal just a few days before. As we headed out to the Pennsylvania Turnpike, I saw a Dunkin' Donuts just off the main drag and the lure of caffeine summoned me. It was a few minutes past five o'clock, but I was willing to risk trouble sleeping later to make sure I didn't nod off on the turnpike. Those December days are among the shortest of the year in the Northeast, which meant we would be driving in darkness.

"Can I get you something?" I asked as I pulled into the drive-through.

"I only want some water. I just want to get home."

As we waited in the drive-through lane at Dunkin Donuts, I thought of the list of things I wanted to say I was sorry for.

I'm sorry that today was such a long day.

I'm sorry that your dad and I are getting divorced.

I'm sorry if I have forced you to do this activity that you don't really want to do.

I'm sorry that I didn't realize your clothes don't fit anymore.

I'm sorry that I didn't know what kind of shirt you were supposed to wear.

I'm sorry that sometimes I push you too hard.

I'm sorry if someday you wish I had pushed you harder.

I only managed to get out the first of the apologies; the rest would have to wait. Haydon said quickly, "It's okay, mom." We pulled out of the Dunkin' Donuts drive-through—me with my coffee, him with his water—and within minutes we were back on the highway.

"Do you want to listen to music?" I asked, hopefully.

He did not answer.

CHAPTER 8

Mother Nature Has Them by the Throat

By the start of 2020, I had begun to understand why we often refer to a boy's voice change as "breaking." Haydon's voice had developed an unpredictable edge that reminded me of a honking goose. He'd also sprouted a faint, Frida Kahlo–esque mustache on his upper lip, and I had learned to avert my eyes if he walked around shirtless, lest I catch a disconcerting glimpse of the hair now emerging from his armpits. I didn't know exactly when this unsettling growth appeared, but it must have happened sometime in the fall because I distinctly remember being with Ellen at the town pool during the previous summer and catching sight of her son bare chested. At the time I was startled to see that he'd grown armpit hair since the previous summer and felt privately relieved that Haydon was still unmarked by this early herald of puberty. I hadn't said anything, but Ellen must have registered the mixture of surprise and disgust that I hadn't fully disguised on my face.

"Yeah, the armpit hair," she said stoically, a moment after the boys left our encampment on the lawn.

"Let's never speak of it again," I suggested.

Now, six months later, Haydon has learned at fourteen and a half that he can catch me unaware and lift his arms so that I'm forced to see what's growing there—he knows that it makes me uncomfortable, and it's one of our inside jokes. Although we never discussed it openly, he seemed to understand that these new bodily manifestations of manhood gave him a power that's simultaneously playful and needling. "Cover your eyes!" I yelled one night to my daughter when he walked into my bedroom after a shower, wearing only his flannel pajama pants. "You'll never be the same after you're forced to see Haydon's armpit hair!"

The three of us laughed long and hard about this, and the laughter felt restorative, even medicinal, since there hadn't been nearly enough laughter in the several months that had passed since their dad moved out. I was glad to know that we were still capable of a family joke, even if it came at Haydon's expense. The quiet emptiness of a house that once held four people kept reminding me that the number of adults in my house had been completely and irreparably cut in half. There were no men here anymore, only a woman and her children.

Except I wasn't sure that it was still accurate to call Haydon a child, even as he flopped himself face down onto my bed, saying just as he did when he was about five years old, "Will you scratch my back?" His back, thankfully, was devoid of hair, and I could indulge him in the physical ritual that was part of his childhood bedtime routine for years. But I also had to admit that it was starting to feel weird to do this—some boys his age had girlfriends now; he even knew another boy in the eighth grade who claimed to have had sex—but I decided to take my cues from him. There was no father there who might criticize this fleeting, intimate moment between mother and son or to covet that closeness for himself. Haydon rarely chose to show me anything that resembled childlike vulnerability these days. The little boy who used to beg me to sit with him when he was scared of the dark was only occasionally visible now, inside an unfamiliar, changing body.

More often Haydon and I found ourselves in a conflict over something, and his continued singing in the boy choir was at the top of this list of things we argued about. For the time being, we had brokered a tentative truce: he would keep singing through the end of eighth grade, after which point he would decide for himself whether to join the changed-voice Graduates. The terms of our armistice weren't ones that I was entirely happy about because I had secured this cooperation only by allowing him to play video games for as long as he wanted to on Saturday afternoons after choir rehearsal. Unfortunately, this inflamed another perpetual source of conflict, which is how I think he should generally spend *less* time in digital settings. In my view, a critical role played in the "Parenting Successfully" performance is The One Who Monitors Screen Time. The script doesn't assign this part to a particular gender, but I suspect it almost always falls to a woman.

"What if I join band at school?" Haydon asked me one day, as I was cleaning up the dishes in the kitchen after dinner. "Then would you let me quit choir?"

I paused to give this suggestion some thought. "What would you play, exactly?" I replied, making little effort to hide my skepticism. Aside from a short-lived relationship with an alto sax in fifth grade, Haydon played only the piano, and last time I checked there wasn't a pianist in the band.

"I talked to the band director today about starting percussion," Haydon said, with an air of resolve that felt new and determined. "I can go to rehearsals starting next week."

It was not lost on me that he had picked the one instrument that doesn't involve contorting your mouth into an awkward shape but instead gave one license to hit things and make loud noises.

But his proposal intrigued me, and so I decided to give the answer that all parents give when they aren't sure yet if they'll give in or not: "We'll see."

He was momentarily satisfied with my response and even helped me load the dishwasher without being asked. When we were finished, he skipped out of the kitchen and gave a little jump to touch the top of the doorframe with his left hand. It used to give him a thrill to jump high enough to reach the wood with his fingertips. But it seemed he had forgotten, at least for a moment, that this ceased to be a challenge many months ago. Now he was tall enough that this movement was little more than a lazy stretch.

Thinking and talking about bodies like this makes me uncomfortable, and it's not just because of the armpit hair. The field of sociology, in fact, has generally been more inclined to talk about gender as a theoretical concept than something that lives in actual human bodies.[1] This is partly because the larger paradigm of socially constructed gender endorses the notion that gender is something that we do, that we achieve, that we create through interactions with others.[2] It's easier to achieve gendered status when a body conforms to certain gendered expectations, but thinking about gender as a social construction inadvertently relegates the body to an afterthought, even an obstacle, to the social work of being classified as a man or a woman or a person who identifies as nonbinary. But the physical changes that happen during puberty put the body front and center, forcing the question of how one will be seen and gendered by others. The changes of puberty happen slowly and then, somehow, all at once, whether we want them to or not.

These physical changes of puberty mirror other, less visible shifts in how power and vulnerability are intertwined. For instance, as mother and son, Haydon and I were constantly negotiating his desire for more independence—to ride his bike farther away, along busier streets; to spend time with new friends whose parents I haven't met; to be liberated from the parental controls on his phone or be allowed to watch R-rated movies; to live without the burden of my compulsive desire for him to keep his room neat and tidy or my rule that he finish his homework before playing video games. Of course, all children are in positions of subordination regardless of their gender—under the thumb of parents, perhaps especially their mothers, and subservient to the rules and strictures of institutions and organizations. On this point, one boy choir director quipped, "Men may rule the world, but ten-year-old boys do not." But I didn't need reminding that Haydon wasn't ten years old anymore. When he was younger, it was easy to pick him up and put him into "time out" when he was misbehaving. But it had been years since I attempted to physically compel him to do anything. Instead, we'd fallen into these elaborate webs of negotiation in which my main source of power lay in my ability to turn off the Wi-Fi.

In fact, I realized that I rarely touched my son anymore, a confession I shared with Ellen on one of our weekend runs. We agreed that this is a problem that feels specific to being the mother of teenaged boys, and Ellen told me about how she was recently driving with her son in the passenger seat and was momentarily unnerved by how much his hairy legs looked like her husband's. We also agreed that things felt different with our daughters, who are only two years behind our sons in age. Something about our relationship with them seemed more open-ended, more filled with possibilities, than the emotional world that we were now entering with our adolescent sons. When our daughters went through puberty, they would be joining a sorority in which we are already members, their monthly periods a continual reminder of how we were bound together by the constraints of motherhood, past, present, and potential future. But seeing a son go through puberty felt more like watching him enter a sketchy secret society whose hazing rituals were known only within the world of men.

My conversation with Ellen reminded me of something my mother told me when I was a child, when we were on the way home from a Thanksgiving weekend with my dad's family.

"Why does Grandma seem to be so much closer to Aunt Anne than to Dad?" I had asked my mother as our enormous, aging Suburban fought its way home through the post-Thanksgiving interstate traffic.

I couldn't have been more than eight or nine years old at the time, but somehow I'd been able to perceive that my grandmother had a closer relationship with my dad's sister than with my father, something that came with a host of intangible goodies that I couldn't quite name but that I knew I wanted to access. My grandmother seemed so at ease around my aunt, so knowingly comfortable with my cousins, that it exposed an impoverished dimension of her relationship with us that I felt warranted an explanation. I knew that my grandmother loved us, of course—that wasn't ever the question. But she didn't seem to inhabit our emotional space with the same presence and comfort that she did my aunt's family. When she came to visit us, it was clear that she was a guest, our interactions unfolding in a manner that resembled a respectful series of interviews rather than a cozy reacquainting of intimates.

My mother shrugged it off with an unconcerned air of resignation. "You know what they say," she said, rolling her eyes ever so slightly. "Your son is your son until he finds a wife, your daughter is your daughter for the rest of your life." I didn't fully understand this until I became a mother and understood for myself how mothers have an easier time staying emotionally connected with their daughters, while boys seem destined to grow up to become some other woman's emotional territory. This isn't to say that the emotional dynamics of mother-daughter relationships aren't complicated—often, they are far *more* complicated than the relationships that mothers have with their grown sons. But that's the point. Mothers and daughters tend to remain emotionally enmeshed throughout their lives in ways that generally unfold differently than they do for mothers and sons.

Although my mother didn't realize it, she was also summarizing some of the arguments developed by Nancy Chodorow, the feminist psychologist best known for her book *The Reproduction of Mothering*, published during the apotheosis of second-wave feminism when my own mother was washing cloth diapers as a stay-at-home mom in the Texas suburbs. Chodorow published the book in 1978 before she herself became a mother but felt she knew something of motherhood because she had been a daughter. The roots of gender inequality, she argued, began with the emotional dynamics of a nuclear family, in which it meant something different to mother a daughter than to mother a son.[3] Chodorow's analysis traced these divergent pathways with the precision of a brain surgeon identifying the origins of a metastatic tumor, starting with a feminist reading of Freud's concept of the oedipal phase. Freud's theory posited that although both boys and girls both long for physical touch from their caregivers, boys eventually realize that a sustained erotic attachment to their mother is out of bounds and reject her in favor of an identification with their father, and with him the more traditional elements of masculinity. Boys sense as young children that to do otherwise would mean metaphorical castration—losing their masculinity if they continue to identify with their mother—and so they equate being masculine with anything that is *not* associated with femininity. This offers one reason for why boys learn to be uncomfortable with emotional displays and have a stronger need than girls to differentiate themselves from all that their mother represents, especially control and dependency. "In theory, a boy resolves his Oedipus complex by repressing his attachment to his mother," Chodorow explains. "He is therefore ready in adulthood to find a primary relationship with someone *like* his mother."[4]

In her view, much of what we recognize as male dominance and misogyny find their origins in the unconscious emotional dynamics of the mother-son relationship.[5] When he turns away from his mother and starts to see his attachment to her as an obstacle to his masculinity, a boy looks outward to the heteronormativity and patriarchy that characterize the larger society.[6] These are weapons, in a way, that a boy can wield against his mother: he will eventually have social power that she does not, even though it requires the painful work of rejecting her. Because men are often more remote in the family—either because of work pressures or emotional constraint or because mothers still do most of the hands-on work of parenting young children—Chodorow reasons that boys' development of a masculine identity is less rooted in identification with the actual person of their father than in turning away from their mother and all that she represents, including her futile attempts to control them.[7]

Chodorow eventually shifted her attention from psychology to psychoanalysis, engaging in clinical work with patients to mine the depths of the human psyche. But she found that these gendered patterns of childhood emotional connection and separation, of loss and longing, were useful ways of interpreting her patients' emotional lives as adults.[8] Her ideas also help explain why it felt like so much was at stake in my son's impending voice change and why the two of us were locked in a battle of wills over whether or not he would continue singing. For starters, it's worth acknowledging that the only way I could guarantee his ability to keep singing as a treble would be, quite literally, some form of castration. The voice change had started to feel like a metaphor for all the ways that my son was leaving childhood behind, joining the world of men to which I am barred entry. His treble voice was the last part of his body that betrayed the vulnerability of femininity and, with it, some lingering testament of his ability to stay connected to me.

It didn't surprise me, then, when one choral director told me about a singer in the boy choir she directed whose voice had fully changed by the time he was a ninth grader in high school. She assigned him a baritone part, assuming that he would want to sing with the changed voice ensemble. "But I could tell something was off," as the rehearsals began, because "he was just having a hard time." She asked the singer privately what was going on, and tears began to fall as he explained how he wanted to continue singing in his high voice instead of using his new baritone range. "It is glorious," she explained of his treble voice, "it is a beautiful falsetto sound. It doesn't sound falsetto, it's still so close because he's so freshly changed." She saw his immediate relief when she reassured him that he could continue singing in his treble range if that was what he wanted.

"What do you think that was about for him?" I asked.

She paused for a moment before saying that she thought it was really about his relationship with his mother, a professional musician who had praised his soprano voice through childhood. "She was just so in love with that ability that he had. I think that was such a point of connection for them."

Suddenly, the director abruptly checked herself, hesitant to interpret someone else's emotional experience. "I mean, honestly, I don't know if that's what it is," she quickly qualified. But after a pause she added, "I just really think he didn't want to lose that connection with his mom."

Later, I found myself thinking about that boy and what his mother may have done differently that made him want to cling to the very connection that my son seemed so determined to sever. Whether it's a change that a boy desires or dreads, it may have the same significance: the voice break can mean an emotional break, too.

I was also starting to realize that even though I'd told myself that being involved in the arts was a way of helping my son develop a more emotionally engaged form of manhood, there was also another, more self-serving part of that agenda.

I want him to grow up staying emotionally engaged with me.

―――

The changed emotional dynamics that come along with puberty stem from changes that happen in bodies—changes that are a constant, unavoidable reminder of the fact that a child is, in fact, a separate and distinct person who will have their own identity and desires that aren't fully amenable to a parent's manipulation. Wayne Koestenbaum writes in his memoir-informed exploration of gender, sexuality, and opera *The Queen's Throat* that "puberty represents a moment of reckoning.... In puberty, the *real* erupts: acne, Adam's apple, sperm, breasts, blood."[9] These physical markers—what are technically called "secondary sex characteristics"—are meaningful precisely because they carry a currency in the larger world, signaling something about the bodies in which they appear. Part of what makes puberty such a seismic transition for parents and children is that these physical changes herald the beginning of a different way of being in the world, one in which sex starts to enter the picture. I can attempt to ignore these changes, of course, but I'm going to have to reckon with them at some point. For all the micromanaging of my son's life that I've successfully carried off thus far, I am finding myself particularly ill-equipped to know how and how much to intervene, now that he's starting to look and sound like a man.

Even though it's announced by the dreaded voice "crack" of the early teenaged years, the voice change for boys actually proceeds in two phases over a period of time than can extend until age twenty.[10] In the first stage, testosterone changes the soft cartilage of the larynx, creating the "Adam's apple" that provides a protective casing for the vocal folds inside. This initial wave of testosterone also causes the vocal folds to expand and lengthen, just as the bass strings inside a piano are the longest and thickest of the instrument. This early stage is when the voice change is most unwieldy, and when a boy's voice is hardest for him to control. But as puberty continues, the cartilage eventually starts to stabilize and harden, giving the vocal folds sustained protection as they grow and lengthen over a period of several years. Although a boy's voice typically drops at least an octave in the initial phase of this change, the second part of the transition is when the voice finally stabilizes, and most male voices find a final resting place in the range of a tenor, baritone, or bass.

When Haydon began choir, I had assumed that boys' singing voices would drop gradually, the way that their speaking voices generally do— steadily sliding lower and lower as an intact, two-octave range until they reach their final resting place. Although the voice change does happen this way for a small portion of boys, the majority have a voice change more like the one that Haydon was experiencing: they keep their treble range in the head voice, begin to acquire a lower range in the chest voice, but have nothing in the middle because they've yet to develop the ability to sing in *passagio*, which means controlling the part of their vocal range that mixes chest voice and head voice across what is called "the break." It's a cruel tease on the part of Mother Nature, giving a boy two voices at once as if challenging him to think he could choose one over the other. Ironically, the in-between range that aligns with the rest of my son's body is precisely the place where his voice is most uncomfortable, stuck inside of an androgynous way station. It's awkward, its tone amorphous and unpredictable, an in-between place where no tune would want to linger.

Even though boys in middle and early high school are dealing with an unwieldy vocal instrument, it is KSB's policy to keep the boys singing as trebles as long as possible, something that aligns with recent developments in vocal pedagogy that encourage directors to keep boys singing through the voice change. Vincent Oakes, who directs the Chattanooga Boys Choir, has focused his research as a scholar and teacher upon various dynamics of vocal change in adolescents, with a particular focus on boys. Oakes explained to me that "the school of thought a hundred years ago was that when your voice starts to change, just give it up for a while, leave singing and come back to it when you're grown or your voice has finished breaking . . . that horrible term breaking," he added. As a result, generations of boy choristers were routinely ejected from choirs the moment their voices started to shift. Instead, Oakes now consciously works to give the boys in his choir special encouragement and attention when, in his words, "they are snap, crackle and pop all over the place."

Explicitly acknowledging the awkwardness of the voice change represents a departure from how we typically think about puberty, especially for boys. As with the boy choristers of a hundred years ago who were cast out of singing until their voices were fully changed, I expect that most mothers would prefer to avert their eyes from the awkward embodiments of male puberty that unfold during this time, disrupting the peaceful safety of childhood. As Ellen and I agreed at the town pool that summer, no woman wants to see your teenaged son's armpit hair revealed publicly in all its glory—even your most devoted best friend. And yet puberty has a way of making bodies seen, whether we want them to be or not. The effects of testosterone on the vocal folds are also permanent, one component of puberty that can't be undone later with hormone therapy or gender-affirming surgery. For the voice at least, the well-worn path through male puberty is still a one-way street.

This means that the changed voice is also one of the most prominent ways that a body can signal male gender to others. After all, even though both males and females grow darker hair on their legs and armpits during puberty, hair can be easily removed by both men and women. The voice, on the other hand, betrays gender in ways that are harder to camouflage. As Koestenbaum writes, "Just as breath surges out through the voice box into the ambient air, so our unmarked, unformed soul loses its imaginary innocence and becomes branded for life with a gender and a sexuality."[11] One former chorister described the unchanged treble voice as "the least gendered" form of singing. But after puberty, he observed, "the voice change attaches gender to the music that you're making." That gender may in fact be one that is embraced and welcomed by the singer. But this presentation of gender is also one that means something to others, who begin to see that voice as belonging not to a child but to a man.

For his part, my son understood the contours of this signaling perfectly. He seemed to want to exercise his new voice primarily by refusing to do what I wanted him to do with it.

"We agreed," I said to him after yet another confrontation about quitting choir, "that you would keep singing until the end of eighth grade."

He'd begun having more frequent voice checks with Mr. Fitz that spring, which was the standard practice for boys in the choir once their voices started to change. After that disastrous Christmas performance a few months previously, I'd suggested to the program coordinator that maybe Haydon could start singing with the older boys in the changed voice group, where perhaps he would be more engaged—looking up to older peers rather than chafing at being with younger ones. But although his recent voice check confirmed that he was beginning to develop a range of lower, chest voice notes, he didn't have enough of the lower range to sing any of the changed voice parts in full. He was stuck with the trebles, at least for the rest of the semester.

Now Haydon sat on the couch, arms crossed at his chest, his face stony and sullen, offering only silence as an answer.

"It's just a few more months," I hastened to add quickly, thinking to myself that Haydon wasn't the only one with an eye on the calendar. I was counting these months, too, desperate for the summer respite during which we would hopefully be able to declare an extended ceasefire before high school started.

"There's always the chance that you might decide that you want to join the Grad Choir next year on your own," I suggested hopefully. "And even if you don't, you only have one more concert."

Whatever the outcome of his decision, I was looking forward to that final opportunity to hear him sing with other trebles in early May. It was admittedly going to be hard for the choir to top the previous year's spring performance, when they sang the entirety of "Bohemian Rhapsody" a cappella, but they'd turned their attention that year to the music of another gender-bending Brit, Elton John. In my opinion, their spring concert was going to have a promising repertoire.

"You know," I attempted to shift the conversation into a more positive direction, "my mom used to listen to Elton John when I was growing up."

His new man-voice replied flatly, "I hate 'Rocket Man.'"

Negotiating the boundary between my power and my son's agency is one that has become harder to discern in the past few months, and most of our arguments are about things more significant than the merits of Elton John. The fantasy that I can still shape the major contours of his life through my mothering—by somehow micromanaging all aspects of his interests, talents, decisions—seems only to increase the more that he resists my meddling. And yet during these battles, another, more powerful mother was calling the shots. It is nature that determines when a voice fully changes as well as the kind of voice it becomes. I might want Haydon to continue singing into high school, might even imagine him having some kind of career as a professional musician, but it's a biological reality that boys who have soloist-quality voices as unchanged trebles have no assurance that they will become solo-quality singers as adults. Some aspects of being a successful musician carry over as boys navigate puberty—musicianship skills, a good ear, an interest in music—but having a voice that's appropriate for solo work is something that is determined by one's body, over which the individual has little actual control. Part of it is about the singer's natural range, but the quality of a voice is also determined by a singer's physiology, and how the structure of their mature larynx and nasal cavities give color and shape to sound. Many alums of ABS learned this the hard way—hoping and planning to become operatic tenors only to find that their voice just didn't have the qualities required of a soloist or that their natural range was as a bass or baritone, which offered fewer opportunities for solo performance. One former chorister remembers speaking a painful truth to a friend from ABS when they were both in their thirties, reflecting on the ebbs and flows of their often-frustrated attempts to forge successful solo careers: "You know, we peaked at like thirteen, fourteen, right?"

Much of our lived experience has to do with how our bodies are received by others—how they are categorized, how they are valued, what kind of access they grant us in the watching world. This seems to capture what's at stake right now with my son: he's ready to be seen as someone who is becoming a man, but as his mother I'm not yet willing to surrender him to what I fear awaits him on that distant stage. I'd like to keep him a child for just a bit longer because quite frankly I have no idea how to be a mother to someone in a masculine body. He's still betwixt and between, which gives me the illusion of having a bit more time to continue to mold him in my image, or at least in the image that I had imagined for him.

And yet the desire to be recognized as a particular gender is perhaps even *more* pronounced when aspects of our bodies are changing, blurring the boundaries between male and female, binary and nonbinary, child and adult. Thinking about male puberty this way suggests that we might see it as a kind of gender transition, one in which a person asks for their body to be received in a way that denotes a particular kind of change or evolution. As British cultural theorist Jacqueline Rose has suggested, a gender transition means that "something has to be acknowledged by the watching world, even if, as can also be the case, transition does not mean so much crossing from one side to the other as hovering in the space in between."[12]

The experience of being seen as a man in the eyes of others is the part of the voice change that choristers often *do* welcome and may even wish for depending on how long the voice change takes in coming. One such singer was a chorister in Vincent Oakes's Chattanooga Boys Choir whom I'll call Jim because he didn't want to use his real name. He got his start singing at church, at the request of his minister—something that led to merciless teasing on the part of his two older brothers. "They said at one point, 'you're not allowed to sing at church anymore, because you embarrassed us so much. You sound like a woman,'" Jim recalled, wincing at this early memory of realizing that there was a stigma attached to a boy who sings in a treble range. But a chance discovery of the Chattanooga Boys Choir's summer camp changed all of that when he was starting middle school. Jim joined other boys for a week away from home on a university campus that was filled with rehearsals along with sports, arts, and other activities. "I was just blown away," he recalled. "Because it felt like everyone there was like me, that we all shared this passion or this hobby. It really was a big thing for me."

His voice change started relatively late—at fifteen—even though the rest of his body had already been marked by the hormones of puberty. "It was a high voice," he said. "My speaking voice is still high tenor," he added, before grimacing at the memory of his teenaged awkwardness, "I mean, I sounded like my mother." This led to myriad other humiliations for a teenaged boy: "When you answer the phone, or go through a drive-through, everyone calls you, ma'am, that sort of thing," he remembered. "I was starting high school, and I was six feet tall and like a refrigerator compared to these children singing the same [treble] part as me." These uneven markers of gender lingered in his body far longer than he would have preferred; he finally joined the tenor section in the high school choir just to save face, even though his voice change lagged behind the rest of his body's development. "It was embarrassing to be as tall as I was, and around so many people that had already gone through a change, and I was still there with the highest voice you could imagine." By the time the voice change finally came, Jim welcomed it because it meant this uncomfortable period of feeling out of place was finally over.

Jim's teenaged experience of having a treble voice and a masculine body isn't all that unusual. A quick glance around a KSB rehearsal would find more than one treble with a faint mustache and other signs of puberty on their bodies. They're usually on the back row because they're the tallest, with unkempt hair and slightly bad behavior. Their bodies are starting to look like men's, but their singing voices still sound like women's. The fluidity of these bodily markers underscores the inadequacies of the gender binary; puberty's changes are generally more ambiguous than they are determinative. Singing in a tenor or baritone voice doesn't necessarily signify that one is a man, just as a boy who sings in a treble voice may not consider this kind of singing to be particularly feminine. In fact, many choir directors were quick to assure me that they didn't see this kind of singing as feminine, either. Masculine and feminine are categories that need not be limited to male or female bodies—even if it is easier to pull off masculinity when one has a body that's male, and vice versa.[13] These complexities point to a slightly different way of thinking about the relationship between gender and the body, a perspective that is becoming dominant in choral work and voice studies. This moves away from identifying singers by gender but instead by their voice part. Just a few years ago the Whiffenpoofs at Yale, the country's oldest and previously all-male collegiate a cappella group, agreed to accept women, provided they could sing the tenor parts.[14] It's no longer an all-male vocal group; instead it's a group for basses, baritones, and first and second tenors.

Interestingly, this shift in nomenclature is a way of degendering singers that still relies on placing various kinds of bodies into categories—it's just that these categories aren't the fixed, exclusionary columns of male and female. One choral director who was also a former boy chorister explained it by saying that once one was willing to set aside one's preconceived notions or political inclinations, a conductor should "simply look at the voice for the voice. We don't look to see does this person have breasts or not, does this person have, you know, a penis or not? It's irrelevant." He describes himself as being openly accepting of transgender singers, even as he looks to their bodies for clues as to where to place them in the choir. What matters in his view is the voice itself, because even if "up here [he gestures to the head] they want to be a tenor, here [he gestures to the throat] will dictate it."

He also sees this process playing out with cisgender singers in a church choir he directs. For instance, an older female singer might join the choir insisting that she's a soprano or an alto, even though her body's natural aging process has diminished her ability to hit higher notes successfully, which means he must sometimes gently inform an older female alto that she's actually a tenor. Not surprisingly, these conversations can be difficult. Cisgender singers are suddenly forced to reckon with bodies that don't quite align with the public presentations of gender they are accustomed to—after all, they've potentially lived decades without having to think about whether their gender identity matches their body's presentation. But these conversations also highlight commonalities with trans singers, who are similarly reckoning with bodies that don't align with a felt gender identity. In both cases singers have had to acknowledge the determinations of their bodies—either bodies that they want to change or bodies that have changed without their agency or permission—and the ways in which they fail to align with how they want the world to receive them.

In the end, we all struggle with our bodies at some point in our lives, and the body often wins. Sometimes—even oftentimes—our bodies don't line up with how we understand ourselves and how we want to be embodied in the world. In terms of gender identity, things like puberty blockers, hormone therapy, and gender reassignment surgery are options for some, and it's good that they exist for those whose felt experience of gender is so painfully out of alignment with how they wish to be seen in the world. But everyday gender transitions can be painful, too—the older soprano whose aging vocal folds have reassigned her to the tenor section or the boy choristers whose prized instrument had an early expiration date that ushered them out of the soloist's spotlight and into the anonymity of the back row. Things change. Voices break. Our bodies shift. We adjust. It turns out that Mother Nature has all of us, not just the unchanged trebles, by the throat.

One weekend in early March I stood next to a group of other mothers at a lacrosse practice, where we made casual conversation as we watched our kids go through a series of drills and exercises before we ultimately shifted to talking about how we should have worn warmer jackets as we shivered on the sidelines. I always find such conversations challenging because in most cases all that I have in common with these other parents, usually moms, is that our kids happen to be the same age and play the same sport. And however innocently the conversation begins—"How's your spring going?"—it often slips into a kind of conversational battle royale in which even the most self-aware parents feel compelled to boast about their kids. Which private schools they're eyeing for high school, the accelerated math class they're taking next year, or how they're joining a new, more competitive club team in the summer. The kids aren't really the ones competing, of course. We are. It's an unspoken contest intended to document our successful parenting, with our kids' hyperscheduled, achievement-focused childhood a testament to how well we're doing at our jobs, maximizing every potential opportunity and manipulating every single variable to give our kids every possible advantage.

I resisted the urge to say much that day. If I were to offer it, my own update would have been a certain conversation stopper: "I'm getting divorced, I'm stressed about money, and I don't really want to be at this lacrosse field because I'm more interested in forcing my son to be a musician." But of course I didn't say what was really on my mind; this ritualistic chitchat is the essential lubricant that smooths the bumpy gears of our suburban machinery. To throw rocks into that apparatus would threaten the unspoken agreement that we all tacitly made when we had kids and moved here for the good schools, the big back yards, the manicured sports fields: we will subvert our own desires to those of our children, committing approximately two decades of our lives to ensuring that they end up at least slightly happier than we are. Instead, I mostly listened in silence as the cycle shifted from the casual hellos to the humblebrags to the inevitable tedium of talking about the weather.

But that day the chatter migrated away from how cold we were to the strange new virus that seemed to have taken root in China.

"They say it's not any worse than the flu," one mom said with the voice of authority.

"Right!" another responded, nodding her head up and down. "Just send them to school with a bottle of Purell," she added, waving her hand with an air of annoyed dismissal.

"All I care about right now is lacrosse," said a third mom, pointing to where her son was standing on the field. He was finally playing goalie on the "A" team, something that he—or at least, his mother—had been hoping to achieve for the past two years. "And this virus had better not ruin the entire season," she concluded, shaking her head as she folded her arms across her chest.

I didn't say anything, but I knew from what I had been hearing at work that the virus was likely to ruin much more than a kid's lacrosse season. Even so, in those early weeks of the pandemic it was tempting to respond to the news from other parts of the world with a spirit of protest and disbelief. I chose to join them in their spirit of optimism, at least for the time being.

But a few days later, the upcoming week of choir rehearsals was cancelled "out of an abundance of caution," and lacrosse practice was put on pause a few days after. For a short time, there was still some faint hope that the pandemic would be only a short-term disruption and that life would return to normal in a few weeks. But after those early days of caution passed, in-person school was cancelled and we were all marooned at home, where my kids suddenly didn't have nearly enough to do and I started working ten-hour days from my bedroom to help my in-person university pivot to online instruction for the remainder of the spring term. This was a shock to the system that sent my job into hyperdrive; at one point my email inbox contained over one thousand unread messages.

Among the many strange things that happened during that time was how all the commitments that usually kept my kids preoccupied suddenly evaporated. There was no more lacrosse practice, no more choir rehearsal, and schoolwork shifted to pass/fail grading for that semester. At one point Haydon said something that would have been unthinkable just a few months before: "I can't remember the last time I was inside of a car." We weren't driving because we weren't going anywhere, of course, and so we found ourselves with lots of free time—or at least my kids did. This also meant that the all-consuming pressure to be achieving something, to be demonstrating accomplishment, had been temporarily put on pause, too. My carefully micromanaged family routine was completely upended by the pandemic, and it became very clear who was—and who wasn't—calling the shots. I am one hell of a hypercontrolling mother, but I was no match for Mother Nature.

KSB shifted to Zoom rehearsals indefinitely in April, signaling a painful resignation to the reality of a global event that would keep its choristers from singing together for well over a year. Around the country, most choirs did the same, only to realize that the connection problems and time lag that inevitably come with a video format made it impossible to hear each other effectively. This was clear in the remote "rehearsals" that Haydon participated in from his bedroom—any attempts to sing were quickly derailed by difficulties hearing the other singers, distractions in the background, or the boys' utter lack of enthusiasm for making music in this format. "There's amazingly problematic problems with trying to rehearse ensembles via Zoom," one director recounted of those early pandemic months. "It just didn't work. So those sessions became more music theory and engagement activities." Other choirs considered replacing group rehearsals with individual vocal instruction over Zoom, but the reality is that the kinds of things one might work on in an individual vocal lesson—the mechanics of sound production, individual vocal and dynamic control—aren't necessarily the most important skills for a choral singer, who needs to be more attuned to listening to the sounds of other singers and working to blend in. "We're not a training ground for solo singers," one director told me, reflecting in exasperation on the challenges of maintaining programing during the early pandemic. "They are members of the choir, and that is their primary objective."

Pandemic-era research concluded early on that choral singing was particularly risky when it came to COVID. Once it became clear that the virus was transmitted by aerosol droplets, researchers started testing mitigation strategies for use in performing arts settings like singing, instrumental music, and theater performance. One of the most notable early studies was the one commissioned by a coalition of performing arts organizations and led by researchers Shelly Miller and Joanna Srebric at the University of Colorado and the University of Maryland, respectively—what would come to be known as the Colorado Study for short. Their research concluded that these various kinds of breath-producing activities generated aerosol particles that fell somewhere between the extremes of normal speech and active coughing. But the threat was enough to warrant a set of protective protocols for singing, theatrical performance, and instrumental music to resume in schools and community organizations in the following year. Their recommendations endorsed rehearsals in which participants could wear masks or use bell covers for instrumental music, stay at least six feet apart, and limit rehearsals to thirty minutes at a time if they had to be indoors.[15]

Some choral groups found ways to incorporate these recommendations and restart their in-person rehearsals relatively early. One of them was the Tucson Boys Chorus in Arizona, led by Julian Ackerly. In addition to Arizona's warm outdoor weather, they were aided by the fact that the organization owned their own building, which meant that they didn't have to spend time or money looking for a suitable outdoor space in which to hold rehearsals. With the recommendations of the Colorado Study to reassure anxious parents, Ackerly set about reopening that fall, under conditions that aligned with the study recommendations. The choir managed most of the 2020–2021 season that way, although Ackerly admits that this approach, too, was inadequate. Despite their outdoor location, "we were dealing with environmental sounds big time," he said. "We're not far from a major road, so there was traffic noise." Moreover, the problems with hearing extended beyond background noise, because six feet of distance turned out to be just too far apart for singers to be able to hear each other effectively.

Back on the East Coast, it would be months before KSB would start offering modified indoor rehearsals to their choristers, so for the time being all that was available to Haydon were the weekly Zoom sessions that were eventually declared optional. And given a choice, he gladly exercised his own free will not to participate. An eerie silence started to settle into the background of our lives, replacing the frantic rhythm that we had come to accept as a normal state of affairs. There was no rushing to get anywhere, no sense that we needed to maintain our pace in the agitated race of daily life. For most of my kids' childhoods we had been quite literally focused on getting somewhere—to a practice, to a lesson, to some set of demonstrable achievements that would certify their exceptionalism and my success as a parent. But now the enormous kitchen chalkboard that once detailed the week's commitments became an open canvas awaiting an idle moment of artistic inspiration. The kids' "online school," a term we should use generously, upon retrospect, was all asynchronous, and so there was no need for them to get up at the crack of dawn. Instead, they stayed up as late as they wanted, watching TV or talking to their friends who were doing the same. They began sleeping until midmorning on weekdays, which felt like an indefensible indulgence, except that I couldn't quite come up with a reason that they shouldn't get to do this. When I tried to articulate a rationale for maintaining what was once a nonnegotiable rule in my house—no staying up until midnight on a school night playing Fortnite with your friends—I was surprisingly stumped when I couldn't come up with one.

"Literally, why can't I stay up?" Haydon said to me one evening, with a spirit of calmness and rationality that was hard to ignore. He then went on to enumerate how he and his sister had started to take more responsibility around the house because they were home all day with little to do while I was shuttered away at the computer in my home office. They had started making their own breakfast and lunch each day and were even doing their own laundry.

Confronted with this evidence, I found that I had little to offer him in the way of explanation. I also realized that this system benefitted me too, because I had four or five hours in the morning to work quietly before my kids woke up to do what little schooling they'd been assigned via a teacher's email the night before.

"You make a good point," I found myself saying in response. We agreed that I would set the Wi-Fi to turn off at midnight; of course, I would be in bed hours before then.

"Just remember to brush your teeth," I hollered down the hall as I walked to my bedroom to collapse each night. Offering this last, feeble attempt to ensure proper oral hygiene would hopefully convince dentists of the future that I was, in fact, paying attention that year.

Perhaps I should have felt worried about what they were missing, or cheated and shortchanged, like the mom who was afraid of losing her son's chance to play goalie. But what I felt instead was something closer to relief. The idea that I was or had ever been fully in control had been revealed as a ridiculous delusion. None of us moms on the sidelines of the lacrosse field or waiting patiently to drive the kids home from choir practice or scheduling tutors to help with math class could brag, cajole, or plan our way out of this one. And what kind of hubris led us to think that the measure of an adult life should be the success and happiness of a child in the first place? As if we could ever ensure that things would work out as we had promised! This is the insidious lie that perpetuates privilege, the delusion that we actually control our own destinies, along with those of the ones that we love: the world is fair, and we will get what we deserve, and all we need to do is work hard enough, plan in advance, and when necessary bribe our children into compliance.

The only corner of my world that I could still control was a massive, thousand-piece puzzle made up of vintage matchbook covers that I'd bought on a whim at a yard sale a few months previously. I didn't even know if it had all the pieces. We set it out on the dining room table, and every night the kids and I clustered around it for an hour or so, each of us working on our own little contribution to the larger work. There wasn't a lot of scintillating conversation—our slowed-down life had left us little to talk about—but the quiet togetherness was undeniably reassuring. Slowly but surely the puzzle started to come together, little clusters of matchbook covers taking shape in isolated territories spread across the table.

Parts of the picture looked deceptively similar, even though they were situated in completely different parts of the image. One night I stared in exasperation at a cluster of red and blue pieces before me, trying in vain to figure out how they went together. They were tiny, little patriots dressed like an American flag, part of a bicentennial drum and bugle corps picture.

Haydon stood beside me and looked over my shoulder.

"I think these ones goes over here," he said, extracting two tiny little drummers from my collection and fitting them easily into his cluster, which was another patriotic tableau from another location across the table. With my pieces added in, he was able to finish his own little matchbook cover, an intact image ready to be joined up to the whole.

And suddenly I was able to complete my own section more easily, since I wasn't stubbornly trying to force in pieces that don't fit. Looking at them again, from the perspective of a picture that was one step closer to being finished, it was hard to believe that I was so confident that they went together in the first place.

"Nice work," I said, with a smile.

―――

Against this backdrop of the global pandemic, Haydon never got the chance to have his last concert as a treble. Instead, he had a virtual voice check that summer, and we learned that his voice had continued expanding while none of us were paying attention, distracted instead by the weight of the virus, virtual school, and the like.

"Congratulations," said Mr. Fitz, over the FaceTime call, "you're a tenor."

Mr. Fitz explained that it still wasn't clear if Haydon would be a Tenor I or a Tenor II—the Tenor I voices are slightly higher, the others slightly lower—because his voice wouldn't stabilize for a few more years. But Haydon's voice got both deeper and higher during that spring—not only could he now sing low enough in his chest voice to get the notes that fell a full octave below middle C, but he could now sing some of the notes above middle C in his chest voice, too, even though those notes had been inaccessible to him at the previous voice check. "Your upper range has also opened up in the last two months," Mr. Fitz added. "You could almost get that F#, which tells me that you might end up a Tenor I in the end."

A sadness settled over me as I learned that my son's voice ultimately changed when no one was paying attention. There would be no final concert program to put in the scrapbook, no last photo of him being forced to smile in his green jacket. It's a loss that pales in comparison to all the losses accumulated during the pandemic, yet it felt like a gut punch just the same.

But this is the way that the voice change happens for most boys: unobserved, unnoticed, and unremarkable, save for a few particularly embarrassing voice cracks that remain etched in the archives of one's adolescent mortifications. Perhaps it's only because a treble voice means something special to a boy soprano that the voice change signifies something that implies a loss—the more precious the voice, the more painful the sorrow. After all, they've been singing for audiences who value them precisely because their voices are stamped from the beginning with an expiration date. "It was devastating," one former ABS chorister told me about his voice change. "I knew that I lost this precious thing that I couldn't get back." He remembered the realization as an eighth grader that although everyone had a voice, not everyone had "*this* voice." "I knew I was losing 'the thing,'" he recalled, "and then once I stopped being in the choir like that and singing every day in that range, I lost it." There's a cruel irony here: it's precisely because their treble voices have earned them so much praise and admiration from others that the change is one that boy sopranos can grieve. Boy choirs do give these singers a community to call upon as they navigate their vocal transitions, "a support group for the voice change."[16] But they can't stay in that support group forever; sooner or later the boy sopranos become men.

KSB put together a spring virtual concert that pandemic year, mostly powered by voice tracks submitted individually by particularly devoted singers and stitched together to make a video presentation. Haydon didn't choose to submit a recording, and I had little energy to compel him to do so. Those pandemic months gave him a new opportunity to assert his own will within the space formerly managed by all of the institutions that structure modern childhood—teams, lessons, choirs, tutors. This constellation of supporting resources wasn't so much a village as a planned community with precious little green space for the kids to run about and find their own way. But the pandemic offered my son an unexpected opening, and he seized upon it to make his escape. He wanted so desperately to have some measure of independence, to be seen by others as the man he was becoming. I couldn't blame him for wanting so badly to make the most of his big break.

I did insist that the three of us watch KSB's spring video concert as a family, by way of a laptop connected to our living room television. The seniors in the choir got a few seconds of live recognition, and we caught momentary glimpses of their bedrooms in the process, where they'd set up a laptop or a phone to capture their faces as Mr. Fisher read their names, one by one. There was a photo montage of the choir doing things from throughout the past year, set to a recording from a performance given a year or two earlier. It was a good effort, but there was still no denying that the whole thing stank.

It's not that the individual tracks that had been stitched together were bad, or out of tune, or anything like that. It's that they seemed lifeless and sterile, as if the process required to assemble them also scrubbed them free of the little flecks of magic that would have undeniably been there, lingering in the atmosphere along with the COVID aerosol droplets, had the boys been singing together as planned. The excitement of an in-person performance is that it includes mistakes and errors that everyone has to move past or willfully choose to ignore. An audience hears the occasional voice crack, puzzles over the spectacle of boys with mustaches who are still singing soprano, watches the little ones squirming when they're meant to be standing still. Things can go wrong, and it's up to the singers to adjust and an audience to forgive because our attention is focused on the magic of the group performance, not the isolated achievements of individuals. This reminded me of something that Wes Martin, director of the All American Boys Chorus in California, said to me: "There's a magic about music when you perform and sing. There's that listening silence that I always listen for in an audience, because you can tell when you finish a song and they don't applaud straightaway, that they're yearning for more—that is the magic of listening silence. And you know at that point that you've got them."

There was no magic of listening silence that day in my living room, as we wordlessly bore witness to the video performance on the television. In fact, true and honest listening was what had been missing all around. In a live performance, not only would the audience have been listening to the choir, the singers would have been listening to each other, working to blend their individual tones into one, slowly getting louder or softer together, staggering their breathing so as to avoid disrupting the continuous sound. It's not about alternately overpowering or submitting to the voices of others, it's about singing in a way that's informed by what they hear around them, as together they watch the conductor for instructions about what comes next.

The meaning of this metaphor was not lost on me. In all my years as a mother I had viewed myself as the conductor, the one who set the tempo and demanded the attention of the performers—"Keep your eyes on me and the show will go on, kids! Do exactly as I say, and everything will be fine!" But if Mother Nature taught me anything that COVID spring, it was that I am not the one with the baton. The perilous project of hanging my own, adult anxieties upon the achievements of my children was always destined to be a lackluster performance. There's no magic of listening silence in that arrangement, no space to see what unexpected echo might surprise us next. Perhaps it was time that I took my rightful place in the choir, learning to listen and blend my voice with those around me.

"You really don't want to continue with choir?" I said to Haydon one night. We were sitting in the kitchen after dinner, talking about his upcoming freshman year of high school. It still wasn't clear how much would unfold virtually and what would happen in person, but my son's wishes about one thing had been quite clear for some time.

He looked me straight in the face and said, "I really don't want to continue with choir."

I nodded my head in understanding. I had heard him, finally, and not just because he sounded like a man. Something about the pandemic had made me appreciate the power of listening and what it takes to actually hear another voice.

"I want to be on the drum line in the marching band," he said.

I allowed a few seconds of silence to linger in the space between us, and then I smiled at him, saying, "You know, I was in the marching band."

"But I also want to play lacrosse in the spring," he added quickly. He wanted to underline what's different between us. Our gender, yes, but also his interests. His choices. His will. His voice.

"I think that sounds like a good idea, too," I replied.

"You have to do an audition for percussion," he said. "And there's a part of it that you have to play on a marimba. Do you think we can rent one so that I can practice?" he asked hopefully.

"Yes," I said. "Yes, I think we can."

CHAPTER 9

The Child is Father of the Man

My heart leaps up when I behold
A rainbow in the sky:
So was it when my life began;
So is it now I am a man;
So be it when I shall grow old,
Or let me die!
The Child is father of the Man;
And I could wish my days to be
Bound each to each by natural piety.
—William Wordsworth, "The Rainbow" (1802)

Erick Lichte was eight years old when his mother took him to hear the Appleton Boychoir sing at a holiday "Lessons and Carols" service, the first classical music concert he ever remembers attending. His family wasn't particularly musical, but somehow his mother suspected that Lichte would like the choir, and she was right. Even now, at forty-eight, he remembers the impact of seeing the choristers walk out in an orderly line, and how they sang against the backdrop of an enormous, imposing pipe organ in the chapel of Lawrence University. He was mesmerized by the performance. Lichte knew right away that he wanted to audition the following year. His mother's decision to take him to that concert, and his decision to audition, would end up shaping his life in ways that neither of them could have anticipated at the time. He continued singing through high school and college and is now a professional conductor of a Canadian vocal group called Chor Leoni, which had until 2022 been an all-male ensemble. In a way, Lichte grew up to direct a boy choir—just one that was full of grown-ups, like him.

Lichte has plenty of experience with same-gender choral groups, after being a founding member of the ensemble Cantus, which he and three other men established at St. Olaf College in 1995. The group has thrived for three decades, offering paid salaries to its members and enabling them to make singing in a choir a full-time job with benefits, one of only a few such groups in the country. While Cantus was initially created as an all-male ensemble, for the past several years they've moved away from that language and focused instead on describing themselves as a choir for tenors, baritones, and basses, following the same trend as other vocal groups, like Chor Leoni, that now use the language of vocal parts rather than gender identities.

Ensembles like Cantus and Chor Leoni are finding new ways to harness the performative power of gender without using language that reinforces a gender binary. For starters, this means that the words "men" or "male" no longer appear in the groups' websites or press materials. In a 2023 address that reflected on those changes, Lichte observed that the words that have been used as shorthand to describe a person's vocal instrument—a "men's choir" or "all male choir" for instance—no longer accurately describe the way all of the owners of those vocal instruments might understand their gender identity. "In the past 10 years of my tenure with the choir," he told the singers, "it is safe to say that there have been seismic changes in the way gender is understood and expressed in our mainstream culture." Lichte also reported being deeply affected by the experiences of singers in the group who identified as nonbinary, even if their voice fell clearly in the range typically associated with male singers. While Chor Leoni still presents itself as an ensemble primarily for singers with tenor, baritone, and bass vocal ranges, Lichte says that just as he does not ask singers in an audition "about their religion, political affiliation, race, sexual orientation, eye color, or economic status," he also "will not ask about people's gender or gender identity." Instead, he says, "What I care about, and what I drive home in my audition process" is a different question entirely: "will this person live up to the values of this choir—musically and as an individual in this community?"

Even so, some of the choir's core values still have to do with expanding the meaning of masculinity. This, too, is part of Chor Leoni's DNA, as it was initially founded—by a woman, no less—as a male choir that was openly welcoming of both straight and gay singers. As Lichte said in that 2023 address, "In an era of male choirs being usually very straight and conservative, or identifying specifically as a space for queer men, at its founding, Chor Leoni never considered this distinction or divide." This same impulse appears to animate the group's current performances. "One of the things that I'm trying to do with my choir is to work very, very hard on how to sing as sensitively as possible," Lichte told me when we first talked in 2020. In his view, this means defying the trend of what an audience might expect from a group of singers who visually present as male. "What is disarming is when we get invited to go to a fundraiser and they don't know who's coming, and I get sixty men there and we sing beautiful *pianissimos*." He added that "people look at a group of [male-presenting singers] standing there in their tuxes, and all of a sudden, this gentle music is coming out. And it throws people for a loop."

Cantus has approached performances in a similar way, using the implied gender of its singers as a way of highlighting larger reflections about the meaning of masculinity. One recent Cantus concert, called "Brave," included every member of the ensemble speaking to the audience about their own evolving relationship with the concept of masculinity. The group's members talked about things ranging from their relationships with their parents, especially fathers, to "stories about being bullied in school, and about our societal expectations of masculinity," as one singer told me. Even though it was a group performance, these individual narratives made it even more powerful, as performers shared components of their own personal journeys around sexual and gender identity.

These adult ensembles are also expanding the kind of repertoire that low voices can perform. As former Cantus member and composer Timothy C. Takach told me, "I've always been a proponent of highlighting the multifaceted masculine personality through music. And so, I wouldn't write a tenor-bass song and give them a love song text or a pirate song or a sea shanty," although he admits that he's written that kind of repertoire, at times, when it was commissioned from him. "But when given a clean slate," he said, "I would choose to give those tenors and basses texts that they may not get a chance to say out loud all the time. Because I think there's power in saying certain words out loud in front of people. And it makes it easier when you're doing it surrounded by other people doing the same thing." Takach also recognized that the words he chooses have changed over time. "This is not my 2005 definition of what a tenor and bass choir is," he admitted. "So, what words do I give them?" he asked. "What matters to them? How can I access who they are, and give them something with which they identify?" These words matter because, as Takach believes, "rather than just giving people what they want to hear, we're trying to effect positive change."

These groups don't make gender identity a condition of auditioning; the singer must have a vocal range that can comfortably cover the part of a bass, baritone, or tenor. Practically speaking, this means that a handful of women with particularly low alto ranges could audition and that trans men and nonbinary singers are welcome, too. Once they're members of the ensemble, however, the singers become part of a particular kind of social community, one that is self-consciously engaged in a relatively progressive project of masculine identity formation. Just as an audience shares an unspoken understanding about the gender identity of the group's singers, the singers themselves understand that they're choosing to participate in a particular kind of social project, one in which gender is a fundamental component. As Lichte observed, "Not only do we get to make beautiful music, not only do we get to have a certain identity and the camaraderie within all of us, but we also get a chance to shape people. And if we want a better world for women, we need to make men better, period." This is one way that the mostly same-gender composition of these groups can be significant. Just as a boy choir can encourage boys in childhood and adolescence to be comfortable with emotional expression, an all-low voice ensemble can provide adult men with a social setting that reinforces somewhat countercultural notions of what masculinity can and should mean. As Lichte continued, "If we want to make men better, I think the arts are a huge part of that, because of what it opens up to you emotionally. And that can be a place where culture gets changed, if it's done right."

Just as I was finishing this manuscript in the fall of 2024, I opened my email and found an unexpected announcement: Commonwealth Youthchoirs, the umbrella organization that had long sustained the Keystone State Boychoir (KSB) and its sister organization, the Pennsylvania Girlchoir (PG), was about to enter a new partnership with the other major youth choral organizations in Philadelphia, the Philadelphia Boys Choir (PBC) and the Philadelphia Girls Choir (PGC). Commonwealth Youthchoirs would transition to being a mixed-gender singing group for kids and adolescents, while singers who wanted a single-gender experience would be able to pursue that option through the Philadelphia Boys or Philadelphia Girls Choirs. Put simply, however, this meant that KSB and PG were being disbanded. After more than two decades, the choral organization that had been founded by two disaffected Philadelphia Boys Choir directors was coming full circle and would be reabsorbed into its ranks. What would be different this time, however, was that the mixed-gender Commonwealth Youthchoirs would persevere as a new option for singers who didn't feel particularly compelled to sing with a same-gender ensemble. The three groups were planning their first joint performance in December 2024, just as this book was going into production.

Commonwealth Youthchoirs (CY) did not come to this decision overnight. Like many vocal and performing arts groups, COVID hit KSB and PG hard, and recruitment had suffered as a result. On top of the pandemic, Mr. Fisher announced his retirement as artistic director of KSB in the middle of the 2020–2021 season, a decision that surprised many parents and demoralized some of the choristers. Although Haydon had left the group by that point, I watched from a distance as CY's messaging about Fisher's departure attempted to explain a decision that was, by any measure, sudden and unexpected. Fisher had always had a somewhat unpredictable, even mercurial streak—that much had been evident to me since our first rehearsal—but his decision to leave the organization during a vulnerable pandemic moment still came as a shock. KSB immediately began a search for Fisher's replacement, but between the sudden leadership change, the difficulty of maintaining rehearsals and performances during the pandemic, and the soft recruitment seasons that resulted, KSB never fully recovered. The Presbyterian church that had been KSB's rehearsal and performance home had also suffered during COVID, as had so many other religious organizations, struggling with finances and an uptick in public violence in Philadelphia's Germantown neighborhood, which made some parents nervous about continuing rehearsals in that space.

The decision to merge with PBC and PGC in 2024, then, made good sense to the CY board for a number of reasons. Philadelphia probably didn't need two all-boy or all-girl choirs, for starters, especially because the groups would typically end up competing with each other for the same population of singers. And as CY board secretary Peter Kohn explained to me that fall, the different cultures that had initially distinguished PBC and KSB, particularly around emotional expression during performance, had long since diminished. There was also little need to replicate two separate organizational structures, when PBC and PGC had a strong administrative staff and a permanent rehearsal space to offer to the groups. Kohn emphasized to me that both boys and girls would still have the option for a single-gender experience, but added that gender identification would not need to be "the most salient characteristic of these groups." He observed that while there would always be interest in boys-only singing, it was hard to know how much of that was driven by the singers and how much was driven by audience interest. Kohn also added that single-gender singing—at least the kind that makes gender a condition of membership or participation—was clearly being deemphasized currently. On that point, I couldn't argue with him. Groups like Chor Leoni, Cantus, and others had made this change already. But even as they define their membership more broadly and reframe their mission, these all-low-voice organizations were still trying to harness the power of gender in performance to do something unique: contribute to the larger cultural conversation about men and manhood, broadening the meaning of masculinity in the process.

As these examples make clear, the place of boys- or men-only organizations in a society that is still wrestling with how gender should convey membership and access to everything from bathrooms to competitive athletics is far from certain. These groups occupy a delicate position in a new and evolving ecosystem, one in which many institutions are increasingly challenged to deny gendered categorizations based on biological sex differences even as real and significant social problems endure in profoundly different ways based on those same sex characteristics. Responding to an unplanned pregnancy can look and feel very different depending on whether or not one has a uterus; on the other hand, navigating a world in which firearms, pornography, and violent video games are readily available plays out differently for male brains that are more prone to expressing violence and taking risks.[1] We're in difficult and uncharted waters here, as our society simultaneously challenges gendered barriers while also reckoning with the disparate impacts of biological sex characteristics on critical social issues and problems. As Richard Reeves argues, this particular social moment has been especially destabilizing for men and boys because shaping men's purpose and meaning "is an important cultural task in any society, especially during periods of rapid social change like our own." In addition, he thinks that the perpetual fragility of masculinity presents a unique opportunity to approach the cultural processes of identity formation differently for male-identified young people. But he also cautions that "this is not to suggest that there is a single blueprint for making men. To say that men have to be made does not mean there is only one set of instructions."[2]

As I conclude this book and the research that created it, I am more convinced than ever that there's no single set of instructions for shepherding boys into a healthy form of manhood. But a key ingredient does seem to be helping boys and men to express their emotions within the context of close and meaningful relationships. Evidence abounds that far too many boys and men are detached from each other and from the connective tissue that brings human beings into meaningful relationships with other people. It's tempting—and periodically in vogue—to blame this "boy crisis" on institutional neglect of biological sex differences and suggest that boys need more male teachers or revised school curricula that underscore boys' allegedly different developmental needs. But Niobe Way, the NYU social psychologist who has studied emotional connections in boys and young men, cautions that the differences that we often observe between men and women in the depth and range of their social connections don't represent innate, biological differences as much as they do boys' acquired internalization of cultural norms that frame close relationships, particularly with other males, as feminine. As she writes, "The very social and emotional capacities, needs, and desires that are associated with being female and gay are not only the very same skills that are at the foundation of our survival as individuals and as a species; they are also capacities, needs, and desires that boys themselves have and are explicit about if one is willing to listen."[3] Ruth Whippman makes a similar point in her recent book about mothering boys, highlighting the latent sexism inherent in otherwise well-meaning attempts to redefine masculinity as something that can include more stereotypically feminine traits. "If we have to attach the label 'masculine' to a behavior before it can have value to men," she writes, "we are still buying into the basic gender hierarchy in which male is superior, female is lesser, and giving weight to the idea that a man embracing anything feminine is a humiliation."[4]

Without question, boys and men would benefit from being liberated from these constraints. The skills of connection and nurturing are increasingly valuable in a changing labor market, one in which what Reeves calls HEAL jobs—those in the sectors of health, education, administration, and literacy—continue to grow and are mostly filled by women. These are jobs that, Reeves argues, "are focused on people, rather than things, and tend to require more literacy than numeracy skills."[5] They are also the jobs that are less likely to be outsourced to artificial intelligence and where shortages in critical fields like health care and education persist. One way to address this, Reeves argues, is to create school and community programming that makes these jobs more visible and explicitly marketed to boys, much in the same way that STEM-focused programming has been created for girls. Such efforts would also require acknowledging the limiting social messages that young people receive about what boys (and girls) should aspire to do. It's not clear exactly what such programming would look like, but the implication is that this kind of cultural work would be addressed primarily to children and adolescents who identify as boys. Such opportunities could also be open to girls or offered in mixed-gender settings, of course, but they would start by acknowledging that boys' cultural socialization often leaves them at a deficit in acquiring these skills. Boys just don't have as many opportunities as girls to be encouraged and affirmed in showing care, emotional sensitivity, and vulnerability.

I spent years mulling over these ideas while Haydon finished high school, watching from an increasing distance as his identity shifted and evolved as a member of the different groups with which he chose to affiliate. Some of these were mixed-gender, like marching band, and others were boys only, like sports. He would end up playing lacrosse for all four years in high school and being a member of the band for three, first in the marching band's pit section on the marimba, after which he carried a bass drum and then the quad-toms in the marching band his junior year. He elected to quit band for his senior year, reasoning that what he really wanted to do was spend more time making music on his laptop—creations that ranged from electronic sound cloud compositions to rap to a remix of the Taylor Swift song "Enchanted."

Even though I'd been predisposed to question the social benefits of playing lacrosse, at the end of his first year of high school I found myself surprisingly impressed by some of the lessons he was learning on an all-male team. For instance, at the team's end-of-year banquet I marveled at the way that the boys on the team cheered for each other as they were recognized for their contributions and achievements across the year. One particular exchange stood out, at the end of the awards ceremony, when the coach delivered an award called the "Iron Falcon." In contrast to the typical "most improved" or "most valuable player" superlatives, this award recognized a player whose overall contribution to the team most demonstrated consistency, patience, commitment, and building up the team. The graduating senior who received the Iron Falcon award was met with a standing ovation by the team, who applauded for an entire minute as the boy walked up to the podium to receive his award. Sociologist Sherri Grasmuck, in her study of boys' Little League teams, dubbed boys like this "emotional workers," players who may not be the best athletes but who take on the work of keeping up the team's spirits by leading cheers, smoothing over social disagreements, and attending to other kids on a team who may be shy or otherwise unsure of their place in the group.[6] What was remarkable about this incident, therefore, wasn't just the existence of a player with these inclinations, but rather that the coach chose to explicitly name and celebrate those virtues in an all-male athletic setting and that the other boys so heartily celebrated him, too.

Without question, more coaches could choose to recognize and celebrate such qualities among male members of an athletic team—and perhaps this happens more often than I might have realized. But I suspect it's even easier for affirmations like these to occur in settings where displays of emotion are openly encouraged, as is often the case in the performing arts. This may not be part of the "set of instructions" for all boys, but I do think that a particularly compelling case can be made for the role of the arts in helping all children, especially boys, to develop a rich and healthy emotional life. By their very nature, the performing arts invite a wider range of emotional expression than the typical experiences of competitive sports, whether traditional athletics or those in the growing field of e-sports or competitive video gaming, which also appeal primarily to boys. Moreover, these experiences are particularly critical for boys in the years leading up to and during adolescence, when their identities are still developing and when peer networks can play a pivotal role in shaping a young person's sense of connection and identity.[7] Parents, teachers, coaches, and other adults can and should nurture this work in all kinds of settings, with kids of all genders. But same-gender organizations may hold particular promise for this transformational work, especially for young boys.

As a closer look at the world of boy choirs has demonstrated, one of the unique features of a single-gender setting is that it can provide a protective "cover" for boys (or girls) to engage in a broader range of behaviors under the heading of "being a boy" (or "being a girl"). Especially for boys, this has the benefit of decoupling behaviors like showing emotion and vulnerability from a gendered (female) or sexualized (gay) interpretation.[8] And on a practical level, this also gives boys more opportunities for and practice in developing relationships with other boys. It also recognizes the ways in which gender identity is a dynamic, lifelong process that can change and evolve over the course of one's life. Giving school-age and adolescent boys a same-gender space in which to recognize and practice more inclusive expressions of masculinity may well be a tool that helps them transcend gender's limitations when they become adults.

Of course, myriad conflicts around gender and its meanings continue to confront our current society. A brazen resurgence of masculine cultural power has taken hold in our political culture, especially in podcasting and social media. Recent executive orders insist on a gender binary. At the same time, many young people are becoming accustomed to giving their pronouns, understanding gender as a meaningful expression of individual identity that sociologist Tey Meadow describes as an "immutable part of the psychic self that needn't cohere, in any predictable way, with the materiality of the body."[9]

This future is still unfolding. But one consequence of this shifting paradigm is that it leaves us without a clear understanding of how changing understandings of gender identity at the individual level can potentially address structural problems of gender inequality at the larger, societal level. To this point, many scholars are skeptical of the potential for individual-level identity work to create meaningful progress toward gender equality. The sociological research on masculinity, for instance, suggests that "hybrid masculinities"—defined as those that incorporate fragments of "marginalized and subordinated masculinities and, at times, femininities"—can be practiced more openly by men who already enjoy privilege, who are typically white and heterosexual.[10] In other words, for a man to be expressive with his feelings or assume a posture of vulnerability may count for little when that man already enjoys a place of status and structural dominance. Moreover, this research also finds that movements that attempt to critique masculinity from within can ultimately end up reinforcing an understanding of masculinity as fundamentally rooted in a rather conventional understanding of manhood as something that presumes both strength and power.[11] The "Iron Falcon" award described above is a good example of this—it may recognize and celebrate relational work on the lacrosse team, but it uses a classic metaphor for male strength to do so. It may not matter if men perform or celebrate alternatives to hegemonic masculinity when the existing gender hierarchy remains unchallenged. Scholars also point out ways that white, straight men can use hybrid masculinities to perpetuate existing structural inequities. As the sociologists Tristan Bridges and C. J. Pascoe have written, "By framing middle-class, young, straight, white men as both the embodiment and harbinger of feminist change in masculinities, social scientists participate in further marginalizing poor men, working-class men, religious men, undereducated men, rural men, and men of color (among others) as the bearers of uneducated, backwards, toxic patriarchal masculinities."[12]

I hope that this book has not contributed to such a project, but I'd be lying if I said that those words didn't give me an uneasy pause. Even though I've highlighted choral organizations that are working intentionally to incorporate lower-income singers along with boys of color, this world is admittedly one that is mostly inhabited by middle-class families who have time and resources to devote to their sons' musical interests. And while I've argued that the inclusive masculinity promoted by boy choirs is a sign of decreasing homophobia, I've also acknowledged how these organizations reveal a persistent discomfort around adolescent homosexuality. And any skeptic would caution that helping a handful of boy choristers be more emotionally expressive and comfortable with vulnerability does little to advance the emancipation of women, particularly if that training is predicated on the exclusion of girls.

A world without gender might well be one with less inequality. And many of us (and I include myself in this group) would prefer to live without gender's oppressive limitations. Yet gender bedevils us not only because it enshrines certain forms of privilege but also because performing gender provides many of us with meaning, identity, and even enjoyment. As Barbara Risman wrote more than two decades ago, "Doing gender at the individual and interactional levels gives pleasure as well as reproduces inequality, and until we find other socially acceptable means to replace that opportunity for pleasure, we can hardly advocate for its cessation."[13] Performing gender—as well as transgressing its boundaries—can be empowering, exciting, fulfilling, and meaningful. And these performances give us clues for how we can harness the pleasure of "doing gender" without necessarily carrying all its baggage.

Performing gender can, of course, have multiple meanings. In the sociological sense, performing or "doing gender" typically means enacting, reproducing, and sometimes challenging societal expectations of what gender represents—essentialist notions of masculinity or femininity, maleness or femaleness. But performance in the sense of an arena of exhibition—as in a vocal or theatrical performance, where there is an audience and an understanding of actual, dedicated performers—has potential to frame gender somewhat differently. Harnessing gender *in* performance the way that a boy or all-male (or all-low-voice) choir does also has the ability to temporarily show us a different kind of world. It's more poetry than prose, more aspiration than argument. And as feminist performance scholar Jill Dolan has written, some performances "allow fleeting contact with a utopia not stabilized by its own finished perfection, not coercive in its contained, self-reliant, self-determined system, but a utopia always in process, always only partially grasped, as it disappears before us around the corners of narrative and social experience." These performances are also temporary, but that doesn't mean they're insignificant. As she continues, "The utopian performative's fleetingness leaves us melancholy yet cheered, because for however brief a moment, we felt something of what redemption might be like, of what humanism could really mean, of how powerful might be a world in which our commonalities would hail us over our differences."[14]

As I wrote these concluding words, Haydon was almost nineteen years old and about to head off to college. The weekend before he was scheduled to leave he asked if we could go shopping together. "I think I'm wanting to upgrade my style a little bit," he said, by which he meant that he would like to find some clothes that weren't sweatpants and didn't have his high school sports team logo on them. Of course, I jumped at this opportunity, and we settled on a plan for me to pick him up from his dad's house that Saturday morning. When he got into the passenger seat of the car it occurred to me that we hadn't driven anywhere together like this in a long time, since he's had his license for almost two years now. It reminded me of all the trips we made to and from Philadelphia back in his boy choir days.

The shopping trip itself was fun. We pulled pants off the rack, and he went off into the fitting room to try them on. I kept myself busy looking through nearby clearance racks, with him whispering every so often, "Psst! Mom!" when he needed my input. By the end of the expedition, he had assembled a pile of four pairs of pants, one pair of shorts, and four T-shirts. None of them said Nike or Under Armor. It truly felt like the end of an era, or rather the start of a new one.

As we started home, I told him that I needed to turn in the book manuscript soon but that I still needed to finish the conclusion. I asked him if he wanted to have the last word in the book, to which he quickly agreed. I was driving, so I handed him my iPhone for him to turn on the voice memo recorder. I started by asking him what he remembered about middle school. "Because I think in some ways, I was kind of pushy," I confessed. "And I feel like I forced you into the boy choir."

"I don't think you forced me," he countered, reasoning that perhaps it was more of a persistent nudge than a forceful push. "I just remember that I hated the drives. And that was the part of it that I really hated. I actually enjoyed myself once I was there. When I look back on KSB, I don't look back on it and think, 'Wow, that was a waste of my time in middle school.' I think I genuinely remember enjoying singing." He quickly added, "And I'm not just saying that because it's for your book. That's the truth!"

I asked him if he thought he got anything out of being in KSB and, if so, what it was, to which he responded, "I think I've always had a special connection to music. I enjoy playing piano. I enjoyed KSB, marching band, now making use of FL Studio. I've always loved music, but I think the one thing that was different was being around all guys in that situation. That was a unique experience."

"What was unique about that?" I asked.

He explained that most of his memories of being together with other boys at those ages came from sports, adding that "the way that sports are structured, you know, you either win or you lose; you're starting or you're not. You either had a good game or you didn't." But in his mind, KSB was "much more group oriented and there wasn't any competition." He added that one of his memories from that time period was of being at the ABS summer camp that got him started singing in the first place, and then attending a lacrosse camp a few months later. Both camps were held on the same private high school campus in Princeton. Even though I had clearly driven him to both places, I hadn't made this connection until he pointed out that both camps were held in the very same location. In his mind, both experiences were fun, but he added that "a lot of people understand that sports are not always kind to all kids. And, you know, being in a boy choir was still giving that sense of being a part of a group with other guys, but it's not nearly as competitive."

I asked him if he would have felt differently about singing if the group had included girls, to which he quickly responded, "Oh yeah, one hundred percent." As he struggled to explain why he started this way: "Because then you're not like—well, this is going to sound stupid," he said. "But if I see a girl walking down the street, I'm going to act differently than if I don't, you understand what I mean? If I'm singing with girls, I feel like it's just a genetic thing, that you just realize there are girls there. And I think that ultimately translates into, well . . . it wouldn't nearly be as expressive, I think."

"And why not?" I prodded.

He fumbled a bit with his answer before he was finally able to explain himself: "I think there's a certain stigma with guys singing as being more feminine, as a more feminine attribute. I'm not saying I think about this, or that I think this way every day in my life. But I think there's definitely a certain stigma that any form of emotional expression is typically considered by society to be more feminine." He quickly shot me a sideways glance, adding, "I don't know if you would agree or not."

I responded that I thought a lot of social scientists would agree with that.

"Right," he replied. "So, what I'm saying is, yes, singing is very expressive and doing that around girls might not get the same result."

"Do you think you'll ever sing again?" I asked.

"Not in the same way," he answered.

The haste with which he delivered this answer sent a current of lament through my gut. Of course, I'm glad that he has developed his own love of music, but I'm sad that he'll never be one of those men singing sensitive lyrics in an all-low-voice ensemble, like Cantus or Chor Leoni. I wondered silently to myself where he would find places that encourage male emotional connection in the future. Will it be a fraternity? A club lacrosse team? Something else? Nowhere else?

But I know better now than to speak any of this aloud or suggest that perhaps he could find an a cappella group in college. Instead, I asked him, "Why not?"

"You know, honestly," he said, "I'm not going to say no to anything, because anything can happen. But my interest in music has changed. The type of music I'm interested in has changed. I still have a lot of love for music," he added quickly, noting that the first thing he did when he woke up that morning was to start laying down chords on his laptop. "But the point I'm making is I don't necessarily see myself singing in a choir like that again," he concluded.

I shifted the conversation toward the question that was most on my mind, as I finish the book and he gets ready to head off to college.

"So, are you glad that I forced you to do it?"

Much to my relief, he answered quickly: "Oh, yeah! One hundred percent!"

He explained, "I think singing in a boy choir is the type of experience that I'm happy I've had. Just because it helped me grow my love for music even more. Especially singing, you know. I would say not everybody who enjoys music is able to sing. And looking back on it, I'm happy I did it. I have memories, like doing 'Bohemian Rhapsody,' and they're good memories in general. I feel like I'm a better person. You know, I'm not the type of person that sees a man expressing emotion and thinks, 'Oh, wow, that's, you know, unmanly.'"

I quickly pointed out that perhaps he was saying this because he knows that this is the thesis of the book. But he insisted: "No, I don't think that's why I'm saying that at all. I think that it's genuinely how I feel."

By this point, we were pulling into his dad's driveway. This particular journey was over. A new one would be starting soon, but my time as the driver had come to an end. We both knew this, and so we sat for a few moments in silence before he moved to open the door. I would have liked to keep this conversation going forever, but I also knew that he was ready to get out of the car. He had packing to do and a graduation party to attend, and of course he wanted to get back to making music on his laptop.

"You know," I said, "I'm really going to miss you."

He looked back at me with an easy smile, the same big grin he's had since he was a kid.

"I'm going to miss you, too."

I'd like to believe that I am sending my children into adulthood in a world that's more just, more equal, and more accepting around questions of sex and gender than the one I brought them into almost two decades ago. But I'm not sure if that's true. Some possibilities seem more open, more injustices laid bare now than they did when they were born in the early aughts, before anyone gave their pronouns or #MeToo had toppled the empires of once-powerful men. That was also before a majority of Americans reelected a president who had been found responsible for sexual assault, the Supreme Court overturned *Roe v. Wade*, and states began adopting legislation to constrain teachers' ability to reference the mere existence of homosexuality. It's hard to know what the next twenty years will bring.

But parenting has a way of making one into an eternal optimist, if only because the alternative is too painful to consider. Maybe one day my children will be sending their own offspring into adult lives where gender has become far less salient in shaping how people think about themselves, their potential, and their opportunities and how others will view acts of caring, strength, and vulnerability. I certainly hope so. I'm also encouraged by the clues left for us within our own bodies. Studying boy choirs and boy sopranos underlines how all of us can activate the registers of male and female, embrace our emotional capacities for expression and vulnerability, along with just how arbitrary the boundaries of masculine and feminine are in the eyes of all-powerful Mother Nature. It also highlights how much potential we have to change things—just as a boy who sings through the voice change can change his voice forever, we all have the potential to see and perform gender in multiple, expansive registers.

Just as with any captivating performance, I can't wait to see what happens next.

Acknowledgments

Many people were early champions of this project, and my Princeton colleagues Mitch Duneier, Jeffrey Edelstein, Brian Herrera, Gabriel Crouch, Joe Stephens, and Stacy Wolf deserve my special thanks. Their words of encouragement and early feedback may have been small moments to them, but their input played an outsized role in shaping this project.

Others read and offered comments on all or part of the manuscript, including Jill Dolan, Hilary Levey Freidman, Craig Denison, Baker Peeples, Susanna Peeples, Kate Stanton, and Ellen Labrecque. Rebecca Graves-Bayazitoglu offered thoughtful input throughout, and I am especially grateful to Amy Reynolds, whose astute and insightful sociological criticism in the final stages made the entire book stronger.

Within the boy choir world, I remain particularly indebted to the former choristers and current directors who spent hours talking with me and helping the project along by opening up their virtual rolodexes and connecting me with a wider array of respondents. I owe a special word of thanks on this score (pun intended) to Kent Jue, Daniel Bates, Jeffrey Tucker, Julian Ackerly, Joe Fitzmartin, Steve Fisher, Matthew Karczewski, Nathan Wadley, and Alan Brown.

Special thanks to my agent Lisa Adams and the team at Rutgers who have so beautifully encouraged this project and seen it through to completion. I am grateful to Kim Guinta and Peggy Solic for their stewardship as editors and to Micah Kleit for his enthusiasm for this project from its earliest beginnings.

To Neil J. Young, my faithful writing partner: This book would not be what it is without you. Throughout the years I spent writing and revising this manuscript, your thoughtful input and steadfast friendship propelled me through draft after draft, chapter after chapter, Zoom after Zoom. As we both learned years ago in the Princeton Writing Program, every writer needs a reader, and Neil, I'm so glad you were willing to be mine.

My parents, David and Emily Peeples, have been tireless enthusiasts for this project and willing readers at every step along the way. Parenting is a lifelong job, it seems, and I'm so lucky that the two of you are still up for everything that entails!

Finally, I am beyond grateful to my children, Haydon and Margaret, and to their father Sam Massengill, for allowing me to write about our shared lives in these pages. Margaret, you were incredibly patient and generous to allow your mother to write about your older brother without ever being resentful or jealous. I hope that the book's dedication helps even things out! And Haydon, thank you for giving me the space and freedom to write about you, our relationship, and all that I learned about myself by being a boy choir mom. I could not be prouder of the man you have become, and I'm so glad that I got to play a role in your story.

Notes

INTRODUCTION

1. Alex Marshall, "After 350 Years of Tradition, a Boys' Choir Now Admits Girls," *New York Times*, July 15, 2022, https://www.nytimes.com/2022/07/15/arts/music/girls-boys-choirs-johns-cambridge.html.

2. See, for instance, Emma Brown, *To Raise a Boy: Classrooms, Locker Rooms, Bedrooms, and the Hidden Struggles of American Boyhood* (New York: Atria / One Signal, 2021); Richard V. Reeves, *Of Boys and Men: Why the Modern Male Is Struggling, Why It Matters, and What to Do about It* (Washington, DC: Brookings Institution Press, 2022); Sonora Jha, *How to Raise a Feminist Son: Motherhood, Masculinity, and the Making of My Family* (Seattle: Sasquatch Books, 2021); Ruth Whippman, *BoyMom: Reimagining Boyhood in the Age of Impossible Masculinity* (New York: Harmony/Rodale, 2024); Michael C. Reichert, *How to Raise a Boy: The Power of Connection to Build Good Men* (New York: TarcherPerigee, 2019).

3. See, for instance, the overview in Douglas Schrock and Michael Schwalbe, "Men, Masculinity, and Manhood Acts," *Annual Review of Sociology* 35 (2009): 277–295.

4. Daniel A. Cox, "Men's Social Circles Are Shrinking" (Survey Center on American Life, June 29, 2021), https://www.americansurveycenter.org/why-mens-social-circles-are-shrinking/. Note that these survey findings reveal similar increases among women, although women still say they have more close friendships than men.

5. Anne Case and Angus Deaton, *Deaths of Despair and the Future of Capitalism* (Princeton, NJ: Princeton University Press, 2020).

6. See, for instance, Nikki McCann Ramirez, "Man Boobs and Raw Eggs: The Most Absurd Moments from Tucker Carlson's Ball-Tanning Special," *Rolling*

Stone, October 5, 2022, https://www.rollingstone.com/politics/politics-news/tucker-carlson-end-of-men-most-absurd-moments-1234606090/.

7. Katharine Khanna and Tey Meadow, "The Fragile Male: An Experimental Study of Transgender Classification and the Durability of Gender Categories," *Gender and Society* 37, no. 4 (2023): 553–583.

8. See, for instance, Danya Lagos, "Hearing Gender: Voice-Based Gender Classification Processes and Transgender Health Inequality," *American Sociological Review* 84, no. 5 (2019): 801–827, 807.

CHAPTER 1 — DO YOU KNOW A BOY WHO LOVES TO SING?

1. See, for instance, Patricia A. Adler, Steven J. Kless, and Peter Adler, "Socialization to Gender Roles: Popularity among Elementary School Boys and Girls," *Sociology of Education* 65, no. 3 (1992): 169–187.

2. Emma Brown, *To Raise a Boy: Classrooms, Locker Rooms, Bedrooms, and the Hidden Struggles of American Boyhood* (New York: Atria / One Signal, 2021), 57.

3. Rosalind Wiseman, *Masterminds and Wingmen: Helping Our Boys Cope with Schoolyard Power, Locker-Room Tests, Girlfriends, and the New Rules of Boy World* (New York: Harmony Books, 2013).

4. William Pollack, *Real Boys: Rescuing Our Sons from the Myths of Boyhood* (New York: Random House, 1998).

5. Judy Chu, *When Boys Become Boys: Development, Relationships, and Masculinity* (New York: New York University Press, 2014).

6. Chu, 144.

7. C. J. Pascoe, *Dude, You're a Fag: Masculinity and Sexuality in High School* (Berkeley: University of California Press, 2007), 54.

8. Niobe Way, *Deep Secrets: Boys' Friendships and the Crisis of Connection* (Cambridge, MA: Harvard University Press, 2013), 7–8.

9. Way, 26.

10. Niobe Way, *Rebels with a Cause: Reimagining Boys, Ourselves, and Our Culture* (New York: Dutton, 2024), 127.

11. Brown, *To Raise a Boy*, 65.

12. Eric Anderson, *Inclusive Masculinity: The Changing Nature of Masculinities* (New York: Routledge, 2009).

13. R. W. Connell, *Gender and Power: Society, the Person and Sexual Politics* (Oxford: Polity Press, 1987).

14. Mimi Schippers, "Recovering the Feminine Other: Masculinity, Femininity, and Gender Hegemony," *Theory and Society* 36, no. 1 (2007): 85–102.

15. See, for instance, Pascoe, *Dude, You're a Fag*.

16. See, for instance, "How Social-Emotional Learning Became a Target for Ron DeSantis and Conservatives," *Fresh Air*, April 28, 2022, https://www.npr.org/2022/04/28/1095042273/ron-desantis-florida-textbooks-social-emotional-learning.

17. Candace West and Don H. Zimmerman, "Doing Gender," *Gender and Society* 1, no. 2 (1987): 125–151.

18. See also Martin Ashley, *How High Should Boys Sing? Gender, Authenticity, and Credibility in the Young Male Voice* (New York: Routledge, 2009).

19. Brown, *To Raise a Boy*; Peggy Orenstein, *Boys and Sex: Young Men on Hookups, Love, Porn, Consent, and Navigating the New Masculinity* (New York: HarperCollins, 2020).

20. Brown, *To Raise a Boy*, 188–189.

21. See Halberstam as cited in Pascoe, *Dude, You're a Fag*, 118.

22. Pascoe, 54.

23. Elizabeth Weil, "Where Have All the Sopranos Gone?," *New York Times Magazine,* November 8, 2013, https://www.nytimes.com/2013/11/10/magazine/where-have-all-the-sopranos-gone.html, para 9.

24. Barbara Risman, "Gender as a Social Structure: Theory Wrestling with Activism," *Gender and Society* 18, no. 4 (2004): 429–450, 446.

25. Michael Cooper, "In a Season of Boys' Choirs, a Question: Why No Girls?," *New York Times*, December 26, 2018, https://www.nytimes.com/2018/12/26/arts/music/boys-choir-vienna-st-thomas-kings-college-cambridge.html.

26. Tobi Thomas, "Lesley Garrett Says King's College Choir Must Accept Girls," *The Guardian*, December 5, 2018, https://www.theguardian.com/music/2018/dec/06/lesley-garrett-says-kings-college-choir-must-accept-girls.

27. Thomas, para. 4.

28. Tey Meadow, *Trans Kids: Being Gendered in the Twenty-First Century* (Berkeley: University of California Press, 2018).

CHAPTER 2 — IT'S LIKE A FINISHING SCHOOL FOR BOYS

1. Philadelphia Boys Choir and Chorale, "About Us." (n.d.), https://pbgcsings.org/pbcc-3/.

2. Hugh Scott, "Our Boys Choir Will Compete in Wales," *Philadelphia Inquirer Magazine*, June 16, 1968, 8.

3. "All-Philadelphia Boys' Choir to Perform in Moscow This July," *Philadelphia Tribune*, May 30, 1970.

4. "Philadelphia Boys Choir in First Documentary," *Philadelphia Tribune*, December 23, 1988, sec. D.

5. Lea Sitton Stanley, "Life Lessons, One Note at a Time: A Boys Choir Finds the Key to Opening Doors Everywhere," *Philadelphia Inquirer*, April 28, 1999, sec. B.

6. Pew Research Center, "Parenting in America: Outlook, Worries, Aspirations Are Strongly Linked to Financial Situation" (December 17, 2015), https://www.pewresearch.org/social-trends/2015/12/17/parenting-in-america/.

7. Aspen Institute, Project Play, "Youth Sports Facts: Participation Rates" (n.d.), https://www.aspenprojectplay.org/youth-sports-facts/participation-rates.

8. Michael Kimmel, *Manhood in America: A Cultural History* (New York: Oxford University Press, 2012), 101–104; see also Eric Anderson, *Inclusive Masculinity: The Changing Nature of Masculinities* (New York: Routledge, 2009), 26–29.

9. Kimmel, *Manhood in America*, 101.

10. See, for instance, Hilary Levey Friedman, *Playing to Win: Raising Children in a Competitive Culture* (Berkeley: University of California Press, 2009).

11. Tucson Arizona Boys Chorus, "History" (n.d.), https://boyschorus.org/history/.

12. See, for instance, Friedman, *Playing to Win*.

13. Cincinnati Boychoir, "History of the Cincinnati Boychoir" (n.d.), https://cincinnatiboychoir.org/history.

14. See Keystone State Boychoir, "South African Medley—Spring Concert 2013" (July 8, 2013), https://www.youtube.com/watch?v=AWjyIdhLc6s.

15. Barrie Thorne, *Gender Play: Girls and Boys in School* (New Brunswick, NJ: Rutgers University Press, 1993). For a more recent example with adolescents in sports, see Michela Musto, "Athletes in the Pool, Girls and Boys on Deck: The Contextual Construction of Gender in Coed Youth Swimming," in *Child's Play: Sport in Kids' Worlds*, ed. Michael A. Messner and Michela Musto (New Brunswick, NJ: Rutgers University Press, 2016).

16. See, for instance, Murray J. N. Drummond, "The Voices of Boys on Sport, Health, and Physical Activity: The Beginning of Life through a Gendered Lens," in Messner and Musto, *Child's Play*, 144–164.

17. Of course, this is not always the case, as Sherri Grasmuck, *Protecting Home: Class, Race, and Masculinity in Boys' Baseball* (New Brunswick, NJ: Rutgers University Press, 2005), illustrates in her ethnography of Little League baseball. Coaching strategies, particularly masculine styles of engagement with players, can run the gamut.

CHAPTER 3—UNCHANGED TREBLES

1. Elizabeth Weil, "Where Have All the Sopranos Gone?," *New York Times Magazine*, November 8, 2013, https://www.nytimes.com/2013/11/10/magazine/where-have-all-the-sopranos-gone.html.

2. Weil.

3. Joshua Goldstein, "A Secular Trend toward Earlier Male Sexual Maturity: Evidence from Shifting Ages of Male Young Adult Mortality," *PLOS ONE*, August 16, 2011, https://doi.org/10.1371/journal.pone.0014826.

4. Martha Feldman, *The Castrato: Reflections on Natures and Kinds* (Berkeley: University of California Press, 2015); Piotr O. Scholz, *Eunuchs and Castrati: A Cultural History*, trans. John A. Broadwin and Shelley L. Frisch (Princeton, NJ: Markus Wiener, 2001).

5. Henry Pleasants, *The Great Singers* (New York: Simon & Schuster, 1966).

6. Pleasants, 44.

7. Leonard Bernstein, "Chichester Psalms: in Three Movements For Mixed Choir, Boy Soloist, and Orchestra (to be sung in Hebrew)" (G. Schrimer, 1965).

8. Donal Henahan, "Review/Music; Bernstein Conducts Bernstein 45 Years after Impromptu Debut," *New York Times*, November 16, 1988, https://www.nytimes.com/1988/11/16/arts/review-music-bernstein-conducts-bernstein-45-years-after-impromptu-debut.html.

9. David M. Howard and Graham F. Welch, "Gendered Voice in the Cathedral Choir," *Psychology of Music* 30, no. 1 (2002): 102–120.

10. Howard and Welch.

11. Lynne Huff-Gackle, "The Young Adolescent Female Voice (Ages 11–15): Classification, Placement, and Development of Tone," *Choral Journal* 25, no. 8 (April 1985): 15–18.

12. Huff-Gackle.

13. Melissa Eddy, "Girl's Quest to Sing with Berlin's Boys Choir Is Dashed," *New York Times*, August 16, 2019, https://www.nytimes.com/2019/08/16/world/europe/berlin-boys-choir-lawsuit.html.

14. Howard and Welch, "Gendered Voice in the Cathedral Choir."

15. Howard and Welch, 106.

16. See also Desmond C. Sergeant, Peta J. Sjolander, and Graham F. Welch, "Listeners' Identification of Gender Differences in Children's Singing," *Research Studies in Music Education* 24 (2005): 28–39.

17. Paul R. Laird, *The Chichester Psalms of Leonard Bernstein* (Hillsdale, NY: Pendragon Press, 2010), 30.

18. "Training a Male Voice with Anthony Roth Costanzo," *New York Times*, July 18, 2017, https://www.facebook.com/nytimes/videos/10151235422724999/.

19. Justin Davidson, "The Pharoah We Need: Countertenor Anthony Roth Costanzo Brings the Sexually Ambiguous Monarch of Philip Glass's Akhnaten to the Met," *Vulture*, September 12, 2019, https://www.vulture.com/2019/09/anthony-roth-costanzo-akhnaten.html.

20. Anne Midgette, "A New Leader and New Sounds at the Met: Philip Glass's Striking 'Akhnaten,'" *Washington Post*, November 17, 2019, https://www.washingtonpost.com/entertainment/music/sing-like-an-egyptian-glasss-akhnaten-strikes-poses-in-new-met-production/2019/11/17/0be2f7da-08c8-11ea-924a-28d87132c7ec_story.html.

21. Anthony Tommasini, "Review: 'Akhnaten' Puts You on Philip Glass Time," *New York Times*, November 10, 2019, https://www.nytimes.com/2019/11/10/arts/music/review-akhnaten-philip-glass-metropolitan-opera.html.

22. "Training a Male Voice with Anthony Roth Costanzo."

23. Anthony Heilbut, *The Gospel Sound: Good News and Bad Times*, 5th ed. (New York: Limelight Editions, 1997), xxiv.

24. See, for instance, Heilbut, 116.

25. Maki Isaka, *Onnagata: A Labyrinth of Gendering in Kabuki Theater* (Seattle: University of Washington Press, 2016), 8.

26. Heilbut, *Gospel Sound*, xxiv.

27. Laird, *Chichester Psalms of Leonard Bernstein*, 35.

28. Laird, 37.

29. Humphrey Burton, as quoted in Laird, 42.

30. Laird, 43.

31. Laura Blen Louis, "Blissfully Unaware of Threat: On Reading Bernstein's Chichester Psalms," *Michigan Quarterly Review* 54, no. 2 (Spring 2015), http://hdl.handle.net/2027/spo.act2080.0054.205.

CHAPTER 4 — DON'T YOU WANT TO SEE THE WORLD?

1. For a thoughtful discussion of gender identity and sports, see Murray J. N. Drummond, "The Voices of Boys on Sport, Health, and Physical Activity: The Beginning of Life through a Gendered Lens," in *Child's Play: Sport in Kids' Worlds*, ed. Michael A. Messner and Michela Musto (New Brunswick, NJ: Rutgers University Press, 2016), 144–164.

2. James S. Coleman, "Social Capital in the Creation of Human Capital," *American Journal of Sociology* 94 (1988): S98.

3. Pierre Bourdieu, "The Forms of Capital," in *Handbook of Theory and Research for the Sociology of Education*, ed. J. G. Richardson (New York: Greenwood, 1986), 241–258.

4. Bourdieu, 245.

5. Raj Chetty et al., "Social Capital II: Determinants of Economic Connectedness," *Nature* 608 (2022): 122–134.

6. Annette Lareau, *Unequal Childhoods: Class, Race, and Family Life* (Berkeley: University of California Press, 2003).

7. See, for instance, Hilary Levey Friedman, *Playing to Win: Raising Children in a Competitive Culture* (Berkeley: University of California Press, 2009), 24.

8. These fears are, of course, coded with racial and economic meanings. See, for instance, Jen McGovern, "The Intersection of Class, Race, Gender and Generation in Shaping Latinas' Sport Experiences," *Sociological Spectrum* 41, no. 1 (December 4, 2020): 96–114; Peter Francis Harvey, "'Everyone Thinks They're Special': How Schools Teach Children Their Social Station," *American Sociological Review* 88, no. 3 (May 6, 2023), https://doi.org/10.1177/00031224231172785; Shamus Rahman Khan, *Privilege: The Making of an Adolescent Elite at St. Paul's School* (Princeton, NJ: Princeton University Press, 2011).

9. Jessica Grose, "Why So Many Kids Are Priced Out of Youth Sports," *New York Times*, February 14, 2024, https://www.nytimes.com/2024/02/14/opinion/youth-sports.html.

10. See C. Ryan Dunn, Travis E. Dorsch, Michael Q. King, and Kevin J. Rothlisberger, "The Impact of Family Financial Investment on Perceived Parent Pressure and Child Enjoyment and Commitment in Organized Youth Sport," *Family Relations* 65 (April 2016): 287, https://doi.org/10.1111/fare.12193.

11. Dunn et al.

12. Linda Flanagan, *Take Back the Game: How Money and Mania Are Ruining Kids' Sports* (New York: Portfolio, 2022).

13. Grose, "Why So Many Kids Are Priced Out of Youth Sports."

14. Carl Jung, attributed in *Boston Magazine*, 1978, https://www.oxfordreference.com/display/10.1093/acref/9780191826719.001.0001/q-oro-ed4-00006107.

15. For a useful summary of class-based differences in parental investments in marriage and child-rearing, see Andrew J. Cherlin, "Degrees of Change: An Assessment of the Deinstitutionalization of Marriage Thesis," *Journal of Marriage and the Family* 82, no. 1 (February 2020): 62–80.

16. See, for instance, Douglas Hartmann and Alex Manning, "Kids of Color in the American Sporting Landscape: Limited, Concentrated, and Controlled," in Messner and Musto, *Child's Play*, 43–60; Michael Messner and Michela Musto, "Introduction: Kids and Sport," in Messner and Musto, *Child's Play*, 1–19.

17. Anne Helen Petersen, "Against Kids' Sports," *Culture Study*, September 12, 2021, https://annehelen.substack.com/p/against-kids-sports.

18. Notably, boys and girls sing together in the choir's primary school, and at the end of fourth grade they can move up to join either the Vienna Boys Choir or the Vienna Girls Choir (grades 5–8). While academic classes are coed during those years, the choirs rehearse and perform separately due to the different vocal changes that each group experiences. From grade 9 to grade 12, boys and girls can choose to continue in the high school and sing together in a mixed-gender choir.

CHAPTER 5 — DRAW THE CIRCLE WIDE

1. See NCES Common Core of Data for American Public Schools, https://nces.ed.gov/ccd. School ID 062223011418 and 063363006168.

2. Jessica McCrory Calarco, "Avoiding Us versus Them: How Schools' Dependence on Privileged 'Helicopter' Parents Influences Enforcement of Rules," *American Sociological Review* 85, no. 2 (2020): 223–246.

3. Stephen Mark Dobbs, "Arts Education in Schools: Private Foundations and Public Responsibility," *Yale Law and Policy Review* 7, no. 2 (1989): 424.

4. Arts Education Data Project, "2019 National Arts Education Status Report Summary" (NAMM Foundation, 2019), https://drive.google.com/file/d/1-603l5cTNDT2nAtffBXfVtysFFO2UVTb/view.

5. Christine Bass, *Where the Boys Are* (DVD, 2012), https://christinebass.com/where-the-boys-are/.

6. Gordon Light and Mark Miller, *Draw the Circle Wide* (Nashville: Abingdon Press, 2008).

7. Although tuition fees vary across the country, most organizations charge an annual fee that ranges anywhere from $900 to $1,500.

8. See data in Jody L. Herman, Andrew R. Flores, and Kathyn K. O'Neill, "How Many Adults and Youth Identify as Transgender in the United States?" (Williams Institute, UCLA School of Law, June 2022), https://williamsinstitute.law.ucla.edu/wp-content/uploads/Trans-Pop-Update-Jun-2022.pdf.

9. Tey Meadow, *Trans Kids: Being Gendered in the Twenty-First Century* (Berkeley: University of California Press, 2018).

10. This is an argument found in the literature on "hybrid masculinities"; e.g. Tristan Bridges, "A Very 'Gay' Straight? Hybrid Masculinities, Sexual Aesthetics, and the Changing Relationship between Masculinity and Homophobia," *Gender and Society* 28, no. 1 (2014): 58–82; Tristan Bridges and C. J. Pascoe, "Hybrid Masculinities: New Directions in the Sociology of Men and Masculinities," *Sociology Compass* 8, no. 3 (2014): 246–258.

11. See, for instance, Douglas Schrock and Michael Schwalbe, "Men, Masculinity, and Manhood Acts," *Annual Review of Sociology* 35 (2009): 277–295, and Eric Anderson, *Inclusive Masculinity: The Changing Nature of Masculinities* (New York: Routledge, 2009).

CHAPTER 6 — CLOSETS

1. Judith Butler, "Performative Acts and Gender Constitution: An Essay in Phenomenology and Feminist Theory," *Theatre Journal* 40, no. 4 (1988): 522.

2. Martin Ashley, *How High Should Boys Sing? Gender, Authenticity, and Credibility in the Young Male Voice* (New York: Routledge, 2009), 82.

3. "St. John's Boys' Choir Staffer Accused of Sexual Misconduct," *WCCO News*, July 26, 2019, https://www.cbsnews.com/minnesota/news/st-johns-boys-choir-sexual-misconduct-allegations/.

4. Mike Stanton, "Bearing Witness: A Man's Recovery of His Sexual Abuse as a Child Part One: Discovery," *Providence Journal*, May 7, 1995, sec. A01.

5. Sharon Otterman, "A Quiet End for Boys Choir of Harlem," *New York Times*, December 22, 2009, https://www.nytimes.com/2009/12/23/nyregion/23choir.html.

6. Diana Jean Schemo, "Years of Sex Abuse Described at Choir School in New Jersey," *New York Times*, April 16, 2002, sec. B1, https://www.nytimes.com/2002/04/16/nyregion/years-of-sex-abuse-described-at-choir-school-in-new-jersey.html; John Heilemann, "The Choirboy," *New York Magazine*, May 19, 2005, https://nymag.com/nymetro/news/features/12061/.

7. Kenneth Kidd, "The Lost Boys," *Toronto Star*, September 25, 2005.

8. Schemo, "Years of Sex Abuse."

9. Heilemann, "Choirboy."

10. Heilemann; Schemo, "Years of Sex Abuse."

11. Schemo, "Years of Sex Abuse."

12. Heilemann, "Choirboy"; Schemo, "Years of Sex Abuse."

13. Schemo, "Years of Sex Abuse."

14. Jennifer S. Hirsch and Shamus Rahman Khan, *Sexual Citizens: A Landmark Study of Sex, Power, and Assault on Campus* (New York: Norton, 2020).

15. Heilemann, "Choirboy."

16. Heilemann.

17. Heilemann.

18. Heilemann.

19. Heilemann.

20. Heilemann; Schemo, "Years of Sex Abuse."

CHAPTER 7 — A CEREMONY OF DISCIPLINE

1. Hilary Levey Friedman, *Playing to Win: Raising Children in a Competitive Culture* (Berkeley: University of California Press, 2009).

2. This perspective is illustrated by the writing of a range of scholars and authors like Lori Gottlieb, "How to Land Your Kid in Therapy," *The Atlantic*, August 2011, https://www.theatlantic.com/magazine/archive/2011/07/how-to-land-your-kid-in-therapy/308555/; Julie Lythcott-Haims, *How to Raise an Adult: Break Free of the Overparenting Trap and Prepare Your Kid for Success* (Stamford, CT: Griffin

Books, 2016); Paul Tough, *How Children Succeed: Grit, Curiosity, and the Hidden Power of Character* (New York: Mariner Books, 2012); Wendy Mogel, *Blessing of a Skinned Knee* (New York: Scribner, 2008).

3. Michael Oliver, *Benjamin Britten* (London: Phaidon Press, 1996), 74.

4. Humphrey Carpenter, *Benjamin Britten: A Biography* (London: Faber, 1992).

5. Neil Powell, *Benjamin Britten: A Life for Music* (London: Hutchinson, 2013), 169.

6. Oliver, *Benjamin Britten*, 90–91; Powell, *Benjamin Britten*, 197–198; Sherill Tippins, *February House* (Boston: Houghton Mifflin, 2005), 234.

7. See, for instance, Powell, *Benjamin Britten*, 138–139, 207; Carpenter, *Benjamin Britten*, 25.

8. As quoted in Oliver, *Benjamin Britten*, 93.

9. Powell, *Benjamin Britten*, 208.

10. Powell, 193; Tippins, *February House*, 117.

11. Carpenter, *Benjamin Britten*.

12. Carpenter, 161.

13. Carpenter, 162; see also Oliver, *Benjamin Britten*, 77.

14. Martin Ashley, *How High Should Boys Sing? Gender, Authenticity, and Credibility in the Young Male Voice* (New York: Routledge, 2009), 83.

15. James Fenton, "How Grimes Became Grim," *The Guardian*, July 2, 2004, https://www.theguardian.com/music/2004/jul/03/classicalmusicandopera.

16. "The Turn of the Screw" (n.d.), https://www.brittenpearsarts.org/music/the-turn-of-the-screw.

17. Carpenter, *Benjamin Britten*, 168.

CHAPTER 8 — MOTHER NATURE HAS THEM BY THE THROAT

1. See, for instance, the discussion in Danya Lagos, "Hearing Gender: Voice-Based Gender Classification Processes and Transgender Health Inequality," *American Sociological Review* 84, no. 5 (2019): 801–827.

2. Candace West and Don H. Zimmerman, "Doing Gender," *Gender and Society* 1, no. 2 (1987): 125–151.

3. Nancy Chodorow, *The Reproduction of Mothering: Psychoanalysis and the Sociology of Gender* (Berkeley: University of California Press, 1978).

4. Nancy Chodorow, "The Psychodynamics of the Family," in *The Second Wave: A Reader in Feminist Theory*, ed. Linda Nicholson (New York: Routledge, 1997), 182.

5. Nancy Chodorow, "Women Mother Daughters: The Reproduction of Mothering after Forty Years," in *Nancy Chodorow and* The Reproduction of Mothering: *Forty Years On*, ed. Petra Bueskens (Cham, Switzerland: Palgrave Macmillan, 2021), 52.

6. Chodorow, *Reproduction of Mothering*, 122.

7. Chodorow, 176.

8. Chodorow, "Women Mother Daughters."

9. Wayne Koestenbaum, *The Queen's Throat: Opera, Homosexuality, and the Mystery of Desire* (New York: Poseidon Press, 1993), 166.

10. Craig Denison and Maria Denison, "Uncovering Meaning and Identity through Voice Change," *Choral Journal* 59, no. 11 (July 2019): 28–37; Lynne Huff-Gackle, "The Young Adolescent Female Voice (Ages 11–15): Classification, Placement, and Development of Tone," *Choral Journal* 25, no. 8 (April 1985): 15–18.

11. Koestenbaum, *Queen's Throat*, 155.

12. Jacqueline Rose, *On Violence and On Violence Against Women* (New York: Farrar, Straus and Giroux, 2021), 88–89.

13. Douglas Schrock and Michael Schwalbe, "Men, Masculinity, and Manhood Acts," *Annual Review of Sociology* 35 (2009): 277–295.

14. David Shimer, "Yale's Famed Whiffenpoofs Singing Group Admits First Woman," *New York Times*, February 20, 2018, https://www.nytimes.com/2018/02/20/nyregion/yale-whiffenpoofs-first-woman.html.

15. James Weaver et al., "International Coalition of Performing Arts Aerosol Study Round 2" (National Federation of State High School Associations, August 6, 2020), https://www.nfhs.org/media/4119369/aerosol-study-prelim-results-round-2-final-updated.pdf.

16. Denison and Denison, "Uncovering Meaning and Identity."

CHAPTER 9 — THE CHILD IS FATHER OF THE MAN

1. See, for example, the recent discussion in Richard V. Reeves, *Of Boys and Men: Why the Modern Male Is Struggling, Why It Matters, and What to Do about It* (Washington, DC: Brookings Institution Press, 2022).

2. Reeves, 96.

3. Niobe Way, *Deep Secrets: Boys' Friendships and the Crisis of Connection* (Cambridge, MA: Harvard University Press, 2013), 265.

4. Ruth Whippman, *BoyMom: Reimagining Boyhood in the Age of Impossible Masculinity* (New York: Harmony/Rodale, 2024), 87.

5. Reeves, *Of Boys and Men*, 152.

6. Sherri Grasmuck, *Protecting Home: Class, Race, and Masculinity in Boys' Baseball* (New Brunswick, NJ: Rutgers University Press, 2005).

7. Way, *Deep Secrets*; Michael C. Reichert, *How to Raise a Boy: The Power of Connection to Build Good Men* (New York: TarcherPerigee, 2019).

8. This is a framework developed by Niobe Way, *Rebels with a Cause: Reimagining Boys, Ourselves, and Our Culture* (New York: Dutton, 2024).

9. Tey Meadow, *Trans Kids: Being Gendered in the Twenty-First Century* (Berkeley: University of California Press, 2018), 215.

10. Tristan Bridges, "A Very 'Gay' Straight? Hybrid Masculinities, Sexual Aesthetics, and the Changing Relationship between Masculinity and Homophobia," *Gender and Society* 28, no. 1 (2014): 59–60.

11. For instance, men who engage in advocacy work against domestic violence "discursively separate 'good' from 'bad' men and fail to account for the ways that presenting strength and power as natural resources for men perpetuates gender and sexual inequality." Tristan Bridges and C. J. Pascoe, "Hybrid Masculinities: New Directions in the Sociology of Men and Masculinities," *Sociology Compass* 8, no. 3 (2014): 251.

12. Bridges and Pascoe, 253.

13. Barbara Risman, "Gender as a Social Structure: Theory Wrestling with Activism," *Gender and Society* 18, no. 4 (2004): 429–450, 446.

14. Jill Dolan, *Utopia in Performance: Finding Hope at the Theater* (Ann Arbor: University of Michigan Press, 2005), 6, 8.

Index

ABS. *See* American Boychoir School
ACDA. *See* American Choral Directors Association
adolescence/puberty (male): significance of physical and emotional transformation, 6, 205–208, 210–211
Akhnaten countertenor role, 87
all-boy choral schools: diminishing number in England, 2; disappearance in the United States, 4
all-male spaces: variability of, 33
American Boychoir School (ABS), 21–22; multiplicity of responses to past abuse, 164–166; past abuse victims' silence as children, 169; period of rebuilding after sex crimes/heterosexual focus, 153–156; policy forbidding sexual contact between students, 156–157; prior sexual abuse scandals, 21, 44, 147, 150–151
American Choral Directors Association (ACDA): policy change for gender inclusion, 136–137
Anderson, Eric: 164; "inclusive masculinity," 30, 56, 148
arts *vs.* sports, 63; education (American public schools)/perception and inequalities, 120; emphasis on collaboration *vs.* competition, 63; as help for boys/men for emotional expression, 4, 9
athletics: and choir participation similarities/differences, 62–63,
252n17; sports metaphors in choirs, 123–124
Auden, W. H.: influence on and friendship with Benjamin Britten, 178–180

"bearded and unbearded" voice, 70
Bernstein, Leonard. See *Chichester Psalms* (Bernstein)
"border work": all-male structure as protective backdrop for discipline and emotional expression, 57, 252n15
Bourdieu, Pierre: on value of cultural capital, 100
boy choirs: access to elite localized cultural prestige, 44–45, 46; benefits of keeping changed-voices boys, 57, 252n15; biologically different voices than girls argument, 35; competition for solos, 76; defining features, 4; Descant status, 71; discipline and self-restraint skills appeal to parents, 176; focus on fleeting voice moments, 72–73; focus on vertical relationships, 76; gender segregation arguments/concerns, 35–36, 65; illustration of masculine/feminine boundaries, 7; impact on trans children, 36; innovations, 56–57; new vision of masculinity propagation, 45, 57; pandemic impact on, 216–218; as protective "cover" expanding behavior range, 237, 259n8; reasons

boy choirs (cont.)
  for declining participation, 44; recruitment strategies, 47–48; safe environment for emotional expression, 33–34; short window for treble voices before adolescence, 39–40. *See also* American Boychoir School (ABS); "border work"; chorister behavior; Vienna Boy Choir (VBC)
boy choirs (new directions), 118; addressing fears of abuse/homosexuality, 148; change opportunities, 140–141; dismantling individual achievement model, 132; inclusive recruitment and its limits, 125–126, 137–140; limitations of aspirational circle, 139, 141, 256n10; school partnerships, 128; singing through voice change, 207; socioeconomic diversity challenges, 141; tour opportunity funding challenges, 131
boys: arts *vs.* sports participation, 43; bullying and choir membership, 110; classic soprano sound, 70; early adolescence and same-gender spaces, 4; early culture lessons in unguarded emotions and masculinity, 27–28; meaning to them of treble voice use and supportive traditions, 3; with music aptitude/discovery, 46–47; sociocultural reasons for joining choirs, 121; vocal range strength, 122; voice and larynx changes, 70, 79–80, 197, 206. *See also* "head voice" tones; treble voices
Britten, Benjamin: *Ceremony of Carols* 178–182; composing roles for countertenors, 86–87; influence of W. H. Auden, 179–180; pedophilia themes in mature work, 180–181; and Peter Pears collaborator/partner, 178–179. See also *Ceremony of Carols*
Butler, Judith: gender as a construction, 146

Cantus and Chor Leoni: expanding meaning of masculinity through music, 229–230; use of language of vocal parts *vs.* gender identities, 228–229

castrati history, 71–72; opera roles disappearance after 1750, 86
Ceremony of Carols, 173–174; musical challenges, 177–178. *See also* Britten, Benjamin
Cheeks, Reverend June: influence on popular music, 88
Cheit, Ross: "recovered memory" of abuse, 149
Chichester Psalms (Bernstein), 74–75; commission, 82; composition/development of, 89–90; performance challenges, 91–92
Chodorow, Nancy: on mother-son relationship, 203; on roots of gender inequality, 202–203
Chor Leoni. *See* Cantus and Chor Leoni; Lichte, Erick (Chor Leoni director/Cantus founding member)
chorister behavior, 58–59
Chu, Judy: on boys' lessons on unguarded emotions, 27–28
club sports for children, 103; criticism of, 113
Colorado Study: COVID and choral singing, 217–218
Commonwealth Youthchoirs (CY): impact of COVID, 232; transition to mixed-gender singing group, 231
"concerted cultivation" by parents, 100
Costanzo, Anthony Roth, 84–88
countertenor, 75, 84; gender and its presentation, 89; modern opera roles, 86; perceptions of outside of Western cultures, 88; vocal forms in contexts of exclusion, 88–89. *See also* Costanzo, Anthony Roth; Deller, Alfred; Kabuki Onnagata; *leo ki`eki`e*
Crouch, Gabriel (Princeton University Glee Club director), 20
cultural capital, 99–100

Deller, Alfred: modern countertenor roles, 86–87
Denison, Craig: on ACDA policy change, 136–137; on ABS, 158–160

INDEX

Dolan, Jill: on performance and humanism, 240

"emotional workers" on boys' Little League teams, 236
empathy: through singing, 60–61

falsettist. *See* countertenor
falsetto. *See* "head voice" tones
"Festival of Nine Lessons and Carols," 1–2
Fisher, Steve (KSB cofounder), 50–52, 68, 143, 146–147; retirement during COVID, 232
Fitzmartin, Joseph ("Mr. Fitz"/KSB cofounder), 50–51
Four Seasons: influence from gospel artists, 88
Friedman, Hilary Levey: parenting as practice for the "tournament of life," 175–176

Garrett, Lesley: criticism of British choral school model, 35–36
gender: and adolescence (focus on), 4; and body relationship perspective, 212; changed voice as signal of, 208; current social conflicts around, 237–238; "doing gender," 239–240; evolving ideas on boys-/men-only organizations, 233; expectations in choral world, 77–78; harnessing *in* performance, 240; identities *vs.* language of vocal parts in vocal groups, 228; and inequality, 239; recognition and puberty, 210–211; as a social construct, 17, 89, 146, 200, 238; sociological emphasis on continuous process *vs.* accomplishment, 31; transitions, 211–214. *See also* puberty
gender inclusion issues: American Choral Directors Association policy change, 136–137; debates/positions about gender nonconforming male singers, 139; debates/positions about trans kids, 137–139; range of opportunities, 135; social meaning of ensembles structured by gender, 137; theoretical *vs.* substantive issue for trans kids, 135–136; uniform/dress code issues, 139, 256n10; *vs.* gender transgressions, 141
girl choirs: focus on horizontal relationships, 76; investment in social experience of choir, 76; training *vs.* urgency of training for boys, 77; views on differences with boy choirs, 75–76
girls: contrasting behavior to boys, 14; encouragement to move beyond submissive femininity, 19; mixed reaction to inclusion in treble voices choir, 2–3, 79; vocal changes during puberty, 79; vocal range strength, 122; *vs.* boys participation in sports, 43–44. *See also* "head voice" tones
Glass, Philip: *Akhnaten* role for countertenor voice, 86

Hanson, Donald: abusive ABS music director, 150, 151, 153; justice avoidance, 165
Hardwicke, John Jr.: ABS abuse suit, 150–151; aftereffects of abuse, 166–169
Harlem Boys Choir: investigations of abuse, 149
"head voice" tones, 79; in Black gospel music, 88; falsetto maintenance, 84–85
HEAL jobs, 235
healthy masculinity: arts as potential support for, 4, 231, 237; enabling by social settings that enforce emotional expression, 231; propagation by boy choirs, 45. *See also* inclusive masculinity
Heilbut, Anthony, 88
Hirsch, Jennifer: research on sexual ethics/sexual assault, 160–161
homosexuality: limits of acceptance, 148; open acceptance of in inclusive masculinity, 148; in ABS child protection policies, 157–159; stigmatization and male fear of misgendering, 29
Howard, David, 78, 79
hybrid masculinity, 238, 260n11; and structural inequalities, 238–239

inclusive masculinity, 30; empathy through choral texts, 60–61; limits to,141; and open acceptance of homosexuality/diminishing homophobia, 148, 164; priority of boys' emotional development, 60; resistance to, 30–31

jock culture. *See* masculinity (traditional/hegemonic)
Jung, Carl: on parents' influence, 104

Kabuki Onnagata, 88
Keystone State Boychoir (KSB): body movement while singing, 51; choir discipline/structure, 53–54; choir ensembles, 52–53; disbanding/new options, 231; emphasis on openness/feelings while singing, 51; gender-bending performance, 143–146; pandemic impact, 216–217, 218; performance for Pope Francis, 52; program growth and success, 52; rehearsal rigors, 90; training goal of cofounders, 50. *See also* Commonwealth Youth Choirs (CY); Pennsylvania Girlchoir
Khan, Shamus: research on sexual ethics/sexual assault, 160–161
King's College, Cambridge: boy choir history, 2; Christmas Eve service, 1–2
Koestenbaum, Wayne: "puberty as a moment of reckoning," 205; on voice change and gender, 208
KSB. *See* Fisher, Steve (KSB cofounder); Fitzmartin, Joseph ("Mr. Fitz"/KSB cofounder); Keystone State Boychoir (KSB)

language of vocal parts in choir identification, 228
Lareau, Annette: on beliefs about good parenting, 174; on "concerted cultivation," 100, 125
leo kiʻekiʻe, 88
Lessig, Lawrence: ABS abuse survivor and lawyer, 150–151, 169
Lichte, Erick (Chor Leoni director/Cantus founding member), 228–231

Litton, Jim: and American Boychoir School "golden age," 171–172

MAGA movement: and gendered lens of political process, 8
masculinity (traditional/hegemonic): centrality in homophobia theory, 30; emotional constraints consequences, 29–30; emotional expression as difference from feminine, 29; expanding meaning through music. *See* Cantus and Chor Leoni. *See also* all-male spaces; healthy masculinity; hybrid masculinity; inclusive masculinity
Meadow, Tey: on understanding gender/individual identity, 238
motherhood challenges of raising a boy, 5, 16, 249n2; American Boychoir School introduction, 22–24; *vs.* emotional connection to daughters, 201–202; emotional labor of parenthood, 18; *vs.* encouraging girls to move beyond cultural confines of submissive femininity, 19; feminist's concerns about same-sex choir, 37–38; goal of rejecting societal gender stereotypes, 17–18; healthy masculinity models in current society, 4; helping to navigate through competing values/goals, 103–104; importance of helping boys/men express emotion in relationships context, 234; mothering work taken for granted, 83; negative consequences of traditional masculinity, 5, 16–17, 35, 249n4; pandemic impact on, 216–217; puberty reactions, 197–198, 200, 204, 210

National Children's Choir (NCC), 12–13

pandemic: choral singing and COVID research/recommendations, 217–218, 220, 224–225; early discussions about, 215; impact on sports/choir rehearsals, 216; influence on group singing, 44
parenting: competitiveness among parents, 214; concerns about social and cultural capital, 101, 255n8;

"concerted cultivation" form, 100, 125; distorted view of influence/importance, 111–112, 255n15; "helicopter," 176, 257–258n2; interventionist, 173–175; and optimism, 244–245. *See also* Lareau, Annette; motherhood challenges of raising a boy

Pascoe, C. J.: study of high school boys' performances of masculinity, 28

Pasek, Benj: emotional expression while singing, 50

PBC. *See* Philadelphia Boys Choir and Chorale (PBC)

Pennsylvania Girlchoir: disbanding/new options, 231; sister choir for KSB, 52

Philadelphia Boys Choir and Chorale (PBC), 39; early roots, 42–43; posture during performance, 50–51. *See also* Commonwealth Youthchoirs (CY); Keystone State Boychoir (KSB) ·

puberty: changed emotional dynamics with, 70, 205; and questions of gender, 200; recognition of son's body changes, 197

Reeves, Richard: destabilizing social moment for men, 233–234; HEAL jobs access for boys and men, 235; warning of men's identity crisis, 6

Risman, Barbara: on "doing gender," 239

same-gender: schooling benefits for boys, 33–34

Schemo, Diana: investigation into ABS abuse, 150, 159–160

sexual orientation and boundaries: addressing fears about homosexuality and abuse, 146–148

social capital, 98–99; behavior guidance for choristers, 110

social-emotional learning initiatives in public schools: reaction to, 30–31

soprano. *See* treble voices

sports participation: boys *vs.* girls, 44

Temptations: influence from gospel artists, 88

"tomboy": as socially acceptable archetype, 34

traditional masculinity. *See* masculinity (traditional/hegemonic)

trans children: choir opportunities for change/equity, 140–141; impact for boys choirs, 36, 135–136; positions on inclusion in same-sex choirs, 137–138

treble voices, 71; boys' *vs.* girls' (varying opinions by experience), 73; changes (feelings about), 221–222; preservation of through singing, 84–85, 89; solo-quality singing and voice changes, 209–210; "unchanged trebles," 35; urgency in training boys' voices, 77. *See also* castrati; "head voice" tones

Vienna Boy Choir (VBC), 113–114; boys' maturity through international tour experiences, 115; members' feelings about, 114–115; partnership with Land of Lakes Choirboys, 105–106; prestige of, 113

Way, Niobe: social connections of men/women, 234; study of emotional vulnerability, 29

Welch, Graham, 78, 79

Whippman, Ruth: on latent sexism in masculinity redefinition, 234–235

Whiffenpoofs (Yale): identifying singers by voice part, 212

About the Author

Rebekah Peeples is associate dean for curriculum and assessment in the Office of the Dean of the College at Princeton University. Her first book, *Walmart Wars: Moral Populism in the Twenty-First Century*, was praised by *Library Journal* as "first-rate sociology, deftly packaged to offer insight for both academic and popular audiences." She has also written for numerous scholarly journals as well *Inside Higher Education* and the *Washington Post*. She lives in Bucks County, Pennsylvania.